Culturally RESPONSIVE TEACHING
in Gifted Education

D1605449

Culturally RESPONSIVE TEACHING

in Gifted Education

Building Cultural
Competence and
Serving Diverse
Student Populations

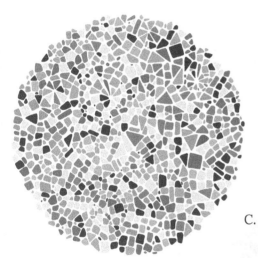

Edited by
C. Matthew Fugate, Ph.D., Wendy A. Behrens, M.A. Ed.,
Cecelia Boswell, Ed.D., & Joy Lawson Davis, Ed.D.

PRUFROCK PRESS INC.
WACO, TEXAS

Library of Congress Cataloging-in-Publication Data

Names: Fugate, C. Matthew, editor. | Behrens, Wendy A., editor. | Boswell,
  Cecelia A., 1949- editor. | Davis, Joy Lawson, 1953- editor.
Title: Culturally responsive teaching in gifted education : building
  cultural competence and serving diverse student populations / edited by
  C. Matthew Fugate, Wendy A. Behrens, Cecelia Boswell, and Joy Lawson
  Davis.
Description: Waco, TX : Prufrock Press Inc., [2021] | Includes
  bibliographical references. | Summary: ""Culturally Responsive Teaching
  in Gifted Education" is a professional learning tool for practitioners
  who are working to create more culturally responsive school and
  classroom environments for gifted and talented students from special
  populations, including those who are culturally, linguistically, and
  economically diverse"-- Provided by publisher.
Identifiers: LCCN 2021006345 (print) | LCCN 2021006346 (ebook) | ISBN
  9781646320899 (paperback) | ISBN 9781646320905 (ebook) | ISBN
  9781646320912 (epub)
Subjects: LCSH: Gifted children--Education--United States. | Culturally
  relevant pedagogy--United States. | Multicultural education--United
  States. | Educational equalization--United States.
Classification: LCC LC3993.9 .C856 2021 (print) | LCC LC3993.9 (ebook) |
  DDC 371.95--dc23
LC record available at https://lccn.loc.gov/2021006345
LC ebook record available at https://lccn.loc.gov/2021006346

Edited by Katy McDowall

Cover and layout design by Allegra Denbo

ISBN-13: 978-1-64632-089-9

Printed in the United States of America.

At the time of this book's publication, all facts and figures cited are the most current available. All telephone numbers, addresses, and website URLs are accurate and active. All publications, organizations, websites, and other resources exist as described in the book, and all have been verified. The authors and Prufrock Press Inc. make no warranty or guarantee concerning the information and materials given out by organizations or content found at websites, and we are not responsible for any changes that occur after this book's publication. If you find an error, please contact Prufrock Press Inc.

Prufrock Press Inc.
P.O. Box 8813
Waco, TX 76714-8813
Phone: (800) 998-2208
Fax: (800) 240-0333
https://www.prufrock.com

This book is dedicated to the practitioners who are tirelessly working to ensure that all students' needs are met and that their voices are heard, recognized, and honored.

Table of Contents

SECTION IV A Call to Action

Acknowledgements

We would like to express our sincere appreciation to the contributors for their tireless work and contributions to this project. Additionally, we would also like to thank Joel McIntosh, Katy McDowall, and the entire team at Prufrock Press for their belief in the importance of this project from the very beginning. Finally, thank you to our families and friends for their unconditional support and unwavering belief in our work.

—*Matt, Wendy, Cecelia, and Joy*

From the Editors

This book has been a journey. When we started out, our intention was to produce a book that addressed the social-emotional needs of special populations of gifted and talented students. However, as the historic events of the summer of 2020 unfolded—and as we delved into our own personal thoughts, self-reflections, and motivations—it dawned on us that this book should be about the need for culturally responsive practices that recognize the gifts and talents that exist among the diversity of students in our nation's schools. In this book, we pay homage to the work of Dr. Gloria Ladson-Billings and Dr. Geneva Gay, eminent scholars on whose shoulders we stand and whose work has shaped our collective insight into the importance of cultural responsiveness in the lives of Black students. Based upon this important understanding, it is our hope that this book helps to broaden and expand their research to the myriad diverse students who bring their own experiences, understandings, and cultures into the classroom.

Each of us brought a unique perspective to this work. The discussions that ensued as we reviewed each essay during our weekly meetings have not only improved the work, but also increased our own personal growth and understanding. We have learned that we never stop learning. The journey toward true cultural responsiveness is neither easy nor ever complete, nor can it be a road taken only by those who are "alike." If the field of gifted education is to move forward, those in the field must invite the voices of everyone who is committed to the vision of equity.

From the very beginning, we knew that engaging the reader in self-reflection would be the most important outcome of this book. Reflection, defined as serious thought or consideration of one's actions, provides one with the opportunity to learn from and through their experiences. As teachers, self-reflection requires us to pay close attention to our daily actions within and outside of the school environment. Self-reflection is a vehicle for continuous improvement and lifelong learning.

HOW TO BECOME A
SELF-REFLECTIVE TEACHER

First, you simply make a conscious effort to do so. You must review your actions, question your methods and decide where and how to improve. Effective teachers must also be students— always learning.

Secondly, find mentors who will support you. They can give you an outsider's viewpoint as you reflect and hold you accountable for your actions. Also, mentors can offer great advice and encouragement. As teachers, our words and actions can reverberate for a lifetime. The importance of our jobs and our training cannot be taken lightly.

Thirdly, challenge yourself. Hidden bias lurks in the darkest corners of our sub-conscious. For this reason, we must become aware of our hidden biases, prejudices and stereotypical thinking. With new awareness, we become better teachers. It can be eye-opening. If we are open-minded to the idea that we may hold prejudices deep inside, it will be effective. This willingness to admit to one's weaknesses is key to becoming a reflective teacher and ultimately, an effective teacher. (Sansbury, 2011, paras. 6–7)

Recommended Uses for This Book

This book is designed to function as a professional learning tool for practitioners working to create more culturally responsive school and classroom environments for their culturally diverse gifted and talented students. By providing readers with a collection of essays by educational advocates for students of traditionally marginalized populations, we hope to increase the cultural competence of teachers and school leaders. Organized in three sections—Culturally Responsive Practices; Race, Ethnicity, and Culture; and Gender, Sex, and Sense of Self—these authors provide their personal insights into the implicit biases that exist within our educational system as a whole, and gifted programs specifically. Lived experiences clearly articulate the critical need to implement culturally responsive teaching and build cultural competence to serve diverse student populations.

This book may be used as a supplementary text for university courses with a focus on gifted, creative, and talented studies, and by practitioners committed to understanding implicit biases as well as the students with whom they work. Educators and school leaders may find it useful in professional learning settings for practitioners (e.g., workshops, book studies, professional learning communities, etc.).

We encourage you to use the reflective questions found on page 12 at the beginning and end of your journey. As a preassessment and postassessment, the questions ask you to reflect on your own personal implicit biases and classroom practices related to the diverse populations of gifted and talented students in our schools. We also ask you to consider how you support all students and nurture agency within your class. The Reflections on Classroom Practice Survey, found in Appendix A on page 252, serves as an evaluation of your current status as a culturally responsive teacher and a road map for students and teachers to becoming lifelong learners.

A printable version of the Reflections on Classroom Practice Survey is available on this book's webpage at https://www.prufrock. com/Culturally-Responsive-Teaching-in-Gifted-Education-Resources.aspx.

As educators, we have to continually reflect upon our own implicit biases and understand how they affect our interactions with students and colleagues, and then we must do the work that is necessary to become a little more woke each and every day. Our students and communities are watching us—they recognize bias and internalize microaggressions. Our actions speak louder than words. We must do better. We can do better. We will do better.

This is our hope for you. As you read these essays, we ask you to reflect deeply on your own journey and how you will continue to grow and understand the value of engaging in culturally responsive practices within your schools and classrooms.

Reference

Sansbury, S. (2011, December 29). *Reflection: Crucial for effective teachers.* Learning for Justice. https://www.learningforjustice.org/magazine/reflection-crucial-for-effective-teachers

Introduction

Acknowledging the Past, Committing to the Future

Joy Lawson Davis

These are pivotal times. On every front, there is turmoil, upheaval, questioning, shifting of views in ways that have the potential to create significant and lasting change to the human condition. As a society, we experienced two distinct, yet overlapping pandemics. For a number of reasons, both pandemics disproportionately affected the lives of groups that we often call disenfranchised, marginalized, or off from the center or majority of our nation's core. These marginalized groups suffer the most when access to resources is limited. Inequitable access then causes limitations on achievement of goals and realization of dreams. The health pandemic and the battle over our democracy have occurred simultaneously, impacting the lives of our most vulnerable communities, families, and students in immeasurable ways. As a result of this upheaval, change is occurring on every front. This book will help educators everywhere gain greater insight into the daily lived experiences of our most vulnerable student populations, the complexities of the multiple identities they hold, and how to reach them in ways that will support their becoming the ingenious, productive, compassionate individuals they were born to be.

The educational arena is in flux. So much has happened in the past few years to bring what we do in the name of schooling to the attention of the general public. Currently, our schools are creating teaching and learning environments in uncharted territories. Virtual learning—where millions of students are using technology at home to learn in unique and challenging ways—and hybrid learning are becoming the norm in schools across the nation in all geographic locations. These new learning modes were precipitated by the need to respond in a healthy manner to the unprecedented COVID-19 pandemic affecting communities worldwide. These changes in learning modalities came at a time when public education was being challenged to be more equitable, to rid itself of generations of systemic racism, sexism, and discriminatory distribution of resources, and during a time of skewed views of students based on skin color, identities, and the size of their parents' bank accounts. When educational policies are challenged in this way, too often the fix is do what appears to be in the best interest of the general public rather than those most in need of public education's attention.

This book will help educators everywhere gain greater insight into the daily lived experiences of our most vulnerable student populations.

As change occurs in these pivotal times, a few questions come to mind: How do we, as educators, equitably and appropriately address the academic and psychosocial strengths of all students while providing support for their individual and group needs? How can we ensure that what we do for one group of students does not place another group at an unfair disadvantage? How can we create teaching and learning environments that empower all students to grow into their destiny with compassion, empathy, and a sense of service to others? How do we ensure that the similarities within groups are valued as much as the distinctions between them? How can we be sure that those students with gifted potential within each group have access to all of the opportunities needed to help them reach their individual goals?

This book has been written to respond to these questions and more. Although this book answers many of these questions, it does not provide all of the answers. As educators, we have learned that our students have the potential to teach us as much as we believe we can teach them. They teach us by the example of their rich heritages, their ethnic and racial traits, their resilience in the face of traumatic circumstances, their historical legacies, and the multiple ways they demonstrate their gifts. They are teaching us how to be sensitive to their gender identities in ways that the previous generations of educators were not equipped for and so much more. This book was written for educators who are willing to learn more about how they can improve their own skills to work with the gifted among the varied populations of students in our schools and to see them, understand them, and value them for who they truly are.

The Critical Need to Address Diversity Equity, Inclusion, and Antiracism

As educators, we are being called on to be more culturally competent to address diversity, equity, inclusion, and antiracism (DEIA) goals in our schools. Gifted students, across groups, are some of the most outspoken, empathetic, and sensitive students in our schools. It is imperative that DEIA goals are fully integrated into comprehensive programming for gifted students. Gifted students are at the forefront of peaceful protesting of the inequities that exist in our society. These ongoing protests are happening worldwide. We are no longer in a time when we can afford to ignore the systemic discrimination, racism, and sexism that has disabled marginalized populations and restricted their access to high-end curriculum and instructional experiences. We know better now how this access can be provided. When we know better, we do better.

It is not simply that there are more students from diverse communities in our schools; what we have become more aware of are the complex differences and needs of these diverse populations. The students for whom we are responsible are different due in part to their race and ethnicity, language, geography, other exceptional conditions, gender identity, and economic backgrounds. Within the gifted education community, some of these students are the ones who are most likely to be among the overlooked and marginalized due to long-term systemic discriminatory practices. They are more likely to be among students disproportionately and unfairly disciplined, be misdiagnosed and placed in special education classrooms, and be victims of bullying. They are less likely to graduate from high school and less likely to enter and complete college. The practices that led to their disenfranchised conditions persist even to this day as more and more students and their advocates are coming forward to overtly express their disdain for discrimination and prejudicial behaviors within school communities.

Culturally Responsive Teaching: Response to Difference That Makes a Difference

The framework for this book comes from the groundbreaking work of Dr. Geneva Gay and Dr. Gloria Ladson-Billings, two Black female scholars who created a foundation for what we know as culturally responsive teaching (CRT), or culturally responsive pedagogies. Both Gay (2000) and Ladson-Billings (1995) provided definitions and descriptions of what educators can do to create culturally responsive teaching and learning environments in schools. In their work, they promoted the alignment of school environments with the cultural norms, traditions, and legacies of students from racially diverse groups, in particular, students of color whose achievement typically has lagged behind that of White peers in schools across the nation.

The constructs that became the foundation for culturally responsive pedagogies more than 4 decades ago continue to provide the foundation for educators and advocates with sensitivity and compassion for underserved, disenfranchised students. Theorists have devoted their lives to the work of teaching the wider community the critical need for culturally responsive practice (e.g., Davis, 2019; Edmin, 2016; Love, 2019).

The essays in this book use CRT to place students at the center of the teaching and learning process. To do this, as educators, we must know our students. We must know their strengths, their needs, their cultural backgrounds, their communities, and their families. We must know all of their multiple identities that shape their every experience.

> ## As educators, we must know our students.

This book has also taken the bold step to expand the use of CRT to include meeting the needs of other marginalized and often overlooked students—those who are twice-exceptional (2e), those from rural communities, and those with varied gender and sexual identities, more commonly known as LGBTQ+ students. 2e students are underachieving in our schools at tragic rates, students from rural communities lack access to enhanced experiences that can be provided by universities, and LGBTQ+ students suffer from victimization in schools because they are misunderstood and disrespected.

The goal in using CRT as a framework for this text is to provide educators—teachers, paraprofessionals, counselors, school staff, and administrators—with firsthand knowledge about the strengths and needs of each student group represented. In doing so, we, the editors, strive to empower educators to build equity-based, culturally responsive programming that will grow our gifted and advanced learner programs into demographically representative spaces that afford each student the best opportunity to develop and grow.

Expanding Culturally Responsive Practice

Ladson-Billings (1995) described the essential components of culturally relevant pedagogy as:

1. a focus on teaching and learning, assuming that children are already equipped with knowledge that teachers can use to build upon;

2. the presumption that knowledge is constructed and can be used toward the eradication of social injustices that students are exposed to, and that the role of the teacher and students is never neutral but situated sociopolitically, socioculturally, and sociohistorically; and

3. the understanding that cultural competence occurs when teachers accept themselves and their students as cultural beings (i.e., teachers must understand and can use their students' cultures as teaching and learning is designed and implemented).

Using the foundation of the early scholars, Davis et al. (2020) further delineated the following as principles of culturally responsive teaching for gifted learners. A culturally responsive educator:

» provides curricular materials developed by and for diverse cultural groups in classrooms/schools (ensuring representational and authentic visual imagery, literature, philosophies, norms, and traditions);

» develops instruction to accentuate/build upon student strengths (i.e., teaching from a strengths perspective);

» disallows use of derogatory, stereotypical, negative phrases and terms to refer to individuals or groups (establishing a microaggression-free environment);

» creates genuine trusting relationships with students by experiencing their families, cultures, and environments through cross-cultural experiences;

» involves parents/families/community leadership as "cultural agents" in the instructional program and partnering on a regular basis (they know their community strengths and can serve as models of gifted individuals who have excelled across domains despite societal challenges); and

» integrates the authentic history of all immigrant and native groups across the disciplines (Native American, African American, Asian American, Caucasian, Hispanic American, Middle Eastern, first generation immigrants from around the world).

As teachers engage with gifted learners across diverse population groups, using culturally responsive teaching pedagogies provides the ideal pathway to promoting and supporting high-end, analytical curriculum experiences that provide opportunities for all students to develop questioning skills, probe deeply while mastering content, respond sensitively and compassionately to the human condition, and create innovative solutions to problems and injustices plaguing their own communities.

Using culturally responsive teaching pedagogies brings students' culture/psychosocial needs and understandings into the classroom, creating instruction that builds on students' prior knowledge and everyday lived experiences. It is this basis that enables educators to expand or broaden the meaning of culturally responsive teaching to include meeting the needs of diverse students based upon income, geography, gender, and/or sexual orientation. For example, a student whose everyday lived experience is impacted by poverty brings to the classroom an understanding of the value of individual effort and creativity that students from other more affluent environments may not equally possess.

> *Using culturally responsive teaching*
> *pedagogies brings students'*
> *culture/psychosocial needs and*
> *understandings into the classroom.*

Gender and Sexual Identities of Gifted Students. Similarly, CRT allows educators to consider the ways that gender and sexual identity affect students' ability, exposure, and achievement. Gender and sexual orientation as a social identity opens the way for the application of psychosocial understandings of how students from various groups view the world. Dispelling myths around gender and sexual identities is critical in order for children and youth to fully experience the value of schooling. Myths surrounding "what boys do" versus "what girls do" can be dispelled when teachers create gender-neutral classroom environments, do not hold students to antiquated views of femininity and masculinity, and allow students to experience and respond to instruction in ways that are most comfortable for them as individuals. This book confronts myths and breaks down barriers regarding gender and sexual identity. Classrooms that are open and available to students across the LGBTQ+ spectrum provide much better opportunities for giftedness to be fully developed outside of the myths of gender and sex. Here again, as educators consider the daily lived experiences of students with varied gender and sexual orientation identities, it is important that students' cultural needs be understood and met in classrooms and schools across the nation. Including gender and sexual orientation as a cultural identity issue in this manner is apropos.

Gifted Students in Rural Communities. In expanding culturally responsive understandings, educators must also recognize the impact of different geographic conditions on students' access to enrichment and acceleration opportunities. In particular, understanding the identity, academic, and psychosocial needs of students from rural communities in America is critical. Rurality in itself is a distinct identity (Chambers et al., 2019). Students who live in rural communities are physically alienated and far too often lack access to academic and enrichment opportunities in which their more urban and suburban counterparts are able to participate (e.g., museums, colleges, universities, business and research centers, hospitals, and more). Being from a rural area does not limit students' intelligence or capacity for understanding complex concepts. Being from a rural area, however, does involve social norms that may shape students' understanding of their place. Additionally, the limitations of resources can impact self-esteem. Ensuring that gifted students from rural communities have access and exposure to advanced instruction, acceleration opportunities, research, and mentoring experiences can greatly impact their chances for success in areas of strengths and interest.

Intersectionality and Culturally Responsive Teaching for Gifted Learners

Creating an expanded vision of culturally responsive teaching is one of this book's key goals. Further, as the editors, we want to highlight the intersectionality of social identities that require educators to be more inclusive and welcoming in their behaviors toward all gifted students. Intersectionality is not a new concept (for review, see Crenshaw, 1989). Crenshaw, a law professor who coined the term in a 1989 article, recently described intersectionality as:

basically a lens, a prism, for seeing the way in which various forms of inequality often operate together and exacerbate each other. We tend to talk about race inequality as separate from inequality based on gender, class, sexuality or immigrant status. What's often missing is how some people are subject to all of these, and the experience is not just the sum of its parts. (Steinmetz, 2020, para. 2)

Gifted students often navigate these multiple worlds of inequity as they develop intellectually, psychosocially, and academically. Without an understanding of the impact of intersectionality on gifted students' experiences, teachers often only consider their intellectual capacity and not how their other identities frame their very existence. For students who have been underserved—whether they are Black, Brown, from a low-income household, or twice-exceptional—their social identities exacerbate the inequities they face daily. For example, a gifted Black female who may be twice-exceptional and living in poverty is less likely than her White male peers to be identified and receive gifted education services due to the impact of racism, sexism, and her school and teachers' lack of understanding of twice-exceptional learners. It is the responsibility of educators to recognize and understand the complexities of the multiple worlds wherein their students exist.

> *For students who have been underserved*
> *... their social identities exacerbate*
> *the inequities they face daily.*

Being gifted and from a low-income background carries with it a number of challenges, as does being twice-exceptional and/or being LGBTQ+, gifted, and from a rural community. Some of the social identities and variables that our student must navigate include:

» income status,
» region (rural, urban, suburban),
» ethnicity and race,
» neighborhood,
» multiple exceptionalities,
» gender identities and sexual orientation,

> » oppressed group status,
> » language, and
> » gifted and talented abilities.

All of these identities impact the functioning of our gifted learners on a daily basis. When working with these students, it is important for educators to recognize and fully understand how these intersectional identities shape a student's experience and how they respond to the world. Just as important, however, is for educators to not get "hung up" on labels and instead ensure that they treat each student individually, appreciating the intellectual, academic, and social-emotional capabilities that they bring to the classroom. We believe that the essays in this book will help readers better understand the needs of all students.

Opportunity to Reflect

This book was written based on the expert authors' personal experiences. We intentionally created the book to help educators recognize their culture and social identities—who they are, what prior experiences shaped their growth and development, and how they continue to evolve as lifelong learners. As the early CRT theorists noted, it is important for all educators to recognize their own cultural identities before they can understand and support the cultural identities of their students. We have high hopes for this book to benefit educators, students, advocates, policymakers, and even the families of our gifted learners as we all work together to improve teaching and learning conditions for the special populations of gifted learners.

The change or shift in behaviors of educators can make the difference for so many students who are intellectually, spiritually, creatively, and academically gifted, particularly those who originate from groups that have been long overlooked and underserved by school programs. Being a member of a racially diverse group, coming from a low-income environment, identifying as LGBTQ+, having other exceptional conditions, or living in a rurally isolated community should not keep highly able students from reaching their promise in any area of human endeavor. More importantly, as educators consider the needs of these students, it is critically important to get to know them as intersectional beings and to be as familiar as possible with the multiple worlds they navigate every day. As educators, it is not enough to focus all of our attention on students' capacity for academic achievement. We must come to understand their multiple and intersectional cultural and social identities, and use their lived experiences to create effective culturally responsive educational environments where they can be their best selves and flourish as they accomplish their goals and become fully whole and accepting of their own true being.

> *It is critically important to get to know [students] as intersectional beings and to be as familiar as possible with the multiple worlds they navigate every day.*

As You Read . . .

Each essay in this book focuses attention on enabling readers to become more culturally responsive as leaders in schools and in their classrooms. In addition, at the end of this book, we have provided tools for your use as you begin to apply what you have learned to your own environment. Our goal is to empower you to become more knowledgeable about, and sensitive to, the impact of culture on the lives of the gifted students you serve. We believe that the expert authors' essays and the resources they provide will help you meet this goal. You can use the Reflection on Self section on the following page as a self-assessment to guide you through thinking about how to use the content in each chapter. The questions are specifically designed to help readers make the best use of the expert content provided throughout the book.

REFLECTION ON SELF

1. In what ways do I acknowledge and address my own implicit bias?

2. In what ways do I address biases that are present in my school?

3. In what ways do I help students understand their own cultural biases?

4. In what ways do I advocate for the diverse representation of students in my school environment?

5. In what ways do I make sure all students have a voice in shaping the school environment?

6. In what ways do I communicate high expectations for all students?

7. In what ways do I make my instruction relevant to students' experiences?

8. In what ways do I encourage students to be respectful of others and their perspectives?

9. In what ways do I foster collaboration among students?

10. In what ways do I engage students in their learning, and in my own learning?

11. In what ways do I encourage students to become problem solvers in their own and the global community?

12. In what ways do I engage the agency of family and community?

13. In what ways do I increase access to opportunities for students both inside and outside of school?

14. In what ways do I incorporate students' lived experiences into my own personal growth?

References

Chambers, C., Crumb, L., & Harris, C. (2019). A call for dreamkeepers in rural United States: Considering the postsecondary aspirations of rural ninth graders. *Theory & Practice in Rural Education, 9*(1), 7–22. https://doi.org/10.3776/tpre.2019.v9n1p7-22

Crenshaw, K. (1989). Demarginalizing the intersection of race and sex: A Black feminist critique of antidiscrimination doctrine, feminist theory and anti-racist politics. *University of Chicago Legal Forum, 1989*(1), 139–167.

Davis, J. L. (2019). Reframing professional learning of teachers working with culturally diverse students. In A. M. Novak & C. L. Weber (Eds.), *Best practices in professional learning and teacher preparation: Special topics for gifted professional development* (Vol. 2, pp. 51–67). Prufrock Press.

Davis, J. L., Floyd, E. F., & Roberson, J. J. (2020, November). The 4Rs: A new framework for teaching diverse learners. *Teaching for High Potential,* 17, 23.

Edmin, C. (2016). *For White folks who teach in the hood . . . and the rest of y'all too: Reality pedagogy and urban education.* Beacon Press.

Gay, G. (2000). *Culturally responsive teaching: Theory, research, and practice.* Teachers College Press.

Ladson-Billings, G. (1995). Toward a theory of culturally relevant pedagogy. *American Educational Research Journal, 32*(3), 465–491. https://doi.org/10.3102/00028312032003465

Love, B. L. (2019). *We want to more than just survive: Abolitionist teaching and the pursuit of educational freedom.* Beacon Press.

Steinmetz, K. (2020, February 20). *She coined the term 'intersectionality' over 30 years ago. Here's what it means to her today.* Time. https://time.com/5786710/kimberle-crenshaw-intersectionality

Culturally Responsive Practices

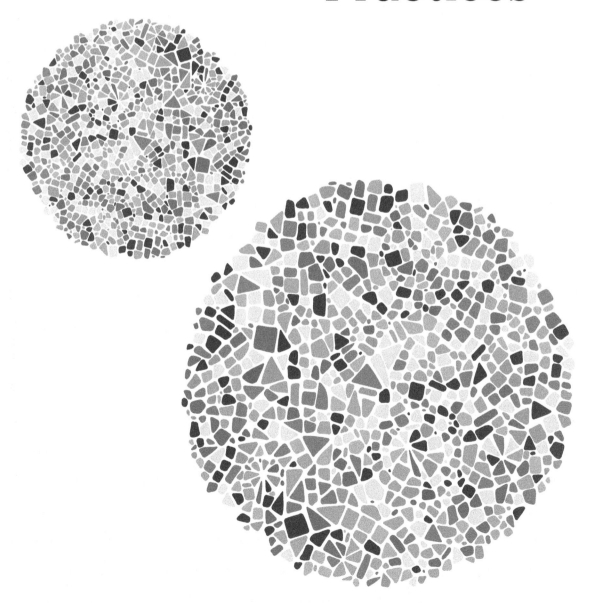

Introduction to Culturally Responsive Teaching Practices

Javetta Jones Roberson

How can we reform education without understanding
the realities of the people we serve?
—Dr. Muhammad Khalifa

Understanding the realities of students served in today's schools
is critical to supporting and meeting students' needs. Education continues to evolve. Schools are not the same as they were 5 years ago.
Educators must face reality and accept that reform and change can be
good for our students and schools. Change can serve as a catalyst for
innovation and spark creativity. Change can present opportunities for

improvement. The essays in this section look at the interconnected shifts that are needed within our educational system to meet the needs of our increasingly diverse populations in schools—shifts in environment, self-refection, perspective, and practice.

A Shift in Environment

Many stakeholders may ask, "What does school climate have to do with gifted services?" Gifted and advanced students are served in schools; therefore, school climate is an essential component of academic success. School climate should reflect the lived experiences of the students, personnel, and parents related to the norms, beliefs, and values that shape their school community (Cohen et al., 2009). A school's climate can support a student's social-emotional health and academic achievement. The reality is that it can either positively or negatively shape students' educational experiences. As educators assess school climate through a culturally responsive lens, it's important to reflect on how the learning environment can affect various student populations. Historically, White students and students of color experience school differently, making it necessary to consider race when assessing school climate (Shirley & Cornell, 2011).

A Shift in Self-Reflection

The presence of implicit bias in our society cannot be denied. Implicit bias has been characterized as an unobservable structure in the mind of an individual that can navigate behavior in an unconscious manner (Amodio & Mendoza, 2010). It may conflict with a person's stated beliefs or values. Implicit biases are often rooted in cultural and racial stereotypes, and their persistence and power have been linked to a strong lack of personal awareness (Devine et al., 2012). Educators who lack personal awareness may also display microaggressions toward students—brief, everyday exchanges that deliver subtle reminders or demeaning messages about racial stereotypes (Sue, 2010). These microaggressions can influence the inequities that exist for racially, culturally, ethnically, and linguistically diverse (RCELD) students in gifted and advanced programs. Educator implicit bias is capable of affecting student outcomes and overall achievement and may influence educators' evaluation of students' academic potential or performance (Papageorge et al., 2016). This deficit perspective can be a detriment to students' educational experience. Therefore, a shift in critical self-reflection must occur to address implicit bias. Being self-reflective involves taking into consideration possible consequences of one's beliefs with the purpose of intentionally changing professional practice (Fook & Askeland, 2007). When biases are removed, educators are left with the ability to base decisions, thoughts, and judgments merely on relationships with students. Further, research suggests that it is possible to recognize implicit bias in oneself and learn techniques to overcome such perceptions and increase positive social interactions (Carter et al., 2017).

A Shift in Perspective

In order to address racial disparities, educators must first acknowledge the systemic racism that exists in education. Being antiracist means increasing self-awareness and speaking out about the causes of these racial inequities. As educators make the journey toward becoming antiracist, they come to understand the varying types of racism. They may also educate peers who may be unaware of their own privilege.

> *Being antiracist means increasing self-awareness and speaking out about the causes of these racial inequities.*

Antiracist educators believe in the power of continuous advocacy for systemic educational change and reform. Their teaching is directly aligned with culturally responsive practice because both are grounded in a social justice pedagogy to ensure teaching practices reflect the realities of students' lived experiences. Antiracist teaching not only acknowledges that racism exists, but also commits itself continuously to the struggle of fighting for racial justice (Love, 2019). These educators understand that the inclusion of texts written by authors from diverse backgrounds alone does little when implemented within a system that still prioritizes racist policies and practices in schools (Neville, 2020).

A Shift in Practice

Culturally responsive pedagogy was developed as a framework to guide and challenge teachers who serve in multicultural educational contexts (Gay, 2018). Culturally responsive pedagogy is foundational in transforming the educational experience of RCELD students. Culturally responsive pedagogy has evolved into systemic practices that incorporate students' cultures and lived experiences to expand learning opportunities across various disciplines. Although culturally responsive practice is instrumental in the academic success of RCELD students, it was never the property of any one ethnic group (Brown-Jeffy & Cooper, 2011). Culturally responsive practice is beneficial for all student groups, as it is meant to empower students by incorporating social, political, and community variables in curriculum and instruction. Culturally responsive practice helps educators and students understand the impact that social oppression has on communities and translates this understanding into engagement and teaching strategies (Blitz et al., 2020). As educators incorporate cultural responsiveness into their teaching and leading practices, their aim is to address systems of oppression head on. These individuals refuse to remain neutral on issues of marginalization and racial injustices. Culturally responsive educators seek to disrupt and resist oppressive practices that are aimed at RCELD students.

The Need for Change

The issues of systemic inequities, racial disparities, and institutional barriers for RCELD students will continue to emerge in our society and our schools. To work to address these inequities, educators must be willing to recognize and acknowledge that these issues exist. Educators must also be a part of conversations, solutions, and interventions to dismantle barriers. The roots of these disparities in our schools and our society are many centuries deep. Implementing strategies such as cultural responsiveness and antiracist teaching as a means to adapt policy, practice, and preparation of educators can help eradicate these disparities.

References

Amodio, D. M., & Mendoza, S. A. (2010). Implicit intergroup bias: Cognitive, affective, and motivational underpinnings. In B. Gawronski & B. K. Payne (Eds.), *Handbook of implicit social cognition: Measurement, theory, and applications* (pp. 353–374). The Guilford Press.

Blitz, L. V., Yull, D., & Clauhs, M. (2020). Bringing sanctuary to school: Assessing school climate as a foundation for culturally responsive trauma-informed approaches for urban schools. *Urban Education, 55*(1), 95–124. https://doi.org/10.1177/0042085916651323

Brown-Jeffy, S., & Cooper, J. E. (2011). Toward a conceptual framework of culturally relevant pedagogy: An overview of the conceptual and theoretical literature. *Teacher Education Quarterly, 38*(1), 65–84.

Carter, P. L., Skiba, R., Arredondo, M. I., & Pollock, M. (2017). You can't fix what you don't look at: Acknowledging race in addressing racial discipline disparities. *Urban Education, 52*(2), 207–235. https://doi.org/10.1177/0042085916660350

Cohen, J., McCabe, L., Michelli, N. M., & Pickeral, T. (2009). School climate: Research, policy, practice, and teacher education. *Teachers College Record, 111*(1), 180–213.

Devine, P. G., Forscher, P. S., Austin, A. J., & Cox, W. T. L. (2012). Long-term reduction in implicit race bias: A prejudice habit-breaking intervention. *Journal of Experimental Social Psychology, 48*(6), 1267–1278. https://doi.org/10.1016/j.jesp.2012.06.003

Fook, J., & Askeland, G. A. (2007). Challenges of critical reflection: "Nothing ventured, nothing gained." *Social Work Education, 26,* 520–533. https://doi.org/10.1080/02615470601118662

Gay, G. (2018). *Culturally responsive teaching: Theory, research, and practice* (3rd ed.). Teachers College Press.

Love, B. L. (2019). *We want to do more than survive: Abolitionist teaching and the pursuit of educational freedom.* Beacon Press.

Neville, M. J. (2020). 'I can't believe I didn't learn this in school': 'Refusing secondly' as an anti-racist English education framework. *Changing English, 27*(2), 193–207.

Papageorge, N. W., Gershenson, S., & Kang, K. (2016, August). Teacher expectations matter. *IZA Discussion Paper Series,* Article 10165. http://ftp.iza.org/dp10165.pdf

Shirley, E. L. M., & Cornell, D. G. (2011). The contribution of student perceptions of school climate to understanding the disproportionate punishment of African American students in a middle school. *School Psychology International, 33*(2), 115–134. https://doi.org/10.1177/0143034311406815

Sue, D. W. (2010). *Microaggressions in everyday life: Race, gender, and sexual orientation.* Wiley.

1

School Climate Change

Requiring Understanding of Our Students and Community

Jeff Danielian

The 21st century has brought to the forefront the issue of climate change. I am not speaking about the ecological phenomenon we now find ourselves grappling with on the planet that we inhabit, but about the change that has been happening in schools across the nation. School climate affects student populations, including many of our nation's high-ability students—and among them capable learners from underserved groups, such as those living in low-income environments, English language learners, and those from racial or minority groups, who all too often go unrecognized. As our student population becomes increasingly diverse, it is imperative that educators understand how to equitably serve students who historically have been underrepresented in gifted education programs and services. The message is clear. All of us must regularly strive to look beyond the surface of what it means to create a positive climate in educational settings. We need this important inclusive perspective in our schools and classrooms, our curriculum, our students, and ourselves. It begins with insight into and understanding of school climate, and it needs to begin now.

The efforts of those involved in education never cease to impress me. From the bottom up or top down, the trials and tribulations faced on every level, and over time, are enough to frazzle even the strongest of resolves. The kindergartner with the oversized backpack becomes the hopeful college freshman. A first-year teacher, lesson plans in hand, blooms into a mentor, guide, and expert educator. Administrators, glassy-eyed and tired amidst mountains of paperwork and decision making, find a way to manage and lead. Advocates press on tirelessly, and writers and researchers alike offer solutions and ideas through the products of years of thought and study. Each situation presents a continuous journey, for all involved play a part in this giant perpetual educational engine, seeking to create a schoolwide culture and climate that takes into consideration both the great diversity of a student body and every aspect of the learning process. The key to success lies in continual commitment, understanding, communication, and an endless pursuit of knowledge of best practices. The educational field needs teachers equipped with the knowledge that at any time, on any occasion, and in a variety of situations, student passions and interests, once observed, can be cultivated into educational success. Couple that with teacher and administrative training focused on the areas of implicit bias, antiracist understandings, and what it means to teach in a culturally responsive way, and you have a recipe for positive climate change.

The key to success lies in continual commitment, understanding, communication, and an endless pursuit of knowledge of best practices.

Defining School Climate

Ross (2013) stated that an equitable school climate responds to the wide range of cultural norms, goals, values, interpersonal relationships, leadership practices, and organizational structures within the broader community. It is my objective here to touch upon these elements, expand upon them, and offer suggestions on how to accomplish the immense but necessary goal of ensuring an equitable school climate. I begin by looking at what it means to create a community where constant and open communication between all parties involved sets the foundation. From there I move to strategies that offer ways to understand and serve individual student needs, with an emphasis on the consideration of cultural norms and values, taking into account each student's varied educational, familial, and social settings. The value of planning and creating a welcoming physical environment follows, and I conclude with a discussion of the significance of culturally relevant curricular planning and the importance of utilizing the alternative methods of delivery available.

School climate sets the stage for the education that will follow. Changing it will not happen overnight, but if those of us involved can approach the task with motivation, knowing that it will take time and an awareness of what is needed to accomplish change, we have made a start.

FIVE KEY ATTRIBUTES TO ACHIEVE HIGH ACADEMIC SUCCESS FOR ALL STUDENTS

(Howard, 2010)

1. Visionary leadership
2. Effective instructional practices
3. Intensive academic interventions
4. Explicit acknowledgement of race
5. Parental and community engagement

Creating a Community

I have always been fascinated by the term *community*. The idea that a group of people with common values, resources, needs, and understandings can live together in an organized and supportive way sounds like the ideal situation for anyone to be a part of. It has been a welcome change in recent years to observe communities opting to "buy local" and "go green," all in an effort to support small business and protect the environment. I'm elated to see Main Street returning, neighbors chatting, and streets safer. I wish I could say the same for our educational communities. Diminished budgets, standardized tests, lowered learning ceilings, and a general neglect for the identification and service of our most highly able students are felt from district to district across the country. For school leaders and educators who know how to properly create a welcoming climate for their students, the challenges they face are often related to support, time, space, resources, and funding. In addition, educators must find ways to combat the ever-changing internal and external factors that can hinder the creation of a sustainable and successful classroom climate and, in turn, the educational growth of their students. High-potential students are in classrooms across our country, but their ability will not be fully realized without teachers who are supported in their efforts to find and cultivate that hidden potential, all in a climate that is conducive to individual growth and success.

Cultural competence requires a commitment from all within the school community. This includes having high expectations and demonstrated respect and value for all students, utilizing student-centered instruction, expanding the classroom to the larger community for understanding and collaboration, and having administrators and school leaders who support a level of experimentation that allows teachers to try new teaching and learning strategies that may not have been approved or considered in the past.

Communication within a community is key to building cultural competence. The use of online classroom and school portals, newsletters, blogs, and town hall forums and meetings as places where cultural conversations and discussions can flourish will only strengthen the relationships between home and school, teacher and student, and parent and teacher. Passing along valuable and up-to-date information, maintaining dialogue, and offering the opportunity for all voices to be heard will ensure that the roots of community will take hold. Educators must come to know and understand the community they serve, and establishing open, honest, and accepting lines of communication ensures that a diverse group of voices can and will be heard.

Frequent distribution of schoolwide climate surveys can serve as a pathway to determining areas of strengths and weaknesses. Knowing how well the school community is addressing cultural competence is important and provides a dual benefit. For those within the school building, it offers feedback from students and parents, who, in turn, can observe firsthand the dedication and commitment of administrators and teachers. Changing the school climate is an ongoing process, evolving as time goes on. Educators should recognize that diversity within a school population is an asset—and one that must be taken seriously.

Community outreach, in and outside of the classroom, can provide opportunities to connect to local businesses, professionals, artists, and advocates, where a wide range of diverse expertise can be shared with the school population, benefiting not only classroom instruction, but also the entire school community. Students can see the value of their extended environment, and the community at large can recognize future leaders. Engaging professionals from similar backgrounds helps students increase their sense of identity and belonging, as well as their potential for success in the future.

Parents and relatives can further contribute to the cultural climate of the school by offering to come into the classroom to share their own cultural experiences, beliefs, and values. It can be very powerful for students to observe that their peers come from different environments and situations. An added bonus is for teachers themselves to share their own stories and histories.

Perhaps it is time to welcome the "local" appeal to education, taking cues from societal shifts occurring in our country. As educators, we can make our schools the places to go to "learn local." We can celebrate diversity and cultural differences in everything we do. We can create the climate change we need.

Understanding Each Student

No matter our situation, as school leaders and educators, we need to be supported in our endeavors to create classroom climates that take into account the immense variation of students present in our schools. The children that make up our classrooms are different in so many ways. Each student requires numerous instructional strategies and personalized responses to ensure that classrooms are places where discovery and experience are the focal point, and where each student is treated and respected as an individual learner, with the potential to succeed in any area. Standards 3 and 4 of the National Association for Gifted Children's (NAGC, 2019) Pre-K–Grade 12 Gifted Programming Standards address responsiveness to diversity and cultural competence by asking educators to focus on the value of language, heritage, and circumstances and the use of positive approaches intended to address social issues, including discrimination and stereotyping. They can serve as a helpful guide.

Students need to feel welcomed, understood, respected, and encouraged to participate.

There are many things I've yet to learn about teaching, and one of the most important is how I can more fully understand each of my student's needs. This involves more than planning and delivering curriculum. For all educators, it means responding to and considering the infinite number of student questions, interests, and experiences that deserve individualized attention and consideration. It means that we need to be listening, and listening intently, because students will tell us what they need. And there will be some students that we just cannot seem to reach, and usually it is the teacher who needs to take a step back and recognize their own implicit biases. Assumptions and stereotypes about race, socioeconomic status, poverty, and language differences need to be recognized and addressed, for they can immediately create a barrier between the student and the teacher. Students need to feel welcomed, understood, respected, and encouraged to participate. Knowing that you may have these biases does not make you a bad educator; rather it allows you to change your perceptions and move in the right direction. This is the only way that the climate can truly improve. If you are unsure about your own implicit biases, a visit to Harvard University's Project Implicit (https://implicit.harvard.edu/implicit) can be quite eye-opening. Users can take a self-test in one of many areas, read research, and uncover truths about themselves they may not have known.

Any dedicated educator will tell you that our vocation involves creating a school and classroom climate that considers culture as well as students' social and emotional and instructional needs. In addition, we recognize that at the end of the day, our students return home to environments beyond our control and at times outside of our understanding. Teaching doesn't start at the first bell and end at dismissal. We think of our students when we get up in the morning and when we lay our heads down to sleep at night. We want them to find success, be able to work with others, understand themselves, problem solve, find solutions, be creative, and find safety and comfort in their classrooms. Davis (2015) noted that the greatest classroom setting that educators can provide is one that allows open discussions and develops resolutions to the problems that afflict society. Educators need to be "well-prepared, confident, and courageous enough to lead the conversations" (p. 5). In the end, we want our students to be the successful individuals we know they can be in the future. Creating a positive school climate also means that students who identify in multiple ways are valued and nurtured, which allows students to feel safer and more connected to their schools (Steele & Cohn-Vargas 2013).

Utilizing interest surveys, or brief questionnaires intended to have the students reflect upon their own passions and interests, provides a great way to start with a new group of students. These surveys allow for conversations to be had, groups to be formed, and connections to be made. In addition, learning style inventories, given with the intent of honing in on how each individual student likes to learn, provides the educator with options for varying the teaching environment so that all students feel connected. Lastly, projects with a directed focus or theme can offer pathways for students to express who they are and what they believe.

The more often students are offered the opportunity to truly be themselves, the more they will add to a positive climate for all. Classroom discussions about current events can reveal opinions and biases, and so it is vital that students and teachers receive instruction, resources, and training in order for them to come to understand and respect the similarities and differences between themselves and others. The outcome is students who possess a love for learning and an appreciation not only for the education they receive, but also for their peers and teachers. In this way, we can truly make education better for every student.

Physical Space Affects Climate

Students come to school with a sense of who they are, where they come from, and with varying expectations, depending on age. From the moment students enter the school building, they also begin to sense their surroundings, and their reactions to what they observe can play a large role in the creation of a climate where success and achievement are priorities. For students to feel welcome in their environment, there are some important things to consider: Do the faculty and staff reflect the diversity of the student population? Will students feel a sense of community and an overall family atmosphere? Do the building and its elements promote and celebrate diversity? Is there a sense of belonging and respect? Answers to these questions can inform administrators as they move forward to create a positive climate for all in the school community.

Faculty and staff hiring policies and practices must change to represent diversity. Positive messages, such as promoting respect and motivation for each individual student in the form of posters and banners, should grace each hallway and common space. Cases displaying trophies, awards, and other materials that celebrate a wide range of accomplishments and multiple standards of excellence should be visible and changed out often. Walls of success, or a hall of fame corridor, showcasing a range of diversity among alumni of the school can only add to a sense of belonging for each student. If schools show that they appreciate and celebrate diversity and individuality, then students will feel more comfortable when they enter the doors of the school and leave with a feeling that they are a part of something bigger.

Within the classroom, when teachers intentionally plan for students to regularly interact with everyone in a variety of ways, we support students' recognition and appreciation for the strengths and values of our increasingly diverse population. For example, in the classroom, desks or tables should be arranged to allow for multiple types of grouping and lots of movement and rotation. Just as teachers come to class with inherent implicit biases, so too do students. By offering opportunities for students to talk, share, and interact with each other, educators can cultivate a classroom climate where every voice, opinion, and belief is valued, respected, and, most importantly, heard.

Prominent individuals from various fields of study should be visible and celebrated. Simply putting posters up of ethnic or gender-specific scientists, for example, during a particular month of the year doesn't cut it. Such displays need to be there all the time and, again, changed out often. Students can be inspired by a wide range of professions and people, even those beyond the specific focus of the year's curriculum. It is our responsibility to offer as much as we can to encourage young minds to wonder and wander.

Curriculum for Change

To the noneducator, the process of teaching evokes images of lectures and note-taking, followed by a little Q&A, and concluded by a graded test. Exams and report cards sum up student understanding each quarter or trimester, and the same sequence of events repeats each year. Although design, delivery, and evaluation of instruction as they relate to curriculum make up a primary function of educators, those of us with dedication and enthusiasm for our profession know otherwise. We know that if we want to change the climate of learning in the classroom, we need to not only be passionate about the material we teach, but also present it and assess it with individuality and positive criticism.

Curricular design and implementation present a lifelong challenge. It is important to note that the strategies used by gifted and talented educators can, and should, be used for all students. We recognize that current events, emerging discoveries, and student questions and opinions constantly challenge the "planned" lesson. Differing levels of student ability, interest, and learning style dictate the language we use, the assignments and choices we give, the grouping choices we make, and the delivery methods of instruction. Evaluation and measure of proficiency take a variety of forms. Written comments or narratives personalize student learning in a way that grades do not. Individualized instruction and assessment allow for individual success. It is our responsibility to positively affirm each student's individual progress so that they feel a sense of accomplishment for themselves, even if there are areas to work on and improve. Assessments should be more about encouragement and less about demand. When students learn to value their own work and not see it as a competition or comparison with others in the class, they learn to respect each other's successes and failures, leveling the playing field and adding to a positive climate for all.

Reworking the curriculum to deliberately include cultural/racial references and supplemental resources from diverse authors can make learning experiences more robust and inclusive. Facilitating discussions about adversity, challenge, and failure, while illustrating the connection to the topics covered, exposes students to the realities of success and achievement. Offering times for students to share their personal stories, experiences, and opinions demonstrates the need for all to be involved and contribute.

Presenting content in a variety of ways can cater to a larger population of students and build their confidence in knowing that they now understand the material.

Differences in student backgrounds and cultural experiences also play a large role in their overall understanding of the concepts and themes covered in class, especially in ones that set high expectations for all students. The result can be students who feel left behind, detached from the conversation, and lost in a sea of unfamiliar terms and anecdotes. Educators can vary teaching styles and approaches to learning so that all students find a connection within a particular lesson or unit. By utilizing problem-solving techniques and critical thinking activities, educators can appeal to the nontraditional student, where imagery, metaphor, and creative thinking may be more valuable to understanding the topic at hand. Presenting content in a variety of ways can cater to a larger population of students and build their confidence in knowing that they now understand the material.

Resources, specifically those intended to change the climate of the classroom, can bring abstract and concrete connections to any curricular unit or class discussion. Accessed, pondered, and eventually presented during a class, these resources, and the lessons they have to teach, begin to take on a life of their own, and what was only imagined as a good idea translates into educational success. Students become enriched, empowered, and excited. The climate of learning changes. There is comfortability in the air.

It is time to discover or rediscover new and existing resources for use in educational environments. Try something innovative and make it yours. Be the awakening for your colleagues and students. Start small, and work toward a longer unit plan. Patience is the key, for these changes cannot take place immediately. It may come in the form of watching a documentary or film, reading a magazine or great book, engaging in a conversation with someone, or introducing these resources during a conference presentation. Curious teachers like me can be found scanning the Internet for other great ideas when time is available. You simply need to begin, recognizing at the start that sometimes things will not go according to plan. Once you begin this shift in practice, you will soon find that your classroom climate has changed, your lessons are better perceived, your teaching is more effective, and your students are better served.

Change Is Here

As often happens when routines become the norm, expectations and assumptions become part of the fabric of our lives. Statements such as, "That's the way it's always been," or "That's how we've always done things" are often the last words of a conversation. There are new developments in education concerning what works best to create a safe and enriching environment for our students. Utilizing them can ensure that students will develop a love for learning in a place they feel comfortable in.

Change is present—not on the horizon or in the proverbial winds, but right now. Change is here. Cultural values, societal issues, and public opinion are at the forefront of media coverage. Debate and conversation, either in person or via social media, communicates to an incalculable audience. Change also has affected the educational environment. You can find it in the positive attitudes regarding what it means to be a teacher in today's classrooms. It is present in the research and subsequent classroom practice inspired by the work of those who have the interests of student achievement at heart. Climate change isn't coming. It is here. New perspectives and initiatives regarding what works best for the students are happening now. It is a great feeling to see the change that has occurred. Now is the time to embrace it and set the standard for what should be.

We have the power to change the climate of our schools, the perspectives of our students, and our entire educational system. We have the power to recognize talent, serve the students identified, and pass on our understanding to other educators. We have the power to advocate—for ourselves, our students, and our profession. I am hopeful for the field of education, and I am hopeful for the future. I have to be. We have to be. Our students are depending on us.

References

Davis, J. L. (2015, Spring). Talking about race in middle and high school classrooms. *Teaching for High Potential,* 5–6.

Howard, T. C. (2010). *Why race and culture matter in schools: Closing the achievement gap in America's classrooms.* Teachers College Press.

National Association for Gifted Children. (2019). *2019 Pre-K–Grade 12 Gifted Programming Standards.* http://www.nagc.org/sites/default/files/standards/Intro%202019%20Programming%20Standards.pdf

Ross, R. (2013). School climate and equity. In T. Dary & T. Pickeral (Eds.), *School climate practices for implementation and sustainability* (School Climate Practice Brief No. 1). National School Climate Center.

Steele, D. M., & Cohn-Vargas, B. (2013). *Identity safe classrooms: Places to belong and learn.* Corwin.

2

Implicit Bias

Challenges in the Classroom

Nina Barbieri and Bernardo Pohl

Implicit bias is a term most of us have heard and something most of us have, unfortunately, experienced. Worse yet, implicit bias relates to thoughts that most of us are reluctant to admit we have had. Implicit biases are unconscious and involuntary thoughts, beliefs, attitudes, or stereotypes toward others based upon social categories such as race, social class, gender, and so forth (Marcucci, 2019). These subconscious beliefs are particularly tricky to uncover and root out, as they tend to operate autonomously and without deliberation (Alderson, 2017; Staats, 2015–2016). Unfortunately, one can quite easily, and unknowingly, internalize negative and harmful stereotypes; these can be undone, but only through intentional effort (Banaji & Greenwald, 2013; The Kirwan Institute, 2012). Of course, that requires one to be aware of their implicit biases.

Although implicit biases are not exclusively indicative of subsequently engaging in biased behaviors, research supports the correlation between implicit thoughts and explicit behaviors (Alderson, 2017). Moreover, there does appear to be a moderating impact dependent upon the type of bias assessed. That is, the relationship between implicit thought and explicit behavior appears to be stronger for political affiliation and race (Rudman, 2004a). This suggests that individuals having high levels of racial bias are more likely to also engage in prejudiced behaviors.

Imagine that you decide to uncover whether you have any implicit biases and take one of the many implicit association tests found online. To your dismay, your results indicate a preference to White people over Black people, or males over females, or some other partiality. What does this information tell you? And more importantly, does this information have an impact on subsequent behaviors when you interact with people in these demographics? Nina recently had her university students complete such an assignment, and to her intrigue, every student was absolutely appalled at the notion they had a preference. Their primary concern was whether it was possible that they had actually harmed another individual in the past. The students were so upset with themselves, as if they had somehow failed their own personal expectations that they had established.

General Impacts

Our actions are the social product of who we are, shaped by our experiences and the environment. Our world has contextualized our understanding of our surroundings. Implicit bias is the foundational attitude that directs our unconscious selves of our understanding and actions (Haslam, 2018; The Kirwan Institute, 2012). Implicit biases are not beliefs or actions we purposely (explicitly) choose. According to Haslam (2018), these are the messages and information that have been fueling our beliefs and attitudes since our early days, which, over time, we have come to accept as truth. Greenwald and Krieger (2006) referred to this as part of our "implicit cognition," which they defined as memory records that implicitly guide our subconscious actions, especially in the area of attitudes and stereotypes (pp. 946–948).

The origin of implicit bias is hard to pinpoint. However, there are several factors that are believed to contribute to a person's implicit bias. Rudman (2004a) categorized implicit bias as automatic social responses that are often not controllable without deep self-conscious examination. However, as we saw with Nina's students, even those willing to engage in the act of this introspection were so horrified at the implication of their results that it significantly impeded the ability to even have a conversation without some damage control.

Biases are part of our social norms. Biases also guide us with regard to the kind of social groups we belong to, and, at times, this can yield favorable results. We tend to act more favorably with people we can relate to. Consider, for example, teachers who pay more attention to students who remind them of their own children or people who show more empathy toward others who share similar backgrounds to them (Haslam, 2018). However, biases can have negative effects as well. These effects can manifest in a negative attitude toward a group of people or circumstances we do not understand (Galli et al., 2015).

> *Because implicit learned behavior is not a conscious act, it is believed that implicit bias is an emotionally learned behavior.*

According to Rudman (2004b), most of our implicit behavior is learned through early experiences, mostly during our preverbal years. This is an extension of Greenwald and Banaji's (1995) argument that our developmental events act as foundational bases that later serve as informational sources for our explicit conscious actions. This is what Rudman (2004b) referred to as "nonconscious sources" (p. 79). As such, we develop emotional, affective, and cultural implicit behaviors that are shaped by our experiences, fueling our implicit responses.

Because implicit learned behavior is not a conscious act, it is believed that implicit bias is an emotionally learned behavior. For instance, people tend to prefer women more than men if they were more attached to their mother during their early years. Studies have shown that White college students tend to have a more favorable view of Black students and feel less threatened after enrolling in a class with a Black professor (Rudman, 2004a, 2004b). In their research, Galli et al. (2015) found that wheelchair users among people who suffered a spinal cord injury tended to see each other positively as members of an exclusive group, yet they continued to associate the wheelchair with barriers and have negative feelings about their disability. Meanwhile, people who have had a disability their entire lives tend to see their disability more positively as a character-building instrument and less as a roadblock (Erevelles, 2006; Gabel & Danforth, 2002).

Lastly, some suggest that implicit bias is a social behavior that often forms through crowd membership and situational moments. Payne et al. (2017) defined this form of implicit bias as the "bias of crowds" (pp. 236–237). In this instance, subconscious behavior is shaped by our situational moments with the people who surround us, such as eating a full breakfast or heavy dinners with others when we travel and attend conferences, while at home we get through the morning with a simple cup of coffee and a small piece of toast or eat a simple salad for dinner. Gawronski and Bodenhausen (2017) argued that implicit bias can be attributed to "association activation" (pp. 268–269). In this case, implicit bias is activated by the environment, such as developing a more favorable view of a Black jazz singer at a night club and a less favorable impression of a Black person standing in a dark alley. Lastly, Rivers et al. (2017) looked at implicit bias as a series of intergroup behaviors, communicated over times, which can shape group outcomes or group rules over time.

In the end, it is clear that implicit bias is a learned behavior, although the exact conditions of how, when, and where it occurs and evolves have been harder to define. It is safe to conclude, therefore, that implicit bias has many factors and can occur under different circumstances, for instance, unexplained preferences that we have since our early age, automatic emotional triggers that make us prefer one person over other, or crowd association that makes us impulsively follow behaviors such as the wave at a sport event.

Impact in Education

Few would deny the impact and importance of education on a child's overall well-being. However, research suggests that implicit biases are noticeable as early as kindergarten. Further, we tend to see these implicit thoughts play out as disparate rates of disciplinary referrals, suspensions, and expulsions, primarily among young boys of color and students in lower socioeconomic brackets (Whitford & Emerson, 2019). What does this mean? It means our students from marginalized groups are at a significantly higher risk of punitive treatment within the school setting. This, in turn, places them at a higher risk of engagement with the juvenile justice system, detachment from school, dropping out, and involvement with the adult criminal justice system. These early experiences lay the foundation for these young people's lives.

Whitford and Emerson (2019) speculated a few reasons why we may see these discriminatory behaviors. The first is a stark absence of diversity across teachers and administrators. This discontinuity between students' life experiences and the teachers (which by extension impact classroom norms and management) results in conflicting ideals that could result in discriminatory punishment. Secondly, and as mentioned earlier, there is a general lack of understanding on the pervasiveness of implicit biases. Without this, many people go through life without moments of introspection to gauge their behaviors. This allows for biased actions to be unexamined. Lastly, teachers tend to base school discipline problems on factors outside of the school, such as poverty, neighborhood, or family structure. This hyperfocus on, and inclination to blame, urban environments absolves the school and its staff of any responsibility, which, in turn, can create misguided problem-solving initiatives.

Implicit Bias in Group Settings

Some recent findings suggest that behaviors caused by implicit bias appear to be situational rather than personal (e.g., Gawronski & Bodenhausen, 2017), meaning that one's level of bias might be contingent upon a variety of social cues at the macro level and is strongly influenced by a confluence of social cues and other cultural elements (Payne et al., 2017). Classrooms are unique spaces, and teachers hold a very special role at the front of the classroom. Teachers not only are tasked with teaching grade-specific content, but also are responsible for shepherding our children along the ever-important road of socialization.

Essentially, socialization refers to the process in which children learn about the larger societal norms, values, and behaviors. Within psychology and related fields, this process has been accompanied with the application of social learning theory, particularly during adolescence. Social learning contends that behaviors are learned through interpersonal interactions (i.e., observing, mimicking, imitating, or otherwise reinforcing the behaviors of another). Teachers have both the obligation to resolve any student misbehaviors rooted in prejudice or otherwise, and the power to wield their own acts of discrimination.

BERNARDO'S NARRATIVE

I grew up Latino and disabled in an environment that did not allow me the benefits of being "Latino" and "disabled." Unfortunately, the aesthetics of privilege and suburban comfort do not tell my family's full story and my journey into experiencing urban education later in my life. By all accounts, and despite the illusions of relative wealth and comfort, I was supposed to be part of the statistics of academic underachievement through the suburban special education pipeline, which contrary to urban education, does grant the benefits of earning a high school diploma in the lower academic tier while aggressively promoting the vocational track for postsecondary education. My counselors and teachers severely discouraged college education in favor of vocational labor training for the service industry, which would have rendered the possibility of never achieving financial security, personal wealth, or property. With all honesty, I can confidently say that I would have never earned a college education if I had listened and followed the advice of my counselors and teachers.

Unfortunately, my disability and ethnicity perpetually fueled this narrative of a person like me never achieving the academic skills and education to transcend and transform the institutional and social structure of a marginalized upbringing. This is a narrative bolstered by messages, including those coming from the media that focus on reinforcing the negative and problematic images of Latinos as gangsters and the images of poor intellectual performance and underachievement for disabled individuals. Unfortunately, this meant encountering several teachers and school administrators throughout my elementary and secondary education who embraced this narrative uncritically. For instance, I had one high school counselor, who, during our annual Individualized Educational Program (IEP) meeting, openly embraced the possibility of sending me to vocational school over college, citing the belief that she did not think I was "cut out" for higher education. Although my parents and I contended this view, for students who have a weak sense of efficacy and few academic opportunities, these kinds of experiences can have profound negative effects. Unfortunately, several of these experiences went unnoticed or unanalyzed until I attended graduate school. During high school, I was preoccupied with trying to survive with the only tool available to me—education.

Contrary to my school experiences, my parents worked really hard to provide my siblings and I with the opportunity to develop a better narrative of ourselves. This was, in part, due to their own experiences when growing up. My mom grew up homeless and in foster care after being thrown out of the house at the age of 9 by her mother and stepfather. My maternal grandfather died before my mom was born; he was a horse breeder in southern Chile and died during a horse stampede after he lost control of his horse. His body was literally destroyed into pieces. Since she was little, my mom had a sour relationship with her own mother and had never gotten along with her stepfather. He was a high-ranking military officer in the Chilean Air Force, and for several years, he reported directly to Pinochet (a Chilean Army General and military dictator who ruled Chile from 1973–1990).

One day, after defending herself with a cricket bat against abuse from her stepfather, my mother was thrown out of the house in the dead of winter and spent 3 days roaming the snowy streets and alleys until child protective services found her. Initially, she was placed under the care of the children's court, and eventually, the court helped her to leave for Argentina for safety reasons. Once in Argentina, she was then under the guardianship of a judge for minors who ultimately placed her under the care of her foster parents, Grandma Josefa and Grandpa Juan. It was not until she started living with them that she had a real home. Since I was little, they have been my real grandparents, and I have very fond memories of them. My siblings and I never had any relationship with our biological grandparents from either side of the family.

My dad grew up under the aggressive and abusive personality of my grandfather—a well-known and respected chemist and academic in Argentina, but one who forced my dad to study what my grandfather wanted. Despite his professional prestige, my grandfather was a schizophrenic and he forced my dad from the age of 4 to assist him in his chemistry lab. It was not uncommon for my dad to pull all-nighters at that early age when assisting my grandfather in his lab. For this reason, my dad spent a significant portion of his childhood and teenage years living with his maternal grandparents and aunts, and away from my grandfather. My dad went on to college to study his passion, physics and electrical engineering, which made my grandfather very angry. He wanted my dad to be a chemist like him. The two of them had an estranged relationship until the day my grandfather passed away.

When my parents met, they decided to work hard and provide my siblings and I with the one thing that was missing from their lives—a stable home with two loving and committed parents. For my mother, because education was taken away from her, she made sure that we would enjoy all of the benefits that schooling would bring. For my father, because education was imposed on him, he would guide us to discover our passions and what made us tick. When my older sister started to draw and paint, they spent an insane amount of money on art supplies. At one point, my sister had more than 200 tubes of tempera. Since I was a child, I dreamed of becoming an architect. My dad built me my first small drafting table, and I spent entire afternoons drafting in his lab. When my brother was 10, he started to show interest in building electrical circuits. When he was 13, he built his first computer. He has never bought a computer from a box. He has built all of his computers from scratch and spare parts.

My parents love the arts, and we grew up reading and listening to music. For example, my dad had the entire collection of the Argentine version of The Beatles' records, which was unique because the sleeves were from the EMI Records collection, not the Capitol Records collection. When I was a little boy, I spent entire afternoons arranging and cataloging my dad's vinyl collection. When we moved to Houston, TX, my dad would take us to the main downtown branch of the public library. We loved going there while he worked in his office. We always had a "project" or "report" to do. On our way home, we would stop at Cactus Records, where my dad started his collection of the American version of The Beatles' albums. I started my own collection of albums by The Smiths and U2.

As a student in high school, special education was not a good experience for me. Before arriving in the United States, the concept of special education was foreign to me. I did receive some assistance—like my friends taking notes for me or my teachers giving me extra time for an assignment—however, I was required to perform, make the grade, and be successful like everyone else. There were no classroom pull-outs, modified tests, or fewer math or science problems. And to be honest, that gave me a huge sense of accomplishment. I was not fluent in English, but I could defend myself. I spoke mostly British English because my teachers were from the Caribbean and England. I could also hold conversations in Italian, Portuguese, and basic German, in addition to Spanish. I played competitive volleyball and soccer in the school's intramural league.

But everything changed when I arrived in Houston. My official label as a special education student rendered me incapable. I was tracked. I was placed in adaptive PE, which for me, was detrimental. Instead of playing soccer as a goalie, I was spending the time playing chess and cards because other stuff was not "safe." My official classification as an English as a second language (ESL) student felt synonymous with illiteracy. When I told my teachers that in my previous school I read *Don Quixote*, they thought I was lying. When I started to recite the lines I memorized for a play, they were baffled.

My years in school can best be described as survival. I wanted to achieve, but I was not allowed to. I wanted to be part of the honor track like my siblings, but I was told "no." By my junior year, I became depressed, and I closed myself in my own world. When at home, especially on the weekends, I would stay in my room reading, writing, or building something. If my brother was writing a science report, I was writing one, too, even if there was no class to turn in that report. The mere act of "doing" made me feel accomplished. My images of myself at home opposed those of my teachers' expectations for me at school. At home, I developed a keen interest in learning, drawing, and reading. At school, I received messages of limitations and inability, which ran in contrast to what I was experiencing with my family. Eventually, I did attend architecture school and earned an architecture degree. However, by the time I graduated, I was so emotionally drained that I remained a shift manager at the grocery store that I had worked at since high school. I never practiced architecture as a professional.

By necessity, I became a substitute teacher and, later, a certified teacher. I taught special education and social studies for 10 years. The act of becoming a certified teacher and attending college classes again left me with the desire for more. It was refreshing for me to be in an academic setting again. I found it inspiring and motivating. Therefore, I decided to pursue a master's degree and doctorate in education. Going to graduate school was more than earning another degree. For me, the process of earning a doctorate was an opportunity that allowed me to discover the inequities and bias that I experienced in my life. For the most part, getting a master's degree was not that difficult; I attended classes and earned the grades. However, the experience of studying under the leadership of Drs. Cameron White and Tony Talber encouraged me to pursue a doctorate.

Making the transition to earn a doctorate was a difficult experience. I was severely criticized for staying at the same university where I earned my bachelor's and master's degrees, but that did not matter to me. Earning a doctorate under the supervision of Dr. Cameron White and the guidance of Dr. Cheryl Craig (currently Texas A&M University) was something I could not pass up. Early on, I was immediately and strongly discouraged. In particular, there was a prominent professor who was also the dean of the College of Education during the 1980s, who told me that my work was not of doctoral quality. I was also discouraged from applying to the program by the director of graduate studies at the time, who told me that my GRE scores were not good enough. Despite everything, I decided to apply for the doctoral program in social studies education and was admitted in the fall of 2003.

My doctoral experience was unique. It was there where I found my biggest inspiration and most revealing moments. I became a fan of the work from Paulo Freire, Henry Giroux, Peter McLaren, and David Purpel. I had amazing experiences, such as asking Joe Kincheloe for an autograph at the American Educational Research Association (AERA) conference in San Francisco in 2006, and later having him agree to sit on my doctoral committee and sponsor the publication of my dissertation. Unfortunately, Joe passed away 2 months before my doctoral defense, but the publication of my dissertation was eventually sponsored by his widow, Dr. Shirley Steinberg.

During my doctoral work, one of my biggest influences was the work of Dr. Cheryl Craig in narrative inquiry. I took several courses with her, including research methodology, but narrative inquiry was particularly intriguing for me, as it was a way to explore our souls. However, I never knew the extent of how deep that influence would go. Soon, I found myself, for the first time, confronting what it meant to be disabled, unearthing my previous memories and experiences of my life. At times, it was a painful and emotionally draining process. It was not easy to confront my disability and what it meant to me. It was not pleasant to unearth my frustrations and anger. It was very hard to uncover all the effort that went with every successful moment. These were things that previously went unnoticed, and for once, they were exposed.

The process of confronting my disability was not easy, but it was important for me to do because I felt the need to share this knowledge with those less fortunate than me—my students. I was experiencing the same educational system that rendered me incapable years ago, the same system that continually placed roadblocks in my way, but this time, I was the teacher. This time, I needed to do something about it. Ultimately, it was at the college level, not at the high school where I was teaching, that I had the opportunity. After earning my doctorate, I started to teach at a university in the evening as a part-time instructor, and eventually, there was a tenure-track opportunity that allowed me to work there full-time. I wanted to be part of a place that allowed me to grow, with the chance of creating a different kind of new teacher and educator—a kind who cared about and cherished their students.

The opportunity to interact with preservice teachers has been very revealing for me. I have been able to explore with them the perils and anguish of our lives. My students are unique. I work in a Hispanic-/minority-serving institution. Seventy percent of our students are Latino or African American. Many of them are first-generation college students, DACA Dreamers, and/or parents working full-time. Many of them share similar stories to my story. For them, this is also the opportunity for a better future. They encountered the roadblocks I encountered, and I encountered theirs.

As an academic, I know that there might be others with higher prestige whose voice might carry more weight. They are the people who so profoundly influenced me. However, my experiences are the product of encountering barriers and difficulties. I do not think I was a particularly successful teacher. But I was, however, a source of comfort for my special education students. With my college students, we have learned to mutually engage in a reflective dialogue. As the years pass by, my memories have become old and distant. Some details are vague. My students' experiences as immigrants, first-generation college students, and full-time working parents are what keep my own memories fresh, embarking together in a journey to explore what makes us unique—to build a future of hope.

Food for Thought

Most educators get into this career because of a desire to help—and certainly a wish to help all students equally. Unfortunately, the inadvertent and yet potentially insidious nature of implicit biases poses a particular challenge. With that in mind, in this section, we offer some suggestions on ways to ensure an inclusive learning environment. The Kirwan Institute for the Study of Race and Ethnicity at Ohio State University provides a series of practical strategies to implement meaningful change at both the organizational and individual level (see Capatosto, 2015). These include considering:

1. *Culturally representative schools.* Messages of belongingness and inclusion can be conveyed through a variety of modalities. This includes not only the diversity of the teachers, staff, and administrators, but also the materials used within the classroom, decorations in the hallways, the images within textbooks, and even the examples used in assignments or homework. Although hiring decisions are made well outside of many of our purviews, a teacher could consider the use of music or books to promote multicultural awareness and values.

2. *Intergroup contact.* Although many students balk at the thought of group assignments, inclusive pedagogical strategies, such as well-structured peer work, promotes cross-cultural learning. Students from different backgrounds are able to communicate with each other and establish friendships, which may, in turn, reduce their own implicit biases.

3. *Mindfulness.* Consider alternative ways to teach students how to mediate their stress, anger, or frustration. This may alleviate the emotional response from transforming into a misbehavior.

4. *Clear and consistent discipline.* There is a fine line between zero-tolerance policies that allow for zero discretion and a subjective set of rules open to interpretation. What is perhaps the

most important component is the clarity in the language used within school behavioral policies, clearly defining misbehaviors and correlated punishments, and ensuring that all language is free of vagueness.

Considering the reaction from Nina's university students, it's important to understand that implicit biases are not inherently an egregious thing, although there is a very real potential for this internal thought process to become externalized behaviors, actions, and differential treatment of others. Recognizing that we have these types of thoughts is the first step in intervening before these biased thoughts have the potential to form into harmful behaviors.

References

Alderson, N. (2017). Defining agency after implicit bias. *Philosophical Psychology, 30*(5), 645–656. https://doi.org/10.1080/09515089.2017.1296565

Banaji, M. R., & Greenwald, A. G. (2013). *Blind spot: Hidden biases of good people.* Bantam Books.

Capatosto, K. (2015). *Strategies for addressing implicit bias in early childhood education.* Kirwan Institute for the Study of Race and Ethnicity. https://kirwaninstitute.osu.edu/wp-content/uploads/2015/06/implicit-bias-strategies.pdf

Erevelles, N. (2006). Deconstructing difference: Doing disability studies in multicultural educational context. In S. Danforth & S. Gabel (Eds.), *Vital questions facing disability studies in education* (pp. 363–378). Lang.

Gabel, S., & Danforth, S. (2002). Disability studies in education: Seizing the moment of opportunity. *Disability, Culture and Education, 1,* 1–3.

Galli, G., Lenggenhager, B., Scivoletto, G., Molinari, M., & Pazzaglia, M. (2015). Don't look at my wheelchair! The plasticity of longlasting prejudice. *Medical Education, 49*(12), 1239–1247. https://doi.org/10.1111/medu.12834

Gawronski, B., & Bodenhausen, G. V. (2017). Beyond persons and situations: An interactionist approach to understanding implicit bias.

Psychological Inquiry, 28(4), 268–272. https://doi.org/10.1080/1047840X.2017.1373546

Greenwald, A. G., & Banaji, M. R. (1995). Implicit social cognition: Attitudes, self-esteem, and stereotypes. *Psychological Review, 102*(1), 4–27. https://doi.org/10.1037/0033-295X.102.1.4

Greenwald, A. G., & Krieger, L. H. (2006). Implicit bias: Scientific foundations. *California Law Review, 94*(4), 945–967. https://doi.org/10.2307/20439056

Haslam, R. E. (2018). Checking our bias at the door: Centering our core values in the classroom. *Literacy Today, 36*(1), 24–26.

The Kirwan Institute. (2012). *Understanding implicit bias.* The Ohio State University, Kirwan Institute for the Study of Race and Ethnicity. https://kirwaninstitute.osu.edu/article/understanding-implicit-bias

Marcucci, O. (2019). Implicit bias in the era of social desirability: Understanding antiblackness in rehabilitative and punitive school discipline. *The Urban Review, 52,* 47–74. https://doi.org/10.1007/s11256-019-00512-7

Payne, B. K., Vuletich, H. A., & Lundberg, K. B. (2017). The bias of crowds: How implicit bias bridges personal and systemic prejudice. *Psychological Inquiry, 28*(4), 233–248. https://doi.org/10.1080/1047840X.2017.1335568

Rivers, A. M., Rees, H. R., Calanchini, J., & Sherman, J. W. (2017). Implicit bias reflects the personal and the social. *Psychological Inquiry, 28*(4), 301–305. https://doi.org/10.1080/1047840X.2017.1373549

Rudman, L. A. (2004a). Social justice in our minds, homes, and society: The nature, causes, and consequences of implicit bias. *Social Justice Research, 17*(2), 129–142. https://doi.org/10.1023/B:SORE.0000027406.32604.f6

Rudman, L. A. (2004b). Sources of implicit attitudes. *Current Direction in Psychological Science, 13*(2), 79–82. https://doi.org/10.1111/j.0963-7214.2004.00279.x

Staats, C. (2015–2016, Winter). Understanding implicit bias: What educators should know. *American Educator,* 29–43.

Whitford, D. K., & Emerson, A. M. (2019). Empathy intervention to reduce implicit bias in pre-service teachers. *Psychological Reports, 122*(2), 670–688. https://doi.org/10.1177/0033294118767435

3

Promoting Antiracism

Through the Eyes of a Black Mother

Michelle Frazier Trotman Scott

I talk to myself, every day, after my alarm goes off.

> Alright, Shelli, you've got to get up. You've got work to
> do. Didn't you hear me? Get up! You can't just lay in the
> bed and wish things away. YOU HAVE WORK TO DO!

I have used these phrases as tools of encouragement—a lot, lately—just to get out of the bed. As soon as I rise, I prepare myself to face "it" . . . whatever "it" is. Despite all that is going on around me, I have learned that it is important to press through and remain strong.

But I am exhausted.

As I reach for my cell phone, I say a quick prayer.

> Dear Lord, thank you for allowing me to see another day. Give me strength and wisdom as I embark on whatever journey you have prepared for me today. I pray that there are no reports about someone who died at the hand of the police via brutality or was murdered due to racist vigilantes. I need Your help, I need Your guidance, I need Your wisdom, I need You. Amen.

Swipe . . .

At the time of my authoring of this essay, we were in the midst of a global pandemic. More than 200,000 deaths and counting in the United States were attributed to the relentless coronavirus (estimates put this figure at more than 560,000 as the publication date of this book approaches), and unemployment rates were at an all-time high. The extended unemployment payments were under threat, and many people were facing eviction from their homes. Civil unrest was running rampant, and Black people were being killed and injured by police at alarming rates. One murder, the murder of George Floyd on May 25, 2020, via the knee of a police officer on his neck, was recorded and shared widely on social media—and this particular murder struck the nerve of people worldwide. The words Black Lives Matter were seen on signs and posters during protests across the globe. But these words were not met without objection. Chants and signs with the phrases All Lives Matter and Blue Lives Matter were amidst those that were seen and heard during protests, causing people to clash. Racism was rearing its ugly head, and although some of the perpetrators knew exactly what they were representing, there were others who were completely unaware that they were promoting racist ideology.

A spectrum of racist practices exists, and when the practices are muddled with macroaggressions, microaggressions, prejudice, and discrimination, those who are on the opposing end are often met with disregard, disdain, and hate. On the flip side, others are striving to place antiracism practices, or behaviors and beliefs that are neutral, meaning there is "nothing behaviorally wrong or right—inferior or superior with any racial groups" (Kendi, 2019, p. 105), at the forefront. An antiracist is able to assign individual behaviors and belief systems to an individual, and not their race as a whole. The work of Merton (1949) brilliantly describes prejudice and discriminatory beliefs using a table divided into four quadrants, with each quadrant representing the type of treatment and action that is displayed upon specific groups. Although Merton's typology did not include race, it can be extended to include race. It provides an accurate description of the behaviors that are emulated by the dominant culture and is reflective of the continuum of discriminatory and prejudice practices that are depicted.

> *An antiracist is able to assign individual behaviors and belief systems to an individual, and not their race as a whole.*

I have adapted Merton's (1949) typology and have color-coded the typology to reflect the color levels utilized by the U.S. Homeland Security Advisory System (see Figure 3.1). (*Editor's Note.* The figure appears in grayscale here, but the quadrants have been labeled by color for readers' reference.)

The red All-Weather Illiberal (Active Bigot) quadrant refers to a person who is prejudiced and discriminatory. This person feels a specific way about a particular group of people, and they make decisions based on their feelings. The orange Fair-Weather Illiberal (Timid Bigot) quadrant refers to a person who is prejudiced but does not discriminate. This is a person who feels a particular way about particular groups of people but does not act upon their feelings because they realize that their feelings are not politically correct. The blue Fair-Weather Liberal quadrant refers to a person who is not prejudiced but participates in discriminatory behavior, while the green All-Weather Liberal quadrant refers to a person who is not prejudiced and does not discriminate.

With Merton's (1949) typology at the forefront of my mind, I can't help but think about the excessive punishment and force that is currently being used on Black children and adults across the country. As a Christian, citizen, wife, mother, teacher, and scholar, I watch and listen in horror at the videos and/or reports of Black people being arrested by police using excessive and unnecessary force, and in some cases, being killed by the hands and guns of those who were sworn to protect

FIGURE 3.1

Color-Coded Levels of Merton's (1949) Typology

Low Risk (Green)	General Risk (Blue)
The Unprejudiced Nondiscriminator	**The Unprejudiced Discriminator**
All-Weather Liberal	Fair-Weather Liberal
High Risk (Orange)	Severe Risk (Red)
The Prejudiced Nondiscriminator	**The Prejudiced Discriminator**
Fair-Weather Illiberal (Timid Bigot)	All-Weather Illiberal (Active Bigot)

Note. Adapted from "Discrimination and the American Creed," by R. K. Merton, in R. MacIver (Ed.), *Discrimination and the National Welfare* (pp. 99–126), 1949, Institute for Religious and Social Studies.

and serve. I cringe when I look at the suspension and expulsion reports showing that Black and Brown students receive more punitive punishment than their White counterparts, and I shake my head in disbelief when I see data that reflect the overrepresentation of Black students in special education and the underrepresentation of the same population in gifted education (see Office of Civil Rights, https://ocrdata.ed.gov, for review). I am also bewildered at the fact that many teacher preparation programs barely scratch the surface when it comes to issues of cultural competency in education, and as a result, programs send their students into classrooms for which they are not fully prepared. I have shared only a few of my grievances, but I am sure you get the gist, so with that said, it is important and necessary to discuss the need for one to possess an understanding of antiracism.

The term *racism* is often used synonymously with *macroaggression, microaggression, prejudice,* and *discrimination.* However, we must be mindful that microaggressions, prejudice, and discrimination are terms that can be used alone, while racism can be connected with each of the terms to describe how a person feels or treats another person based on their belief that they are superior to the other person due to their race. I frequently deal with implicit and explicit racial bias, and I have had to learn how to navigate the racial terrains that I commonly face.

I was identified as gifted when I was in the third grade. I was pulled out of class on a weekly basis to attend my gifted and talented education (GATE) classes. I was placed in the "highest" reading, spelling, and math groups, and I was miserable. I was the only Black student in each group, and I was typically by myself. My Black classmates taunted me, and my teachers did not understand me. I felt alone when I was in school . . . but I eventually learned how to survive in both (Black and gifted) worlds. However, it was exhausting. When I entered my doctoral program and formally learned about cultural characteristics, things began to make sense. Giving my teachers the benefit of the doubt, I believed that they lacked cultural competence and did not understand my energy and my way of thinking. But as time progressed and I learned more, I realized that some may have felt as if I did not belong in the gifted space.

> *We must be mindful that microaggressions, prejudice, and discrimination are terms that can be used alone, while racism can be connected with each of the terms to describe how a person feels or treats another person.*

Fast-forward to when I became a mother of a child with a dark complexion. I knew that I had to be intentional in my approach toward teaching her to have racial pride. As a matter of fact, the first time I laid my eyes on her, I knew that I would have to encourage her with words of affirmation that would serve as a reminder that she was loved, that her skin tone was beautiful, and that she was a kindhearted and intelligent girl. This was necessary, not only because she was Black, but also because skin preferences are taught. Children are able to identify racial differences as early as 6 months old (Pauker et al., 2016), and it is up to the adults who surround them to mold how they interpret and embrace such differences. Doing so is imperative because research shows that students with darker skin tones may be considered less attractive, less intelligent, and not as motivated (lazy) as those who are White and/

or lighter skinned. Although these premises are untrue, they are the reality for young children attending preschool and elementary school (for a review, see Clark & Clark, 1947; Davis, 2005; Spencer, 2008), and to make matters worse, these perceptions persist into adulthood (for a review, see Ben-Zeev et al., 2014; Edwards et al., 2004; Graham, 2006), including for my daughter.

When one becomes a teacher, they are expected to uphold ethical codes and principles. As such, the Code of Ethics for Educators adopted by the National Education Association (NEA) in 1975, and used in portion today, indicates that educators, including education support staff, "should adhere to the highest ethical standards and should guarantee an equal educational opportunity for all students" (NEA, 2020, para. 2). More specifically, with regard to the educator's obligation to students, the code of ethics indicates that educators:

> Shall not on the basis of race, color, creed, sex, national origin, marital status, political or religious beliefs, family, social or cultural background, or sexual orientation, unfairly—
> a. Exclude any student from participation in any program
> b. Deny benefits to any student
> c. Grant any advantage to any student (NEA, 2020, Principle I, para. 8)

Although all educators are expected to follow this ethical charge, data show that exclusion is happening on many levels, and although it may be unintentional, the outcome does not change. Many students with gifts and talents go unnoticed because they are misunderstood, misplaced, and sometimes even misdiagnosed by educators who lack cultural competency and possess deficit mindsets (Trotman Scott, 2014).

The Road to Identification

My daughter was overlooked for gifted services three times—once in first grade, a second time in third, and another time in fifth grade. In two instances, she scored extremely well on achievement tests, well enough to be identified as gifted, and although her cognitive abilities tests were high, they were not high enough to be automatically referred to the gifted program. So, she was at the mercy of her teachers who had to evaluate her in the areas of motivation and creativity using a checklist, and each time, she was denied entry because she was not rated high enough.

> *Many students with gifts and talents go unnoticed because they are misunderstood, misplaced, and sometimes even misdiagnosed.*

First Grade

The Incident. My daughter's first-grade teacher was fresh out of college. She was excited to be teaching but was somewhat overwhelmed by all of the paperwork. She was there long enough for her class to take the norm-referenced test that was administered early within the first 3 months of school, but she was unsure of the stanine score meanings, so she did not submit my daughter's name for GATE consideration. The teacher got engaged to be married and moved before the winter break, so she was replaced by a seasoned teacher, but by that time, identification had taken place and we were notified that we had to wait until my daughter entered third grade before she could be evaluated again. Although I was not happy about her not being able to move along in the identification process, I chalked it up to the fact that the teacher was new and ill-informed. I was already providing my daughter with enrichment activities at home, so her needs were being met. But she was having to do double the work in order for that to happen. Nonetheless, I was optimistic about what was to come.

Typology and Ethics. Using Merton's (1949) typology, the first-grade teacher posed a general risk as a Fair-Weather Liberal. The teacher believed that my daughter was smart, but because she was unaware of the referral criteria, she did not submit my daughter's name for further review. As a result, the teacher denied my daughter the opportunity to be considered for the academic benefits of GATE, which is a violation of the NEA code of ethics.

Antiracist Strategies. An effective antiracist approach with this teacher would have been for the gifted coordinator, district diversity officer, or another appointed person of authority to provide the teacher with the referral criteria and answer any questions that she may have had. Building demographics and GATE demographics should also have been shared, emphasizing trends and inequities that may have existed. Ford's (2013) equity model should also have been shared as a tool that could have helped the teacher determine if equity was an issue. A final discussion could have mentioned other tools (e.g., portfolios) that could have been used for GATE referral.

Third Grade

The Incident. My daughter's third-grade teacher was a veteran teacher. As in first grade, my daughter, along with her classmates, took a norm-referenced test in early October. Prior to the results of the test, I attended a parent-teacher conference to speak with the teacher about my daughter's progress. I was excited that she had this particular teacher because I knew the teacher had been teaching for a number of years and was familiar with the GATE assessment process. But I quickly realized that the teacher lacked cultural competence and held a deficit mindset. During the conference, it was clear that she misinterpreted my daughter's communal behaviors, oral tradition, and movement (Boykin et al., 2005) as excitability, inability to keep still, and social dependence and neediness (American Psychiatric Association, 2000). I allowed the teacher to speak without interruption because I wanted to see where she stood. The teacher went as far as to tell me that my daughter was "not at the top, not at the bottom, but in the middle" and that she was "easily distracted and a distraction to others."

When the teacher finished, I pointed out that my daughter scored in the highest level on all of the statewide tests during the past 2 years and that she seemed to be progressing well in her third-grade class. But the teacher was not moved. It was clear that she had a deficit mindset and did not care that my daughter was performing well in any area. Instead, she went on to tell me that my daughter frequently left her seat to go to the desks of friends to talk. I later found out that my daughter was actually helping her friends with their work because the teacher ignored them. At that point, I became so frustrated that I abruptly ended the conference.

A few weeks after the parent-teacher conference, the norm-referenced test scores became available. My daughter scored high enough to be evaluated for GATE, again. But what I did not know was that she would be evaluated via a motivation and creativity teacher checklist, and my daughter was denied entry into GATE a second time due to the low marks her teacher provided on the checklist.

Typology and Ethics. Using Merton's (1949) typology, the third-grade teacher posed a severe risk as an Active Bigot. Her macroaggressive statement about my daughter's academic abilities, despite her academic performance, was evidence that she viewed my daughter's behavior through a deficit lens. As a result, the teacher denied my daughter the opportunity to be considered for the academic benefits of GATE, which is yet another violation of the NEA code of ethics.

Antiracist Strategies. An effective antiracist approach with this teacher would have been for the gifted coordinator, district diversity officer, or another appointed person of authority to examine the achievement test data with her and ask why she believed the student was average when the data showed otherwise. It would also have been helpful to share the aspect of the deficit thinking phenomenon and point out how the teacher viewing the student (through a deficit lens) may have been a factor when she completed the motivation and creativity checklist. Suggestions on how to frame statements and questions that focus on student dynamics (positive attributes) should also have taken place.

Guidance on approaches for talking with parents/caregivers and ways to provide positive attributes and concerns that are reflective of the fact that the student has both strengths and areas in need of growth would also have been helpful. A caregiver would be more receptive to, "Your daughter gets along well with others and has great conversational skills. I have to redirect her to her desk often because she leaves her seat to go to the desks of others to talk during class. Her social skills are phenomenal, but it is important for her to stay seated unless given permission," as opposed to, "She frequently leaves her seat to go to the desks of friends to talk." Using the aforementioned approach would have highlighted strengths and shown the caregiver that the teacher was aware that the student exhibited success in some areas. It could have led to additional conversation about the function (the why) of the behavior. A more in-depth conversation would have revealed that the students felt that the teacher ignored their raised hands. It would have also revealed that the student understood the course content and was being asked by her classmates for help, which in turn, may have changed the way the teacher viewed her as a GATE student.

Finally, research discussing the characteristics of students from different cultures should have been shared with the teacher. The teacher should have been encouraged to refer to the research as she was evaluating students as a way to determine if she was viewing each student through a deficit lens, using a Eurocentric view, or with implicit/explicit biases in play.

Fifth Grade

The Incident. Up to this point, I chose to use words of affirmation to remind my daughter that she was smart, beautiful, and kind. But by third grade, I had to have the hard conversation about microaggressions, macroaggressions, racial prejudice, and discrimination with her. It was necessary to discuss the racial prejudices and discrimination that she had faced and would continue to face because of the color of her skin. She longed to be in the gifted program, and she shared her desire with her teacher, but the third-grade teacher could not see her brilliance for what was deemed as a distraction.

By the time my daughter entered fifth grade, she was acutely aware of the dynamic of race. This time, she realized that she was the only Black student in her class who was evaluated and the only student who was not identified. She was devastated, and there was not much that I could do to console her. I scheduled a meeting with her teacher, but I knew that it would not change the outcome. But this time, I decided to put on my professional hat, and I called a meeting with the teacher, the counselor, and the gifted coordinator to discuss what my daughter encountered. I pointed out the disparities that my daughter had experienced and how the creativity and motivation checklists served as roadblocks to her identification. I also shared how the checklist responses were reflective of a deficit mindset and a misunderstanding of cultural differences that led to a misinterpretation of behaviors and abilities. Finally, I pointed out that my daughter was the only Black student who was evaluated and the only student not identified. During the meeting, her teacher professed that he was ignorant of the process and was unaware of the fact that the checklist responses were what prevented my daughter from being identified. He went on to state that he did not believe that a subjective test should have been used to determine eligibility and that he would have preferred to provide a professional opinion of her. The teacher apologized and accepted fault, but that did not change the outcome . . . for my daughter. Yet, his response gave me hope and led me to believe that his renewed awareness was key and that he would be reminded to think differently and approach things with a different type of intentionally.

Typology and Ethics. Using Merton's (1949) typology, my daughter's fifth-grade teacher posed a general risk as a Fair-Weather Liberal. He believed that my daughter was smart, but his lack of understanding as it pertained to how the teacher checklist played in the evaluation process prevented my daughter from qualifying for GATE. As a result, the teacher denied her the opportunity to be considered for the academic benefits of GATE, which is a violation of the NEA code of ethics.

On the account of my daughter not being identified for GATE, her fifth-grade teacher did not recommend her for accelerated grade courses in middle school, which led to yet another NEA code of ethics violation because she was excluded from participation in the accelerated grade program (course), which in turn, led to the final NEA violation of granting an advantage to other students because my daughter was at a disadvantage when she was appropriately placed in the accelerated grade program her seventh-grade year.

Antiracist Strategies. An effective antiracist approach with this teacher would have been a combination of what was provided to the first- and third-grade teachers—that is, for an appropriate figure of authority to have provided him with the referral criteria, making sure that he understood each step and the role that he served in the process, and to have answered any questions that he may have had. Tools that are less utilized (e.g., portfolios) that are appropriate for use in the GATE referral process should also have been discussed. Finally, the sharing of research that discusses characteristics of students from different cultures would have been helpful. The teacher should have been encouraged to refer to the research as he was evaluating students to ensure that each student was being evaluated in a nonbiased manner.

A Glimpse of the Effects

At the end of my daughter's fifth-grade year, it was no surprise that she earned every academic achievement award available. It was also no surprise (to us) that out of the entire fifth-grade class, she earned the best musician award and the best artist award. As families often do, we made lunch plans so that we could celebrate her accomplishments, but she was not in full celebration mode, as she referenced how she was seen as not being motivated or creative by her third- and fifth-grade teachers on more than one occasion. She could not fully enjoy or appreciate her success because she was haunted by how she was perceived by her teachers. I tried to lighten the mood by telling her that she didn't need to be identified as gifted. I pointed out that her test scores were high enough and that I would advocate for her to be placed in accelerated classes in middle school, and she would continue to excel. She accepted that approach and added that all of her friends knew that she was smart, so she didn't care what her teachers thought. She also pointed out that it was clear that their evaluation of her was erroneous and that they were the one with the issue, not her.

Sixth/Seventh Grade

The Incident. My daughter was finally identified as gifted when she entered the seventh grade. It is important to point out that this was the first time that she had teachers that were not of the dominant culture (White). Her middle school teachers were astonished when they realized that she was not identified as gifted. One teacher reached out to me to inform me that there were higher level courses in which she believed that my daughter should have been enrolled. She provided me with next steps on how to ensure that she was in the correct class the following school year. She even offered tutoring in the event that my daughter needed help getting up to speed because she missed a portion of instruction because she was not referred for grade acceleration courses by her fifth-grade teachers.

Typology and Ethics. My daughter's sixth- and seventh-grade teachers would be considered All-Weather Liberals on Merton's (1949) typology. They believed she was intelligent and was not appropriately placed. They provided information needed to ensure that she was placed in the accelerated grade courses, and they put provisions in place (tutoring) in the event she needed additional support. The teachers also referred her for GATE evaluation, and she was subsequently identified.

> *She could not fully enjoy or appreciate her success because she was haunted by how she was perceived by her teachers.*

Antiracist Strategies. These teachers used an effective antiracist approach and should have been encouraged to share their approach of intention with their colleagues in order to show how they viewed students who were once viewed through a deficit lens through a dynamic lens.

Ninth Grade

The Incident. My daughter's euphoria ended when she entered ninth grade and was met with yet another teacher who possessed a deficit mindset. On the first day of class, the teacher asked each student to state their name and the middle school they attended. Afterward, she called my daughter up to her desk and suggested that she enroll in another class that was on what was called the "discrete" track. The discrete track did not cover two courses in one class across one semester. Instead, the track would require her to take the two separate courses over two semesters. The teacher's reasoning was that "students who came from your middle school typically struggle in my class." The teacher emailed me with the same story, but I quickly declined and told her that my daughter would remain in the course and would have help if it were deemed necessary. My daughter did well in the course until the final day of the semester when the teacher decided to give a four-question exam, of which my daughter missed two of the questions. That one exam caused her grade to go down a letter grade. My daughter was devastated and was convinced that the teacher did this to be spiteful.

Typology and Ethics. Using Merton's (1949) typology, I would consider the ninth-grade teacher to be an Active Bigot. Her macroaggressive statement about students who came from the middle school that my daughter attended (which happened to be a Title I school) showed that the teacher believed that my daughter would not be capable of being successful in her class. Had my daughter accepted her suggestion to move to the discrete track courses, my daughter would have been excluded from participation in the accelerated program, and she would have been at a disadvantage when compared to her peers who remained in the program, both of which are violations of the NEA code of ethics.

Antiracist Strategies. An effective antiracist approach with this teacher would have been for a person of authority to point out that she prejudged my daughter based solely on school attendance, and that macroaggressive statements such as the one that she used could prove to break the spirit of students. A discussion about where gifts and talents are found (i.e., in all races, ethnicities, and socioeconomic demographics) should also have ensued.

The Outcome

My daughter prevailed. Her journey left her bruised, but she was not broken. She had a family who was supportive and who provided her with encouragement and strength during her times of discouragement. She held multiple leadership positions in school, earned academic awards, and earned an academic and athletic scholarship to college. But it was not without a fight.

As a mother, I had to advocate for my daughter. She faced microaggressions, macroaggressions, discrimination, and prejudice with and without racial undertones throughout her K–12 education and will continue to do so. I had frequent conversations with offenders so that I could point out their offenses, but I did it in such a way that many of them were receptive and willing to put in the work to make the change. My daughter also learned how to advocate and speak up for herself along the way. To be antiracist is to promote equity, promote autonomy, point out biases, and transform racially systemic practices. And I do my best to do what is necessary to eliminate all barriers.

References

American Psychiatric Association. (2000). *Diagnostic and statistical manual of mental disorders* (4th ed.).

Ben-Zeev, A., Dennehy, T. C., Goodrich, R. I., Kolarik, B. S., & Geisler, M. W. (2014). When an "educated" Black man becomes lighter in the mind's eye: Evidence for a skin tone memory bias. *SAGE Open, 4*(1). https://doi.org/10.1177/2158244013516770

Boykin, A. W., Tyler, K. M., & Miller, O. (2005). In search of cultural themes and their expressions in the dynamics of classroom life. *Urban Education, 40,* 521–549. https://doi.org/10.1177/004208590 5278179

Clark, K. B., & Clark, M. K. (1947). Racial identification and preference among Negro children. In T. M. Newcomb & E. L. Hartley (Eds.), *Readings in social psychology* (pp. 169–178). Holt, Reinhart, and Winston.

Davis, K. (Director). (2005). *A girl like me* [Film]. Reel Works Teen Filmmaking.

Edwards, K., Carter-Tellison, K., & Herring, C. (2004). For richer, for poorer, whether dark or light: Skin tone, marital status, and spouse's earnings. In C. Herring, V. M. Keith, & H. D. Horton (Eds.), *Skin deep: How race and complexion matter in in the 'color-blind' era* (pp. 65–81). University of Illinois Press.

Ford, D. Y. (2013). *Recruiting and retaining culturally different students in gifted education.* Prufrock Press.

Graham, L. O. (2006). *The senator and the socialite: The true story of America's first Black dynasty.* HarperCollins.

Kendi, I. X. (2019). *How to be an antiracist.* Penguin Random House.

Merton, R. K. (1949). Discrimination and the American creed. In R. MacIver (Ed.), *Discrimination and the national welfare* (pp. 99–126). Institute for Religious and Social Studies.

National Education Association. (2020). *Code of ethics for educators.* https://www.nea.org/resource-library/code-ethics

Pauker, K., Williams, A., & Steele, J. R. (2016). Children's racial categorization in context. *Child Development Perspectives, 10*(1), 33–38. https://doi.org/10.1111/cdep.12155

Spencer, M. B. (2008). Fourth annual Brown lecture in educational research: Lessons learned and opportunities ignored since *Brown vs. Board of Education*: Youth development and the myth of a color-blind society. *Educational Researcher, 37*(5), 253–266. https://doi.org/10.3102/0013189X08322767

Trotman Scott, M. (2014). Resisting dark chocolate: A journey through racial identity and deficit thinking: A case study and solutions. *Interdisciplinary Journal of Teaching and Learning, 4*(1), 43–55.

4

The Need for Culturally Responsive Gifted Educators

Javetta Jones Roberson

Underrepresented populations in gifted and advanced programs have faced and continue to face discrimination, bias, and barriers to services. Gifted educators have a responsibility to not only address and bring awareness to the structural inequities that plague our educational system, but also stand and fight those inequities with practices that promote academic success for all students. The practice of cultural responsiveness in gifted education is one of the many solutions needed to bring equitable practices to serving racially, culturally, ethnically, and linguistically diverse (RCELD) students.

To be clear, there is no *one* checklist, template, rubric, or list of "to-dos" to check off and proclaim, "I'm now culturally competent" or "culturally responsive." Culturally responsive pedagogy (CRP) is a continual cycle and process that requires a paradigm shift in thinking and awareness of your own practices. Being culturally responsive in the classroom means that as the educator, you are willing to find multiple ways to include, respect, and honor all cultures represented by your students by valuing their history and experience within your teaching, instructional, and curricular practices. It means not just focusing on a particular student's background, but understanding and embedding student identities, family experiences, and cultural norms in everything you do. It means setting high expectations for all students, regardless of background, and providing the support to match those expectations. As educators, we must celebrate students' voices and let them know they matter and hold value in our classroom.

Foundations of Culturally Responsive Pedagogy

To understand the journey to becoming a culturally responsive educator of the gifted, I believe it is important to understand the foundations of culturally responsive pedagogy. Culturally relevant/responsive pedagogy was developed in the early 1990s as a framework to guide educators who connected with diverse student populations in schools and organizations. Dr. Gloria Ladson-Billings (culturally relevant pedagogy) and Dr. Geneva Gay (culturally responsive teaching) are the two researchers who merged the research and practice of culturally responsive pedagogy. Culturally relevant pedagogy, as defined by Ladson-Billings (2009), "empowers students intellectually, socially, emotionally, and politically using cultural referents to impart knowledge, skills, and attitudes" (p. 20).

When educators are culturally relevant, they focus on the collective empowerment of students. They are inclusive of all students and build on the cultural assets and knowledge students bring to the classroom. Inclusivity is expressed through the curriculum and instructional support of students. Culturally relevant educators bridge those cultural assets and connect them to academic skills and concepts, making learning for all students relevant to their everyday lived experiences. Culturally relevant educators make sure that students learn about their own culture and the culture of others, creating a sense of pride in diverse students. These educators fight for social justice for all students and work to dismantle oppressive systems.

> *Culturally relevant educators make sure that students learn about their own culture and the culture of others, creating a sense of pride in diverse students.*

Gay's (2002) culturally responsive teaching (CRT) work pushes the aforementioned attributes further through inclusive teaching practices. Culturally responsive teaching uses the "cultural knowledge, prior experiences, frames of reference, and performance styles of ethnically diverse students to make learning encounters more relevant to and effective for them" (Gay, 2010, p. 31).

SIX GUIDING PRINCIPLES OF CULTURALLY RESPONSIVE TEACHING

- Culturally responsive teachers are socially and academically empowering by setting high expectations for students with a commitment to every student's success;
- Culturally responsive teachers are multidimensional because they engage cultural knowledge, experiences, contributions, and perspectives;
- Culturally responsive teachers validate every student's culture, bridging gaps between school and home through diversified instructional strategies and multicultural curricula;

- Culturally responsive teachers are socially, emotionally, and politically comprehensive as they seek to educate the whole child;

- Culturally responsive teachers transform schools and societies by using students' existing strengths to drive instruction, assessment, and curriculum design; and

- Culturally responsive teachers emancipate and liberate from oppressive educational practices and ideologies. (Aronson & Laughter, 2016, p. 165; Gay, 2010)

The framework for culturally responsive pedagogy is meaningful for all student populations. This framework can have an particularly positive impact on students who are traditionally marginalized in schools—those who are Black, Hispanic, Native American, first generation immigrants, from low-income backgrounds, and others. These practices can benefit the lived educational experiences of students who haven't been acknowledged or who feel as though they are invisible.

There is a need for an inclusive pedagogy that connects and appreciates diversity, builds critical thinking skills, and opens doors for students to reach their potential. In an educational system riddled with inequities, the absence of an inclusive pedagogy can have a detrimental effect on learning outcomes for these students. Culturally responsive teaching is one major way educators can work to combat inequities and build on students' academic abilities.

Fostering Culturally Responsive Curriculum and Instructional Practices

A truly culturally responsive curriculum in the gifted classroom is learner-centered, inclusive of all student backgrounds, and rigorous and relevant to everyday student life. The curriculum welcomes the students' prior knowledge, experiences, language, and identity, making them an integral part of instruction. The curriculum in a culturally responsive gifted classroom is authentic, rigorous, and relevant; allows for student connections; and reflects various cultural experiences. A curriculum that does not ensure that all students feel valued has failed everyone. Therefore, it is critical that gifted educators support the implementation of a culturally responsive curriculum in gifted and advanced programs.

The way the curriculum is taught in a culturally responsive gifted classroom falls under many of the aforementioned characteristics. I believe one of the major ways that educators can create meaningful learning experiences for their students is by building relationships. How can you know what to include in teaching practices if you have no clue who your students are? The answer is . . . you can't. Accessing firsthand knowledge of each student's personal experiences, recognizing their family and community connections, and involving them in the learning process support culturally responsive teaching practices.

Using a color-blind approach with students is problematic. All students come to the classroom with specific cultures and identities that make them who they are. Using color-blind statements, such as, "I don't see color when I teach my students," "I treat all of my students the same because their culture/color doesn't matter to me," or "I don't see race," as well-intentioned as they may be, communicates that you do not see your students. Additionally, you are not recognizing the systemic inequities that plague an institution that was never built in favor of these students. Being culturally responsive means you are at the forefront of combating the many injustices that students face. You are teaching students through a social justice lens, meaning you are constantly finding ways to combat structures that negatively discriminate and target students in your classroom, while positively building students up in the process. You are communicating frequently with them and setting high expectations for their learning with the support to mirror that expectation. You frequently pour positivity into your students through actions, not just words. You care about your students. Culturally responsive educators look to break the glass ceiling and view all students as having untapped potential.

As an educator of the gifted, I often thought of ways in which I could incorporate my students' culture in my everyday classroom environment. My fellow teachers and I were given a curriculum framework to use to make sure we understood the state standards that needed to be covered for grade-level readiness. The framework served as a guide, and I was lucky to have a principal who didn't want us to use a scripted curriculum. We had creative freedom in how we taught our students. There were some nonnegotiables with our state standards, as they covered grade-level content readiness. Our leaders wanted us to teach beyond grade-level readiness "through" the standards, rather than "to" the standards. Although there was still much emphasis on standardized testing and accountability, the support I received from campus leadership in creating meaningful connections through the "how" and "what" of curriculum spoke volumes. Our campus leadership saw past the politics of teaching to the standardized test and placed our students' needs first. This, however, is not currently the case in many schools. Culturally responsive gifted educators must find ways to balance high-stakes accountability while maintaining fidelity in gifted programming and meeting students' needs.

Commitment to Being a Lifelong Learner Through Cultural Responsiveness

The continual process of being culturally responsive deals most with the development of educators. I believe a key component in being culturally responsive is that, first, you must be culturally competent. Cultural competence is possessing the necessary skills and disposition to successfully collaborate and communicate with individuals from different cultural backgrounds (Kohli et al., 2009). When educators are culturally competent, they go beyond monthly cultural celebrations to truly embed culture in their classroom's DNA. They make diversity a priority in everything they do. Culturally competent educators are able to understand, recognize, and appreciate cultural diversity, and they demonstrate a willingness to fight any oppressive systems created to discriminate against the most vulnerable of populations. Cultural competence serves as the gateway to being culturally responsive.

Professional learning that is intentional and planned with equity at the forefront is capable of supporting lifelong learning. The reality is that many educators are underprepared to meet the demands of the rapidly growing racially, culturally, ethnically, and linguistically diverse student population. The lack of knowledge and training in serving diverse student populations has also had a "gatekeeper" effect on students' identification, recruitment, and retention in gifted and advanced courses. Having continuous professional learning that addresses misconceptions and current research on these brilliant minds can help alleviate many gatekeeper issues. Setting professional learning goals that are more than content and standards and that address social-emotional needs and cultural responsiveness support a growth mindset in educators. Simply put, the same energy and effort put in learning and growing in your content area should also be reflected in your cultural responsiveness journey.

Culturally competent educators are able to understand, recognize, and appreciate cultural diversity.

The Value of Incorporating Student Culture and Language in the Classroom

Over the years as an educator and leader in gifted and advanced learning, I have made it my priority to encourage advanced-level teachers to understand the importance of creating learning experiences for students that they can relate to. Real-world experiences and aspects of students' community and culture should be embedded in the heart of lesson planning. Many do not realize this important step in building a culturally responsive classroom. For our gifted learners, specifically gifted students of color, the need to see their culture mirrored in the everyday practices of a culturally responsive classroom is critical to them taking ownership of their learning and using it for conceptual connections. Whether this occurs in a core subject classroom (math, science, social studies, English language arts) or an elective course (fine arts, career and technical education, etc.), students need to know that their culture, family traditions, community, and language are valued and appreciated. This can be done through incorporating them in everyday teaching and curricular practices. Quick-write activities about community awareness, blended learning activities with visuals and vocabulary in station rotations, and project-based learning that focuses on real-world scenarios are all ways students' language and culture can add value to learning.

Family and Community Connections

As a culturally responsive educator of gifted students, you have a responsibility to honor the families and communities that your students come from. You have to put the energy into connecting with your students' families and communities. The phrase "it takes a village to raise a child" may be cliché, but in the realm of cultural responsiveness, the village helps support your classroom efforts. Student factors, including family socioeconomic backgrounds, parental support, and community cultural values, all play a part in gifted educators connecting with families and aiding student success. Cultural responsiveness in gifted education cannot occur if educators do not know the students they serve or the families and communities that they come from. For this very reason, relationships must be forged for the betterment of the gifted student. Educators should form partnerships with families and community members. Communicating classroom goals and expectations for students, conducting parent nights to help with understanding of gifted and advanced classes, and assisting parents with at-home resources for support are all great ways a culturally responsive educator can keep families and communities connected with schools. All students thrive when stakeholders within and outside advanced-level programs are involved and their input is received as a tool to build students' positive self-concepts. Educators can learn so much simply by communicating and partnering with families on the achievement goals of their students. Culturally responsive gifted educators going the extra mile in understanding their students' communal contexts can adjust their classroom environment, making learning even more inclusive and of value to the student.

Culturally Responsive Leadership in Gifted Education

When I speak of gifted educators, I am also including leaders in the conversation, as the pathway to school and district leadership in gifted education starts in the classroom. Educators never lose the title of "educator" even when they have made the shift into leadership roles.

As we focus a great deal on culturally responsive gifted educators in the classroom, there is also a need for culturally responsive gifted educators who are in leadership roles. Leaders of gifted and advanced programs can utilize culturally responsive leadership practices in building equitable programs designed to support family and communities of students, professional learning opportunities for continuous improvement, and promoting inclusive pedagogy as a whole. Culturally responsive leadership (CRL) practices are characterized by (a) being critically self-reflective; (b) developing and sustaining culturally responsive teachers and curricula; (c) promoting inclusive, anti-oppressive school contexts; and (d) engaging students' indigenous (or local neighborhood) community contexts (Khalifa, 2018).

Culturally responsive gifted leaders make a valiant effort to use their program data to guide their decision making in ways that do not perpetuate inequity.

Culturally responsive leadership, just like CRT, is a continual process not to be checked off on a to-do list, but practiced in behaviors that are displayed based on data received from organizations being served. Culturally responsive leadership includes the leader focusing on pedagogy, curriculum, and instruction for traditionally marginalized students and advocating for them in all educational contexts (Roberson, 2020). Gifted and advanced education leaders who are culturally responsive have an awareness of the student populations served in their programs. They are critically self-reflective of their own leadership practices, their culture, and the culture, biases, and misconceptions of others. Culturally responsive gifted leaders make a valiant effort to use their program data to guide their decision making in ways that do not perpetuate inequity. They recognize and understand the many barriers gifted and advanced students face and input systems to counter those negative effects.

Simply put, there is a critical need for gifted school and district leaders to operate in cultural responsiveness. Educators in the classroom cannot do this work alone. It takes gifted educators committed to the cause of CRT and CRL while fostering academic excellence among all students. It is possible that if culturally responsive practices are not put in place in gifted and advanced programs, the oppressive structures and systemic injustices built within them will continue to be reproduced.

The Blessing and Burden of Advocacy

In the line of work for equity through teaching and leading practices, I often consider this a true work of the heart, but it can be burdensome. Something has to lie within you to continue this work, as lives and livelihoods depend on it. Anytime you face work that is meant to dismantle barriers of systemic inequalities for marginalized student populations that have been in place since the early beginnings of the U.S. educational system, it will cause you to think about how you can promote positive change through your own actions. I believe being a culturally responsive gifted educator is an action because it is something you do. There is no "saying" you're being culturally responsive in gifted education without any action taking place, as that defeats the purpose of the work you are striving to accomplish every day. Being a culturally responsive gifted educator is, in my opinion, a blessing and a burden. All aspects require a paradigm shift in thinking and involve some form of advocacy. Advocating for students, especially those most vulnerable in gifted and advanced courses, is a work of the heart. You have to be prepared for roadblocks. Continual roadblocks will confront you. We must recall that when gifted and advanced placement programs first began, students of color were never in the equation for consideration. So, to even connect culturally responsive practices in these programs is a blessing and burden in its own right. Advocacy will be a major part of this work. You will have to continue to go against the status quo. There will be times you will have to rise against decision makers in school systems who want a "quick fix" to equity issues in education. You will have to rise against self-proclaimed researchers who use deficit think-ing models as an easy way to address various issues with students from diverse backgrounds. You will have to speak up against curricula that are too "White-washed" or centrally focused on one majority culture.

My suggestion for your advocacy efforts is to be solution oriented. As a culturally responsive gifted educator, you don't know everything. That's the joy in having a continuous improvement mindset in being culturally responsive because you want to continue to learn and to help others learn in the process. It's not about a checklist. It's not about a set list of strategies. It's about having the mindset of growing through cul-tural competence and helping others do the same. I entered the field of education because I loved kids. I wanted to make a difference. I wanted to help them reach goals and beyond. But most importantly, I wanted to challenge their thinking. I looked at how the world viewed certain students and thought less of them. I looked at our nation's history of our educational system. The system has so many flaws. I wanted and needed to help students navigate through a system never built for them. In gifted education, there are even more disparities. However, I made advocacy my priority. Gifted educators who are committed to ensur-ing equity in gifted education advocate for all students as a culturally responsive practice.

References

Aronson, B., & Laughter, J. (2016). The theory and practice of culturally relevant education: A synthesis of research across content areas. *Review of Educational Research, 86*(1), 163–206. https://doi.org/10.3102/0034654315582066

Gay, G. (2002). Preparing for culturally responsive teaching. *Journal of Teacher Education, 53*(2), 106–116. https://doi.org/10.1177/002248 7102053002003

Gay, G. (2010). *Culturally responsive teaching: Theory, research and practice* (2nd ed.). Teachers College Press.

Khalifa, M. (2018). *Culturally responsive school leadership*. Harvard Education Press.

Kohli, H. K., Kohli, A. S., Huber, R., & Faul, A. C. (2009). Assessing cultural competence in graduating students. *International Journal of Progressive Education, 6*(1), 6–27.

Ladson-Billings, G. (2009). *The dreamkeepers: Successful teachers of African American children* (2nd ed.). Jossey-Bass.

Roberson, J. J. (2020). *The voices of leaders: Examining the underrepresentation of diverse students in advanced academic programs through a culturally responsive leadership lens* (Publication No. 27961393) [Doctoral dissertation, Texas A&M University-Commerce]. Pro Quest Dissertations & Theses Global.

Race, Ethnicity, and Culture

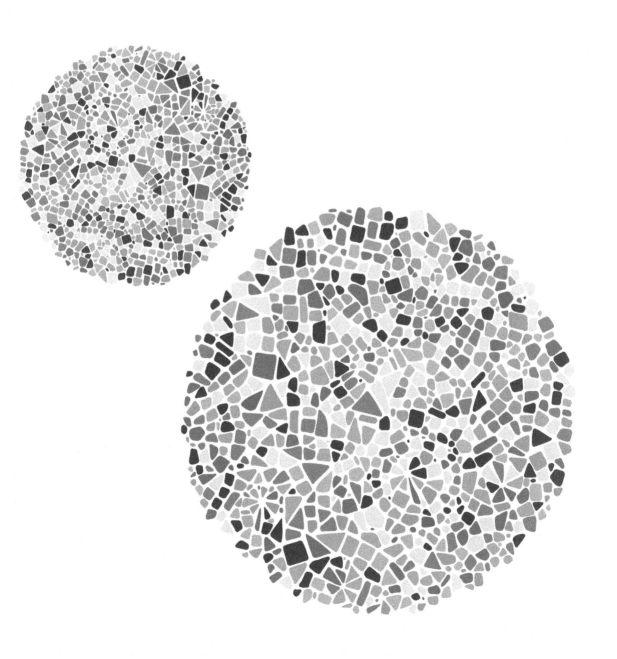

Introduction to Race, Ethnicity, and Culture

Kristina Henry Collins

At best she was invisible, and at worst, she faced low
expectations and misunderstandings from her teachers.
(Gentry & Gray, this volume, p. 117)

This quote from Gentry and Gray's essay on Indigenous youth could
very well be the battle cry for every underrepresented, underserved, and
unidentified student of color with gifted potential, talent, and achievement in America—an all-too-familiar epitaph to their K–12 educational
career. It represents the summation and characterization for the essays
that follow.

Distinctive and unique to this text as a publication in 2021 is that it comes during a period of newfound "wokeness" (see Gentry & Gray, this volume) in America related to race, ethnicity, and culture. The unrest that has grown from 2020's COVID-19 pandemic and the public killing of George Floyd and other victims of police brutality in America has forced people into a reality and sense of awareness like no other since the Civil Rights Movement of the 1960s and 1970s. Because it has been more than a century since the first intelligence tests and the many historical events that have shaped gifted and talented education policy and practices, as educators, we must induce those who still remain "asleep" to see the fallacy of color-blindness and culture-blind ideology and the benefit of culturally responsive, strength-based practices in gifted and talented development for all students. Through research and advocacy presented in the essays in this book, the authors hope to spur collaboration among scholars and practitioners of gifted programs and other educational professionals about the environmental, cultural, and sociological variables that affect equity in access and service for gifted students of color and those of other marginalized populations. Although it is painful to revisit what seem to be the same stories since the inception of gifted education in America, new perspectives give way to hope for sustainable solutions and inspiration to take action within our own institutions.

New perspectives give way to hope for sustainable solutions and inspiration to take action within our own institutions.

Defining the Problem

It can be difficult for gifted education stakeholders to understand what multicultural education should look like. Inclusiveness is often approached as an issue to resolve rather than a pillar to lean on. Gifted education practitioners operating in a state of cultural mindlessness rather than cultural mindfulness have led to myths and erroneous beliefs in an existence of acultural policies and practices that have become partially normalized and standardized.

The solution does not lie in fixing a system that is broken, but instead by understanding that our gifted educational system is operating in the exact way that it was designed—embedded with racist ideology, implicit biases, exclusionary intent, and inequitable desired outcomes. Tearing down the existing system and reframing its purpose with newly aligned taxonomies and program development constructs is necessary to redress institutionalized racism if we are to build cultural competence among educators who are tasked to properly and equitably serve diverse student populations. To do so, we must recognize the myth of acultural policies and practices that have an effect on culturally and linguistically diverse students, students from poverty, and others who have are part of historically marginalized populations that are addressed in this book.

Multilingual Students With High Potential

All too often, cultural biases of language acquisition and expression as an indicator of intelligence exist and present a barrier for the identification of multilingual students with high academic potential. We must challenge the very anti-inclusive nomenclature explicitly embraced and conveyed in American classrooms through the limiting and deficit labeling of traits of multilingual learners and the general perception that students who lack English language proficiency lack intelligence. This American-centered thinking not only harms children, but also perpetuates the deficits that exist in our preparation and training of educators to be equipped to position students—especially students with high potential—to be globally competitive. Even schools that have put forth effort and resources in identifying multilingual students with high academic potential often do not address their academic and linguistic needs, confirming that equity intentions with cultural competence deficits still lead to inequality.

Students of Color and Students From Poverty

Intersectionality of race, poverty, and language encompasses distinct layers of the systemic racial injustices that are prevalent in education and perpetuate a culture of poverty that plagues generations. That culture continues to affect poverty-stricken districts that do not have adequate resources, as well as the existence of cultural disparity between the White middle-class teachers that oftentimes marginalize students, their values, and their experiences. This is evident when the attributes, circumstances, and achievements for students of color in poverty are not compared to other students in poverty of the same age, experience, and environment, but instead to their wealthier counterparts.

Although there is a high concentration of students of color living in poverty, we must caution against the use of low socioeconomic status (SES) as a preferred conversation tool or "code word" to address race and ethnicity, as this can conjoin race to poverty in all circumstances and lead to continued misconceptions that all students of color are from low-income families. I find, too often, when stakeholders are not comfortable confronting the racism in gifted education, they will waywardly focus their attention on poverty as a substitute for race. The discussion and consequences of race on the quality of a student's education warrants its own examination. For example, the institutional racism and systemic bias toward American Indian and Alaskan Natives (AIAN) students represent a story of deliberate marginalization, genocide, and inhumane "erasure" for a whole group of people's perspective, values, and manifestation of gifts and talents out of history.

Redefining the Solutions

When exposing the grave trespasses of the American educational system, we must also offer active solutions and recommendations that can take us forward toward equity in access and service for all students. We must expand our thinking and embrace new, culturally responsive terminologies and practices that debunk deficit thinking. Giftedness must be viewed through the sociocultural cognitive lens to frame critical content knowledge. Doing so positively shapes the cultural competence of professionals' attitudes and mental positions toward culturally and linguistically diverse populations of students. This is the foundation for sustaining culturally and linguistically positive practices that are inclusive and appreciative of the diverse and unique manifestation of gifts and talents by all students.

5

Redressing and Neutralizing Institutional Racism and Systemic Biases in Gifted Education

Kristina Henry Collins

Although polarizing events in America in 2020—COVID-19, political campaigning, police brutality of Blacks—contributed to racial and civil unrest, many organizations, including those in gifted and talented education, began good-faith efforts of translating symbolic, humane support into real action for change, equity, and social justice (Collins, 2020a). I fear, however, that forging actions for change without redressing the institutional racism and systemic biases that exist will inevitably equate to more of the same with only a new label or new name. This chapter represents my own journey trying to understand why we are still having the same conversations about racism in America—and in gifted education. It is my personal and documented examination for meaning-making and conjectured solutions.

Having served in diverse education leadership positions, I find myself questioning the overall impact of my continuous efforts, with seemingly insignificant changes, compared to the overall educational dilemmas that we, as educators, face. Redressing institutional racism and systemic biases compels a shift in strategic thinking and action planning that first recognizes that the solution does not lie in fixing a system that is broken, but in understanding, first and foremost, that the system is operating in the exact way that it was designed—embedded with racist ideology, implicit biases, exclusionary intent, and inequitable desired outcomes. Seeking to find any organization that approaches grievances with this mindset, I discovered that Hong Kong, a former British colony until 1997 when it became a special administrative region of the People's Republic of China, utilizes the Legislative Council Redress System. Its redress system is designed to "receive and handle complaints from members of the public who are aggrieved by Government actions or policies" whereby its members also "undertake 'ward duty' during which they meet with individual members of the public and provide guidance to staff on the processing of cases" (Legislative Council of the Hong Kong Special Administrative Region of the People's Republic of China, n.d., para. 1, 2). I further contend that an examination of policies and practices must include a historical synthesis of their broader purpose, working definition of key concepts, and subsequent processes for any program development.

Redressing institutional racism and systemic biases compels a shift in strategic thinking and action planning.

In 2010, the National Science Foundation (NSF) cited a 2008–2009 survey from the National Association for Gifted Children (NAGC) report that revealed major issues among the 45 states that acknowledged gifted education: inadequate funding, inconsistent reciprocity, inappropriate programming and placement, and inadequate teacher preparation, accountability, and professional development. These issues are just a few of the symptoms and outcomes of institutional racism and systemic biases that have existed since gifted education's inception and continue to exist today. As such, I wanted to revisit gifted education's broader purpose, definition of giftedness, and how its programming came to be. Based on my review, I have devised a table of major events that have shaped gifted education's policies and practices. Although much progress has been made, some of the early efforts yielded and revealed adverse outcomes that disadvantaged gifted students of color from the beginning.

The Broader Purpose and Origins of Gifted and Talented Education

As shown in Table 5.1, the first large-scale gifted education effort was enacted by the passing of the National Defense Education Act without any formal conceptual definition of what it meant to be gifted. The act provided federal funding to ensure trained manpower of sufficient quality and quantity for the sole purpose of meeting the national defense needs of the United States. It aimed primarily at education in science, mathematics, and foreign languages. Subsequently, gifted education has been offered as a plausible approach and process solution for various educational woes. Coupled with the early processes for identifying gifted students that were not inclusive, along with the socially constructed definition of giftedness, I conjecture that institutional racism and systemic biases were inherently embedded in gifted education during the onset of its inception.

Giftedness as a Social Construct

Table 5.1 shows that it was 15 years after the passing of the National Defense Education Act that the first formal federal definition of giftedness was offered—a definition that has been shaped by society and modified over time. However, I imagine that the purpose of gifted education, coupled with the widely known Stanford-Binet IQ test as scientific validation, influenced any practical use of the term prior to a formal definition. More appropriately labeled as scientific racism, the major weaknesses of this IQ test and any subsequent test built upon it

TABLE 5.1
Historical Context for Major Sources That Shaped
Gifted Education Policy and Practices

1916	Adapted from Binet's (1905) psychometric instrument that suggested mental age, the Stanford-Binet Intelligence Scale was published and soon became the standard intelligence test used in the United States (revised in 1937, 1960, 1986, and 2003 using U.S. Census data).
1955	Building on the Stanford-Binet test, the Weschler Adult Intelligence Scale was published. Two versions for use for children were developed.
1957	The Soviet Union successfully launched Sputnik 1, the world's first artificial satellite. The launch ushered in new political, military, technological, and scientific developments. Although the Sputnik launch was a single event, it marked the start of the space age and the U.S.-U.S.S.R. space race. American politicians worried that their educational system was not producing enough scientists and engineers.
1958	The National Defense Education Act passed—the first large-scale gifted education effort.
1964	The Civil Rights Act passed, emphasizing equal opportunities in education.
1972	The 1972 Marland Report with the first formal definition of giftedness was issued: *"Along with academic and intellectual talent, the definition includes leadership ability, visual and performing arts, creative or productive thinking, and [psychomotor] ability."*
1974	The Office of the Gifted and Talented (within the U.S. Department of Education) was given official status.
1975	Public Law 94-142, the Education for All Handicapped Children Act, passed as a federal mandate to serve children with special education needs (excluding gifted and talented children).
1983	*A Nation at Risk* reported scores of America's brightest students.

TABLE 5.1, continued

1988	The Jacob K. Javits Gifted and Talented Students Education Act was passed by Congress.
1990	The National Research Center on the Gifted and Talented (NRC/GT) was established at the University of Connecticut. (It included researchers from the University of Virginia, Yale University, and the University of Georgia; funding ended in 2012.)
1993	*National Excellence: The Case for Developing America's Talent* was published.
1995	NRC/TGT (Frasier et al.) released *A New Window for Looking at Gifted Children* (RM95222).
1998	The Pre-K–Grade 12 Gifted Programming Standards were published by the National Association for Gifted Children (NAGC; revised in 2010 and 2019).
2002	The No Child Left Behind Act (NCLB) was passed. The Javits program was included and expanded to offer competitive statewide grants. The definition of gifted and talented students was modified again: *"Students, children, or youth who give evidence of high achievement capability in areas such as intellectual, creative, artistic, or leadership capacity, or in specific academic fields, and who need services and activities not ordinarily provided by the school in order to fully develop those capabilities."*
2004	*A Nation Deceived: How Schools Hold Back America's Brightest Students*, a national research-based report on acceleration strategies for advanced learners, was published by the Belin-Blank Center at the University of Iowa.
2006	National Gifted Education Standards for Teacher Preparation Programs and Knowledge and Skill Standards were published by NAGC (revised in 2013).

(e.g., Weschler Scale, Army's testing program) were the psychologists' failure to consider the grave, generational impact of omission of cultural differences on tested intelligence and the biases of the developer who subscribed to the Galtonian theory that mental abilities were primarily a product of racial heredity. Unfortunately, such racist scientific advancements served as a cover for political, ethnic, and racial biases. They fabricated various political programs that utilized a goal of science to predict and control—an ideology extended to society at large. Scientific racism established an ideology of differences as the root of scientific research on minorities with an attempt to classify Blacks, specifically, as scientifically inferior. In the case of updated and empirical frameworks, many were new methods and tools to uphold previously held deficit assumptions about Blacks and other people of color.

The first formal definition of giftedness in 1972 positioned academic and intellectual traits as valued, foundational characteristics with added considerations of "other" traits of giftedness (Marland, 1972). It did not situate talent development as a prioritized benefit to the student. Policies and practices for recruitment (identification), programming, and retention were developed and formalized for more than 30 years before an update to the definition was offered in 2002 (No Child Left Behind Act, 2001). It was the first time needs and benefits of the students were even prioritized and purposed.

Program Design That Is Culturally Unresponsive

The oppressive nature under which gifted education was originally purposed and subsequently designed "diminishes the dreams, hopes, and potential contributions" (Grantham et al., 2020) of gifted students of color. Cognitive, individual, and culturally unresponsive programs create an environment that fosters victimization for underrepresented gifted students of color—causing unfair treatment and/or blaming the victim for contributing to the unjust treatment or situations (Collins, 2020a, 2020b).

Based on my work as a gifted program developer and coordinator, I have found that working closely with the families of gifted students of color offers an invaluable cultural resource. Treating parents as equal partners provided me with insight to a social construct of giftedness valued by their community and manifested by the students that informed our program, curriculum, and content. Family and community engagement (with an invitation to parents as informed advocates in decision making and not simply volunteers to meet the school's needs) had positive impact in maximizing gifted students of color's potential, interest, and overall success (Collins & Fields-Smith, 2022). Integration of community customs, beliefs, and values into programming and curriculum cultivated the engagement of gifted students of color's in meaningful and culturally respectful ways; it validated them as gifted students who excel in and out of school.

Implications for Gifted Education Professionals

My work and research have revealed that although there is greater ethnic diversity in public schools and increased inclusion of students of color in gifted and advanced programming, educators still struggle to appropriately cultivate a scholar identity among gifted students of color (Collins, 2018; Rodríguez Amaya et al., 2018). As such, students of color with the highest level of ability and determination often lack the opportunity to develop their talent. So, the question becomes, how do educators neutralize and decrease the negative impact of institutional racism and systemic/individual biases that exist?

Understanding the ramifications of consequential validity—intended purpose, definitions, and development process—the school-within-a-school magnet program and curriculum (Collins & Roberson, 2020) that I designed was built to neutralize and decrease these impacts. We examined our existing policies and practices, correcting them as needed prior to developing and implementing a strength-based, multicultural gifted and talented service and programming model that created positive change and long-lasting impact for students of color as lifelong learners and producers of knowledge. Complementing a socially expanded view of giftedness as a social construct, I relied on Dr. Mary Frasier's groundbreaking work, F-TAP (Frasier's Talent Assessment Protocol) and TABs (Traits, Aptitudes, and Behaviors). Her work offered equitable and timeless principles that were integrated into policy and practice for student recruitment and retention of gifted students of color at the high school level, and increased our number of identified gifted and highly talented students of color who had been overlooked in early grades. Frasier conceptualized four critical components that serve as persistent barriers for recruitment and retention: attitudes, access, assessment, and accommodation, or 4As (Frasier, 1997; Frasier et al., 1995).

Attitude Positively Influenced by Culturally Competent Skill Development

The mental position, feeling, and emotion toward gifted students of color exhibited by regular education and gifted education professionals position them as gatekeepers. This mental position, or attitude, is directly influenced by the quality of educational training that educators complete. However, the formal training and continuing education needed to effectively serve and counsel gifted students of color can be very limited. For the general education professional who is not required to complete any significant gifted and talented training, their attitude may be limited to an interpreted definition of giftedness supported by their own educational experiences. As one of the most common methods for student recommendations to the gifted program, teachers' attitudes represent a major hurdle to recruitment of gifted students of color. Educators must acknowledge this and be willing to advocate for improved teacher training. For practitioners, gifted education training typically includes topics related to the characteristics of giftedness, assessment for giftedness, gifted services, and curriculum and instruction. Responsible for implementation of services and programming to all identified students, their attitudes can have disproportionate influence over retention for gifted students of color (Collins & Kendricks, 2022).

Gifted education professionals must take personal responsibility and be held accountable for developing their own learning about how to best serve and counsel culturally different students.

For both regular education and gifted education professionals, the extent to which they are culturally competent directly impacts the quality of education that gifted students of color receive. All education professionals are in a position to guide the life experiences of all individuals. Gifted education professionals must take personal responsibility and be held accountable for developing their own learning about how to best serve and counsel culturally different students. At minimum, all education professionals, as culturally competent professionals, should possess multiperspective cultural knowledge evident by an appreciation and ability to understand, communicate, interact with, and effectively serve people across cultures. Cultural competency is included in every course and inservice that I provide. Culturally competent professional traits, along with other cultural competencies (not all-inclusive) that I teach, are outlined in Table 5.2. They are presented as critical content knowledge to positively affect educators' mental position, or attitude, toward gifted students of color and prepare them to promote inclusiveness in a culturally competent manner.

Absolute Equity in Access and Assessment

I don't think that implicit cultural biases will ever be completely absent in the attitude of any educator. So, it is important that the ways in which culturally and linguistically diverse groups of students become considered for gifted program placement (access) along with the entire process of evaluating the presence of and degree of giftedness (assessment) is diverse and equitable. Differentiated from equality and beyond the dominant, educational paradigm, equity is the differing treatment that ensures opportunities for gifted students of color that are the same as their White counterparts. However, I have found that even the most culturally competent educator struggles with translating the concept of equity into equitable policies and practices. More often than not, they offer evidence for understanding with proposed equitable policies and practices grounded in deficit thinking that ignores institutional racism and systemic biases, and focus ineffectively on the perceived deficits of the student. Similar to unresponsive program design, deficit-based equitable policies and practices foster victimization for gifted students of color, attributing the situation to the student and further exposing them to unjust treatments from peers.

TABLE 5.2
Critical Content Knowledge That Shapes Culturally Competent Professionals' Attitudes

Term	Description/Definition
Acultural Myth	The belief that something or someone lacks culture and/or cultural influence; "lacking culture" judgment is based on the value of certain culture's beliefs and practices, over another, as important "knowledge."
Culturally Assaultive	Opposite of culturally responsive; an example would be when a teacher discredits, dismisses, and/or does not accept a families' cultural values; a color-blind and broad, homogeneous approach to relating to individuals.
Cultural Characteristics	Void of stereotype, the empirical evidence presented as generalizations of key and/or common core characteristics of a cultural group to guide culturally responsive development of assessments, policies, procedures, practices, etc.
Cultural Conflict Theories	Acknowledge cultural differences with an understanding that distinct, unique cultural beliefs and values can and do conflict with dominant culture; cultural incompatibilities.
Cultural Considerations	Taking into account the positionality (ancestry and heritage) of race-based culturally different groups and how their "American status" came to exist (i.e., involuntary minority, model minority, dominant culture, etc.).
Cultural Deficit Theories	Contend that the culture in which some students are reared is inferior or substandard in comparison to another; paradigms that carry a "blames the victim" orientation.
Cultural Difference Theories	A deficit-muted view of culture, acknowledging and appreciating the diversity of cultures.
Cultural Discontinuity	An experience in patterns of culture that are different from one's own primary or most dominantly influenced culture and posited to inhibit creativity in early development of students.

TABLE 5.2, continued

Term	Description/Definition
Cultural Identity	Pertaining to one's self-concept situated in connection to and/or strong sense of belonging to a cultural group; overlapping identities and experiences resulted from various shared conditions.
Cultural Language	Defined to distinguish itself from slang, language disorders, and/or improper mechanical use of a standardized language (e.g., Standard American English[SAE]) that warrants intervention, it is the speech pattern and language forms resulted from cultural linguistic factors such as vernacular, rule-governed dialect, and dynamic meaning that have distinctive and predictable characteristics.
Culturally Competent Professional	Possessing multiperspective cultural knowledge evident by an appreciation and ability to understand, communicate, interact with, and effectively serve people across cultures.
Culture Shock	Cultural disharmony that occurs when individuals encounter cultural discontinuity in a situation, and they have difficulty making cultural transitions.
Culture Tools	These are shared beliefs, customs, language, knowledge, roles, technology, history, etc., that are developed by people within the culture; *over time* principles of values, survival, sustainability, standards of engagement within and outside of the culture.
Intersectionality of Culture	Intersections of social and cultural power differentials, categorizations and identity markers such as ethnicity, race, class, gender/sex, nationality, geopolitical positioning, religion, sexuality, age, dis/ability, species, and so on; it takes into account people's overlapping cultural identities in order to understand the complexity of advantages, disadvantages, and prejudices they face.
Three Views of Culture	Used to explain the school performance of diverse students that impacts recruitment and retention in gifted and talented education—deficit, different, and conflicted.

Note. The terms and definitions are developed from direct, summative, and/or interpreted information from Ford (2013). For *Cultural Language*, it is important to note that standardized English is not acultural and as a language has its own dominant cultural influence.

When I conduct workshops around the country, I often use Figure 5.1 as a visual aid to help educators understand the potential harm of deficit-based equity solutions and recognize more appropriate equity solutions. In Figure 5.1, the graphic on the left illustrates a deficit-based equity approach whereby the perceived deficits (height) of the student are the apparent reasons equality doesn't work, as evidenced by the offered solution to apply appropriate resources (the boxed crate) to compensate for the perceived or actual deficits/needs of the student. This approach ignores and dismisses the presence of institutional racism and systemic biases, represented by the fence, as the primary source for perceiving the student's characteristic (height) as a deficit in the first place.

Additionally, this approach risks educing a response by others that their "entitled" resources were taken away to be given to the student in need; this misinterpretation creates an even more isolating environment for the student. Alternatively, the graphic on the right illustrates a strength-based approach that recognizes institutional racism and system biases (the track) as the primary issue. This is evident by exemplification of an equalized, strength-based view of different students (equal height) who are strategically positioned to offset, or neutralize, the impact of the inequitable policies and practices that affect them individually. Although, on the surface, both approaches seem to offer adequate short-term solutions, the latter is complemented by culturally responsive practices that promote an equalized opportunity for talent development and positive identity formation.

Equity in access and assessment fosters the social, emotional, and cultural contexts needed to support the identity and talent development of the individual student as a matter of fundamental rights and social justice (Collins, 2019; Ford et al., 2018). More definitively, I theorize that absolute equity, a principle of universal justice, is a noncomparative, responsive treatment tool applied in action to (1) hold culturally accountable, (2) add individualized worthiness to, and (3) ensure affective maximization of a system of learning that is otherwise defected by the necessity of standardization (Collins, 2019), racism, and biases.

FIGURE 5.1

Addressing Equity and Equality that Neutralizes
Institutional Racism and Systemic Biases

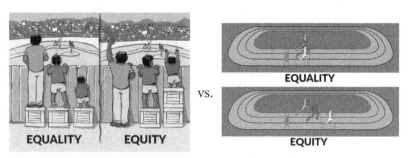

Note. The left-hand image is from "Illustrating Equality vs Equity," illustrated by Angus Maguire, 2016, Interaction Institute for Social Change, https://interaction institute.org/illustrating-equality-vs-equity, http://madewithangus.com. Reprinted with permission of the Interaction Institute for Social Change website. The right-hand image is from "The Problem With That Equity vs. Equality Graphic You're Using," by P. Kuttner, 2016, Cultural Organizing, https://culturalorganizing.org/the-problem-with-that-equity-vs-equality-graphic. Reprinted with permission of P. Kuttner.

Accommodations for Cognitive and Cultural Diversity

It is important that gifted education professionals approach program design and curricular experiences in ways that support students' needs and interests. Referred to as accommodations, an appropriate framework and lens that neutralize the biases that disadvantage students of color utilize a neurodiversity and cognitive diversity lens that build on students' strengths and resist pathologizing their differences. Neurodiversity is a viewpoint that brain differences that are not the result of disease or injury are normal variations in human genome (cognitive diversity), rather than deficits (e.g., autism, Attention Deficit/ Hyperactivity Disorder). Cognitive diversity suggests that differences in perspective, as a byproduct of cultural differences, cultivate creative problem solving and innovation that should be appreciated and valued in formal educational settings, especially in a gifted education setting. Such an approach reduces stigma around learning and thinking differences.

Modeled to account for the consequential impact of institutional racism and systemic biases that create stigma around learning, thinking, and cultural differences, I posit that every gifted student of color, inherently, is a twice-exceptional (2e) learner, and appropriate accommodations should be made for identification and programming services. Figure 5.2 illustrates a cultural context for dual or twice-exceptional (2e) students. Within gifted education, a widely accepted definition for a twice-exceptional learner is a student:

> who exhibits high performance capability in an intellectual, creative, or artistic area; possesses an unusual capacity for leadership; or excels in a specific academic field and who also shows evidence of one or more disabilities as defined by federal or state eligibility criteria such as: learning disabilities; speech and language disorders; emotional/behavioral disorders; physical disabilities; traumatic brain injury; autism spectrum disorder; other health impairment such as ADHD. (Texas Education Agency, n.d.)

It is important to reiterate, however, that giftedness and disability are both social constructs. Other social categories, including race/ethnicity, age, socioeconomic status (SES), language, gender, sexual orientation, religion, physical (dis)abilities, and so on, become cultural exceptionalities—marginalized when more dominant representations of that same category are present or determined to be the norm. The criteria for determining whether someone belongs to any of these categories are created and shaped by society. This cultural lens for addressing exceptionalities is situated within, for the most part, the overarching macroculture of the larger society, revealing an intersecting relationship between exceptionalities that is more complex. For example, an overrepresented classification in special education or the underrepresentation in gifted education for Black and Latinx students is evidence that exceptionality is a social category, as interpreted by this model.

FIGURE 5.2
*The Intersectionality of Gifted, [Dis]Abilities,
and Other Social Categories*

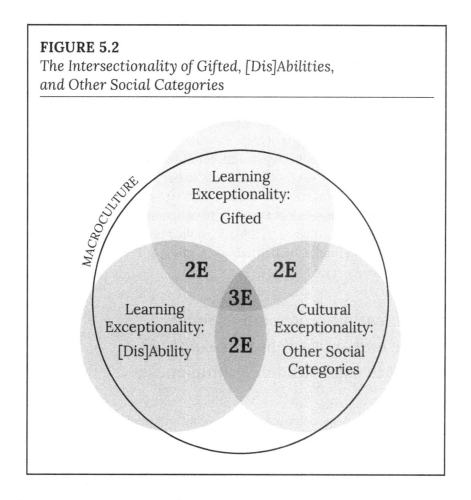

Final Thoughts

Based on almost 30 years of educational leadership, advocacy, and personal experience as an unidentified gifted student, mother of identified gifted students, and community agent, I offer the following as recommendations to further neutralize institutional racism and systemic biases.

As a nonnegotiable, gifted and talented education services and programming must recognize and appreciate diversity as a value-added concept in gifted education. Appreciation includes an explicit and consistent celebration of differences as strengths of the student and to the benefit of the program. Gifted education professionals must prioritize and employ absolute equity as a treatment to value students' uniqueness and to develop students individually while accomplishing gifted education goals. Even though it is not discussed much, at the forefront of identity and talent development in any setting, acknowledgement of the racist positionality toward Black people in America (Collins, 2020a) is critical, and must be countered by antiracist program policy, curriculum design, and instructional strategies. Promotion of a positive, self-image as gifted students of color should be stressed at every stage of development to include positive social, emotional, and cultural support, along with academic success (Collins & Roberson, 2020; Ford et al., 2018). Identify and nurture potential in all types of talent, especially from individuals whose talents may not have manifested and fully translated in academic settings (e.g., athletic, skilled positions that incorporate physical and intellectual giftedness; Collins & Perry, 2018; Dexter et al., in press).

Gifted education professionals must prioritize and employ absolute equity as a treatment to value students' uniqueness.

To promote responsive meaning-making and to offset any detected underachievement, implement "life planning" as an integral part of the curriculum design that compels academic achievement and talent development as a focus of students' lives. For college preparation, a major objective can focus on preparation for the most competitive and highly selective schools in America, and globally as a standard for academic excellence (Collins, 2017; Collins & Perry, 2018). Find ways to infuse students' specific academic and/or STEM interest into every course, enrichment opportunity, competition, etc., for continued development (Collins, 2018; Collins et al., 2019). Include guidance and/or preparation for state and national competitions as real-life, problem-based projects that offer development strategies and expose students to like-minded competitors with the same interest (Collins & Grantham, 2017).

Take responsibility to maximize learning and potential by making students aware of out-of-school opportunities, such as summer school for enrichment, earning credits by exam, taking dual enrollment and online, joint enrollment courses, completing independent courses, and studying abroad (Collins, 2017). Service learning within the student's own community also provides opportunity for in-depth and culturally relevant exploration of subject-based topics and concepts taught in school. It fosters creativity, community engagement, and problem solving as well as leadership development that benefits the student and the connected community.

By no means do these recommendations serve as a replacement for the hard work that must ultimately be facilitated to effect significant change. As a high school math teacher, I like to recite the statement, "You can never reach a true conclusion given a false hypothesis." It is the "false hypotheses" upon which gifted education was built that must be redressed and corrected.

References

Collins, K. H. (2017). From identification to Ivy League: Nurturing multiple interests and multi-potentiality in gifted students. *Parenting for High Potential, 6*(4), 19–22.

Collins, K. H. (2018). Confronting color-blind STEM talent development: Toward a contextual model for Black student STEM identity. *Journal of Advanced Academics 29*(2), 143–168. https://doi.org/10.1177/1932202X18757958

Collins, K. H. (2019, February). *Employing absolute equity to support gifted individuals: A lesson from the learning tree* [Webinar]. Supporting the Emotional Needs of the Gifted.

Collins, K. H. (2020a). Talking about racism in American and in education: The reflections of gifted Black educational professional and mother of gifted Black young adult. *Parenting for High Potential, 9*(3), 3, 5–9.

Collins, K. H. (2020b). Gifted and bullied: Understanding the institutionalized victimization of identified, unidentified, and underserved gifted students. In F. H. R. Piske & K. H. Collins (Eds.), *Identifying, preventing, and combating bullying in gifted education.* Information Age.

Collins, K. H., & Fields-Smith, C. A. (2022). Understanding the cultural capital of Black parent engagement in STEM talent development among gifted Black students [Manuscript under review]. *Journal of Advanced Academics.*

Collins, K. H., & Grantham, T. C. (2017, November). Developing scholar identity: The Dr. Martin Jenkins Scholars Program. *Teaching for High Potential*, 6–9.

Collins, K. H., Joseph, N. M., & Ford, D. Y. (2019). Missing in action: Gifted, Black girls in science, technology, engineering, and mathematics. *Gifted Child Today*, 43(1), 55–63. https://doi.org/10.1177/1076217519880593

Collins, K. H., & Kendricks, T. (2022). Fostering cultural capital for recruitment and retention: A holistic approach to serving gifted, Black students in gifted education. In J. A. Castellano & K. L. Chandler (Eds.), *Identifying and serving diverse gifted learners: Meeting the needs of special populations in gifted education* [Manuscript in preparation]. Prufrock Press.

Collins, K. H., & Perry, A. M. (2018). Crouching talents, hidden gifts: The dualism of academic excellence and athletic development for African American, gifted student-athletes at selective, prestigious, research universities. In L. A. Castenell, T. C. Grantham, & B. J. Hawkins (Eds.), *Recruiting, retaining, and engaging African-American males at select public research universities: Challenges and opportunities in academics and sports* (pp. 175–186). Information Age.

Collins, K. H., & Roberson, J. J. (2020). Developing STEM identity and talent in underrepresented students: Lessons learned from four gifted Black males in a magnet school program. *Gifted Child Today*, 43(4), 218–230. https://doi.org/10.1177/1076217520940767

Dexter, M., Collins, K. H., & Grantham, T. C. (in press). Extending the scholar-baller model to support and cultivate the development of academically gifted Black male student-athletes. *Gifted Child Today*.

Ford, D. Y. (2013). *Recruiting and retaining culturally different students in gifted education*. Prufrock Press.

Ford, D. Y., Grantham, T. C., & Collins, K. H. (2018). Giftedness, racial identity, and social-emotional learning: Challenges and recommendations for culturally responsive practice. In F. H. R. Piske, T. Stolz, C. Costo-Lobo, A. Rocha, & E. Vazquez-Justo (Eds.), *Educação de superdotados e Talentosos - Emoção E criatividade* (pp. 87–102). Jurua.

Frasier, M. (1997). Gifted minority students: Reframing approaches to their identification and education. In N. Colangelo & G. A. Davis (Eds.), *Handbook of gifted education* (2nd ed., pp. 498–515). Allyn & Bacon.

Frasier, M. M., Martin, D., Garcia, J., Finley, V. S., Frank, E., Krisel, S., & King, L. L. (1995). *A new window for looking at gifted children* (RM95222). University of Connecticut, The National Research Center on The Gifted and Talented.

Grantham, T. C., Ford, D. Y., Davis, J. L., Frazier Trotman Scott, M., Dickson, K., Taradash, G., Whiting, G. W., Cotton, C. B., Floyd, E. F., Collins, K. H., Anderson, B. N., Fox, S., & Roberson, J. J. (2020). *Get your knee off our necks: Black scholars speak out to confront racism against Black students in gifted and talented education.* The Consortium for Inclusion of Underrepresented Racial Groups in Gifted Education.

Kuttner, P. (2016). *The problem with that equity vs. equality graphic you're using.* Cultural Organizing. https://culturalorganizing.org/the-problem-with-that-equity-vs-equality-graphic

Legislative Council of the Hong Kong Special Administrative Region of the People's Republic of China. (n.d.). *Legislative council secretariat (handling of complaints).* https://www.legco.gov.hk/general/english/sec/corg_ser/redress.htm

Maguire, A. (2016). *Illustrating equality vs equity.* Interaction Institute for Social Change. https://interactioninstitute.org/illustrating-equality-vs-equity

Marland, S. P., Jr. (1972). *Education of the gifted and talented: Report to the Congress of the United States by the U.S. Commissioner of Education and background papers submitted to the U.S. Office of Education,* 2 vols. U.S. Government Printing Office. (Government Documents, Y4.L 11/2: G36)

National Science Foundation. (2010). *Preparing the next generation of STEM innovators: Identifying and developing our nation's human capital.* https://www.nsf.gov/nsb/publications/2010/nsb1033.pdf

No Child Left Behind Act, 20 U.S.C. §6301 (2001). https://www.congress.gov/107/plaws/publ110/PLAW-107publ110.pdf

Rodríguez Amaya, L., Betancourt, T., Collins, K. H., Hinojosa, O., & Corona, C. (2018). Undergraduate research experiences: Mentoring, awareness, and perceptions—a case study at a Hispanic serving institution. *International Journal for STEM Education* 5(9), 1–13. https://doi.org/10.1186/s40594-018-0105-8

Texas Education Agency. (n.d.). *Twice-exceptional students and G/T services.* Equity in gifted/talented (G/T) education. http://www.gtequity.org/twice.php

6

Culturally and Linguistically Sustaining Practices for Multilingual Learners With High Academic Potential

Nielsen Pereira and Luciana C. de Oliveira

The United States has been a leading nation in the world in welcoming immigrants for centuries. Millions have migrated to the United States since around 1600 when the first Europeans started settling on the east coast. Thus, educating those who immigrate to the country and their children needs to be a priority in U.S. schools. In 2017, approximately 9.6% (4.85 million) of the students enrolled in U.S. public schools were classified as English language learners (ELLs; National Clearinghouse for English Language Acquisition, 2020). Between 2000 and 2017, the population of ELLs increased in 43 states, with some states (e.g., Kentucky and Mississippi) seeing increases of more than 400%. We use the term *multilingual learners* (MLs) to refer to this population of students because it highlights the fact that these students generally already know one or more languages and are becoming multilingual with the addition of English to their linguistic repertoire (de Oliveira, 2019). Most teachers in the United States will, at some point in their careers, have MLs in their classrooms. Preparing educators to teach MLs and to provide any additional support that these students may need is crucial. Within the ML population, a group that has been largely overlooked in U.S. schools, are MLs with gifts and talents or who show high levels of academic potential. These students have been underrepresented in gifted programs (Peters et al., 2019), and the many myths and misconceptions, as well as some terminology issues, have resulted in a lack of research on how to identify and serve MLs with high academic potential. Unfortunately, the focus in educating MLs has long been on teaching them English first and then focusing on the actual content they need, but MLs, especially those with high academic potential, also benefit from additional challenges and programming that address their strengths.

We prefer the term multilingual learners (MLs) because this term emphasizes an asset-based approach to educating this population.

Before we present other issues in identifying and educating MLs who are gifted and talented, as well as solutions to such issues, we need to clarify a few terms, as it is clear that terminology issues exist both in the fields of Teaching English to Speakers of Other Languages (TESOL) and gifted education. The terminology used to describe MLs generally reflects deficit perspectives and the general perception that these are students who lack language proficiency. Terms such as *limited English proficient* (LEP), *non-native English speakers*, and *language-minority students* highlight these students' limited English proficiency as well as the fact that English, which is seen as the language of the majority in the United States, is not their home language. As noted, we prefer the term *multilingual learners* (MLs) because this term emphasizes an asset-based approach to educating this population.

The terminology used to describe students with gifts and talents often reflects the misconception that these are students with extremely high levels of ability and who will do well in school with or without much help from teachers. The use of terms such as *gifted and talented* or *intellectually gifted*, as well as the misconception that gifted students are geniuses, are a disservice to the students and gifted education advocates. In addition, these terms have been used to characterize gifted services as elitist. This terminology may cause issues with identifying students from certain populations as gifted: If a general perception exists that gifted students are those with "exceptional ability," then students who struggle with any aspect of their schooling will likely not be identified as gifted. Alternative terms to describe gifted and talented students include *students with gifts and talents*, *students with high ability*, and *students with high academic potential*. By using the term *multilingual learners with high academic potential*, we reiterate our commitment to strength-based views and broadening access to gifted services. Students who show high academic potential, and not just students with demonstrated ability, should also receive gifted and talented services.

Our Experiences

Our own experiences have led us to focus our research and advocacy endeavors on MLs who have high academic potential. We are transnational scholars who immigrated as young adults to the United States to pursue graduate degrees in education. We both learned and taught English as a foreign language (EFL) in Brazil and grew up speaking Portuguese with our families. We also learned other foreign languages well enough to try to use them in everyday conversation—an experience that is still unusual to many in the United States—but perhaps not well enough to use these languages in academic settings. Our experiences help us understand the experiences and struggles of MLs in U.S. schools. However, because we immigrated to the United States as adults, different sets of issues affected our experiences in academic settings—both of us have very strong skills in our home languages and came to the United States in fairly comfortable situations to study at well-respected educational institutions where we met peers who were, for the most part, welcoming.

Unfortunately, that is not always the case with MLs who immigrate to the United States as children or adolescents. Teachers are the ones who can help these students by making sure that they feel welcome in an educational environment that caters to their needs and emphasizes their strengths. One issue that likely affects teachers' perceptions of MLs is the fact that learning and using a foreign language is not common in the United States because of the dominance of the English language around the world. Most people who live in the United States expect visitors to this country and people involved in the tourism and hospitality industry in other countries to speak at least some English. One of the consequences of this is that many people in the United States have limited experience with how challenging it is to learn a foreign language in a classroom or by immersion. That struggle in itself is something that can create some empathy for those who are learning other languages. Here, again, our own experiences learning foreign languages serve us well and make it easier for us to understand the challenges MLs face in U.S. schools.

As teacher educators, we have interacted with many educators, administrators, and teacher education students who held misconceptions regarding MLs, especially those with high academic potential. We have also encountered many educators and administrators seeking assistance to create procedures to identify more MLs for their gifted and talented programs and find ways to provide the services these students need. We have witnessed schools putting all of their efforts (and financial resources, in some cases) in identifying MLs with high academic potential, then placing these students in programs that did not address their academic and, most importantly, their linguistic needs. We have taught preservice teachers who did not understand how a child who was not completely fluent in English could be gifted or have high academic potential. We have seen many researchers also focus on finding ways to identify MLs with high academic potential; however, studies on effective practices for educating these students are still scarce. All of these issues have led to the current state of research on and practices for MLs with high academic potential. Our goals in writing this essay are to discuss some of these issues and misconceptions, to present a set of culturally and linguistically sustaining practices that work with MLs, and to encourage researchers in the fields of TESOL and gifted education to study existing and new educational practices for MLs with high academic potential. First, we would like to present a few misconceptions regarding MLs with high academic potential.

Misconceptions

One of the biggest misconceptions regarding MLs is that this is a homogeneous population and thus the same strategies and approaches to teaching these students will work with all MLs. Multilingual learners come from many parts of the world, and it is crucial for educators to be aware of cultural and linguistic differences. It is also important for teachers to acknowledge that this diversity makes classrooms culturally rich environments where students learn not only the content, but also about different cultures and languages. Learning to accept students who speak a different language as different and as bringing a wealth of knowledge and experiences to classrooms can help teachers see these students as assets.

> *Multilingual learners come from many parts of the world, and it is crucial for educators to be aware of cultural and linguistic differences.*

Another misconception is that all children who immigrate to the United States are proficient in their home language. One key issue here is that these children may or may not have the literacy base in their home language, so teachers cannot assume that they can read materials in their home language. Many immigrant children are students with interrupted formal education (SIFE), which presents additional challenges. Teachers cannot expect these students to do as well as students who speak English as a first language on tests that have a verbal component, including written directions. Because MLs may not have the literacy base in their home language, testing them in that language may also not be the best option.

Another common misconception in gifted education is that MLs need to be completely fluent in English to be identified as gifted and talented. This is likely one of the reasons why MLs are one of the most disproportionately represented populations in gifted programs. However, using gifted identification practices—such as universal screening, culturally sensitive assessments, multiple pathways to identification, and involving multiple stakeholders, including parents and multilingual teachers—may help improve the representation of MLs in gifted programs (Gubbins et al., 2018). Additionally, the rapidity with which a student acquires the English language could be a sign that a student could benefit from gifted services. Another key to improving identification practices is professional learning. When teachers are finally able to see cultural and linguistic diversity as an asset that they can use in their classrooms and something that they are responsible for sustaining and helping students maintain, they will be better equipped to see potential in MLs and other culturally diverse students.

Culturally and Linguistically Sustaining Practices

Culturally sustaining pedagogies (Paris & Alim, 2017), which expand and perhaps replace the previously widely used concept of culturally responsive teaching (Ladson-Billings, 2014), go beyond being responsive to students' needs or cultures or making sure classroom materials and instruction are relevant to them. Paris (2012) claimed that being responsive or relevant is not enough and that culturally responsive or relevant programs do not necessarily help "sustain and support bi-and multilingualism and bi- and multiculturalism" (p. 95). Culturally sustaining pedagogies address the multiethnic and multilingual nature of many U.S. classrooms and help sustain "the cultural and linguistic competence of their communities while simultaneously offering access to dominant cultural competence" (p. 95). More importantly, one of the goals of culturally sustaining pedagogies is to help perpetuate and foster "linguistic, literate, and cultural pluralism as part of the democratic project of schooling" (Paris, 2012, p. 95), which is a crucial goal in the education of multilingual learners with high academic potential.

In our article published in *Teaching Exceptional Children* (Pereira & de Oliveira, 2015), we discussed qualities of linguistically responsive teachers as well strategies that these teachers can use with MLs with high academic potential, drawing on the work of Lucas and Villegas (2011). In this essay, we combine the notion of linguistically responsive teachers with culturally sustaining pedagogies to frame what teachers need to know and be able to do to teach multilingual learners with high academic potential. We propose that teachers should use culturally and linguistically sustaining practices to address the needs of MLs with high academic potential.

A Knowledge Base for Culturally and Linguistically Sustaining Practices

Teacher preparation and professional learning can help teachers implement culturally and linguistically sustaining practices. Teachers should value linguistic diversity in their classrooms and learn about their students' language backgrounds, experiences, and proficiencies both in English and in their home language (Pereira & de Oliveira, 2015). Teachers need to develop understanding of the factors that influence language use, the connection between language, culture, and identity, and the importance of helping students maintain their home languages and culture. Aspects of all students' cultures can be highlighted in the classroom and used to contrast those with U.S. cultures. This can be accomplished in a variety of ways, such as using books, stories, and movies representing MLs' cultures or incorporating historical events from MLs' countries of origin. It is crucial to check for authenticity of such books, stories, and movies. This will not only make MLs feel included, but it can also teach U.S. students about other cultures and languages. Students who speak a different language are assets and provide learning opportunities for the teacher and other students in the classroom.

Teachers need to be aware that MLs have gifts and talents. In fact, being bilingual should in itself be seen as a gift. Teachers need to be aware that MLs with high academic potential may more quickly develop English language skills. Thus, teachers must find ways to modify, not simplify, instruction to address their needs. Instruction needs to be modified in a variety of ways, such as by changing the way information is presented (e.g., written directions, visuals, nonverbal communication). This also includes differentiating instruction by teaching MLs more nuanced or different ways to complete tasks or present information. For example, students who already know the process of photosynthesis in their home languages only need to learn how the process can be explained in English. The key is that MLs with high academic potential need additional levels of challenge in language and content learning because those are inseparable (de Oliveira, 2016). Because of this, simplifying the language means simplifying the content.

Teachers need to be aware that MLs have gifts and talents.

To support language and content learning, second-language learning strategies should be incorporated. Building a language-rich environment where students have opportunities to listen, read, speak, and write in English provides a challenge for MLs with high academic potential. This environment includes using MLs' home language(s) as resources in the classroom because skills and concepts transfer to the second language. Paying attention to how language is used in the classroom is crucial. Academic language—or the language used in schooling—contrasts with everyday language used for communicative purposes. Using academic language includes a process of making academic dimensions of subject matter transparent for MLs. Bridges between everyday and academic languages are essential for understanding of content (de Oliveira, 2016). We recommend using multimodal strategies—strategies that use multiple modes—to support MLs' academic language and content learning. One such strategy is called Visual Thinking Strategies (VTS). Originally designed for use with museum goers, VTS has been adapted for the classroom and provides MLs with a nonjudgmental space for art discussion where their voices are validated by the teacher facilitating the activity. Classroom implementation takes several steps, which include showing an image to students and asking specific questions that lead students to reflect on the image and make connections to content. The strategies described here help MLs develop advanced language proficiency and content learning.

A Call for Research on Effective Practices for Multilingual Learners With High Academic Potential

To date, most of the research on MLs with high academic potential has focused on identification and underrepresentation issues. The bottom line is: We know identification procedures and instruments that work with MLs and the ones that show promise. We also know that many widely used identification procedures and instruments are biased against MLs, and these should be avoided if the goal is to increase the representation of MLs in gifted programs. Furthermore, the underrepresentation of MLs in gifted programs has been well documented in studies using school district data as well as census data collected by the Office of Civil Rights (e.g., Peters et al., 2019). One area that has not received enough attention from researchers is effective practices for teaching MLs with high academic potential, and, although we know that the field of gifted education has much to learn from the field of second-language teaching, additional research focusing specifically on this population is desperately needed. Studies could focus on schools and programs with a proven track record of meeting the needs of this student population. Intervention studies could be used to investigate if promising practices are actually effective.

Culturally and linguistically sustaining pedagogies, as described in this essay, should be further explored. We hope this essay leads to further conversations between the fields of TESOL and gifted education that could take us in new directions for research and practices with MLs with high academic potential, a critical student population that has been neglected in both fields.

References

de Oliveira, L. C. (2016). A language-based approach to content instruction (LACI) for English language learners: Examples from two elementary teachers. *International Multilingual Research Journal, 10*(3), 217–231. https://doi.org/10.1080/19313152.2016.1185911

de Oliveira, L. C. (Ed.). (2019). *The handbook of TESOL in K–12.* Wiley.

Gubbins, E. J., Siegle, D., Hamilton, R., Peters, P., Carpenter, A. Y., O'Rourke, P., Puryear, J., McCoach, D. B., Long, D., Bloomfield, E., Cross, K., Mun, R. U., Amspaugh, C., Dulong Langley, S., Roberts, A., & Estepar-Garcia, W. (2018). *Exploratory study on the identification of English learners for gifted and talented programs.* University of Connecticut, National Center for Research on Gifted Education.

Ladson-Billings, G. (2014). Culturally relevant pedagogy 2.0: A.k.a. the remix. *Harvard Educational Review, 84*(1), 74–84.

Lucas, T., & Villegas, A. M. (2011). A framework for preparing linguistically responsive teachers. In T. Lucas (Ed.), *Teacher preparation for linguistically diverse classrooms: A resource for teacher educators* (pp. 55–72). Routledge.

National Clearinghouse for English Language Acquisition. (2020). *English learners: Demographic trends.* https://ncela.ed.gov/files/fast_facts/19-0193_Del4.4_ELDemographicTrends_021220_508.pdf

Paris, D. (2012). Culturally sustaining pedagogy: A needed change in stance, terminology, and practice. *Educational Researcher, 41*(3), 93–97.

Paris, D., & Alim, H. S. (Eds.). (2017). *Culturally sustaining pedagogies: Teaching and learning for justice in a changing world.* Teachers College Press.

Pereira, N., & de Oliveira, L. C. (2015). Meeting the linguistic needs of gifted English language learners: What teachers need to know. *Teaching Exceptional Children, 47*(4), 208–215. https://doi.org/10.1177/0040059915569362

Peters, S. J., Gentry, M., Whiting, G. W., & McBee, M. T. (2019). Who gets served in gifted education? Demographic representation and a call for action. *Gifted Child Quarterly, 63*(4), 273–287. https://doi.org/10.1177/0016986219833738

7

Indigenous Youth

See Them, Hear Them, Educate Them

Marcia Gentry and Justyna Gray

We wish to acknowledge and honor the indigenous communities native to these regions and recognize that Purdue University is built on the ancestral and unceded lands of the Potawatomi, Shawnee, Miami, and Delaware peoples. We would like to pay our respect to the elders and descendants who have stewarded these lands and waters since the beginning. We owe them a historical debt for the place on which we work and study.

Positionality and More

The editors of this important book asked me (Gentry) to write this essay on educating indigenous[1] youth, and I have reflected deeply on my connection to and expertise in the area of educating Native American youth. First, as a nonnative scholar, I do not purport to be an expert. Rather I am a deliberate and eager student who seeks to learn and speak up to "get in good trouble, necessary trouble" (Lewis, 2018, as cited in Bote, 2020) to effect positive change. You see, I want to get it right. I want to account for centuries of wrong, for genocide, and for making entire groups of people invisible still today. I want to see the lives and experiences of Indigenous peoples written back into history without the customary whitewashing that is all too common, and I want them to be visible, valued, and included in society today and in the future, without expected assimilation. I want the Indigenous youth in schools today to feel respected, understood, and important. As educators and as part of a country comprised of many equally important cultures, we owe these youth a high-quality education at a minimum. We owe it to them to see them, to hear them, to understand them, and to care about them. And they deserve to be equitably and effectively served in programs for youth with gifts and talents, now and in the future.

We owe these youth a high-quality education at a minimum. . . . they deserve to be equitably and effectively served in programs for youth with gifts and talents.

Because I do not have the firsthand lived experiences of being a Native person, I asked a very wise young woman, still in high school, to coauthor this essay. Justyna Gray has attended school in three very different kinds of communities. First, she attended a poorly funded K–8

---

1   Language is important. First, we acknowledge that the idea of race as a human taxonomy is not based on science or evolutionary biology, but rather is a social construct rooted in prevailing social perceptions (Zack, 2016). Second, we use the terms American Indian, Alaska Native, Indian, and Native youth or peoples interchangeably, recognizing that AIAN is the official federal category, but some peoples prefer different terms. We use Indigenous peoples more broadly to refer to peoples with ancient ancestral ties to colonized lands.

Bureau of Indian Education (BIE) school on the Navajo Nation. Then she attended middle and high school in a medium-sized university town where she was one of only a very few Indigenous students in the schools. In this setting, her grades fell, and for the first time she under-achieved (Desmet et al., 2020). She took the initiative to remove herself from this high school, where at best, she was invisible, and at worst, she faced low expectations and misunderstanding from her teachers. Instead, she chose to finish her last 2 years of high school at Navajo Preparatory School in Farmington, NM, adjacent to the Navajo Nation. So, together, we write this essay in an attempt to bring understand-ing, insights, and inspiration to the many good teachers working with diverse youth across the country. I write in first person, quoting Justyna throughout, and she provides a member check of my text. Neither of us purports to speak for the entirety of Indigenous youth in schools, but what we can do is provide some direction, information, and resources to help teachers continue in their growth and learning as they work with diverse populations.

Teaching from a White perspective or any specific cultural per-spective simply is not good enough for the diverse students who attend school in the United States. All students deserve more, and all benefit from accurate depictions of history, from literature and science inclu-sive of diverse authors (and characters), as well as from diverse teachers (Grissom & Redding, 2016). All students and teachers deserve more, including those from the dominant cultures and those who have been minoritized for decades by this dominant culture. We, as educators, owe it to them to strive to do better—to create inclusive, culturally responsive, nurturing learning environments in which they can develop their strengths, talents, and interests alongside each other.

Purpose

I want to be woke, and I want you to be woke as well. Woke means being alert to injustices in society, especially to racism, and alert to one's own privileges. It is not enough to not be racist. Teachers must be antiracist (Kendi, 2019), they must overtly and actively resist racism, and they must make their classrooms places of refuge for all students, especially those who have been invisible for centuries. To do nothing, to sit by when injustice occurs, to turn away, is—by its very inaction—a racist act. Teachers must be held to be antiracist, step up, and speak up, as anything less can potentially damage the minoritized students with whom they have been entrusted to educate. So, we, the authors, will address the challenges faced by American Indian and Alaska Native (AIAN) youth and actions that can be taken by scholars and educators to mitigate these challenges and to discover, honor, and develop the talents of these diverse and deserving youth.

Context

Teachers, clergy, doctors, and police, by the nature of their professions, must be held to higher standards because of the important work they do. They cannot be racist, classist, ignorant, and judgmental, and be effective in the profession. This essay focuses on educators and the education of American Indian Alaska Native, Native American, Indigenous, and First Nation Peoples because after centuries of genocide, relocation, boarding schools, assimilation, omission, and cultural appropriation, educators can and must do better. We, the authors, believe at our core, we know what is right, but we continue to be amazed at the invisibility of Native youth in our schools and the lack of knowledge, compassion, empathy, and sensitivity to their concerns by teachers, curricula writers, program developers, and the dominant culture.

Access, Underrepresentation, and Missingness of AIAN Youth With Gifts and Talents

Black and Brown lives matter, and their minds matter as well (Grantham et al., 2020). Yet according to my and colleagues' recent analysis of access, equity, and missingness nationally and in every state, Black and Brown youth are woefully underrepresented in and missing from gifted programs (Gentry et al., 2019). AIAN youth have less access to schools that identify youth with gifts and talents than do students from other races, and when they do have access, with very few exceptions, they are woefully underrepresented in gifted programs across the United States.

> *More AIAN students across the country are missing from gifted education than are identified due to a combination of lack of access and underrepresentation.*

In fact, more AIAN students across the country are missing from gifted education than are identified due to a combination of lack of access and underrepresentation in schools where they have access. One especially disturbing trend is that underrepresentation is actually worse, except for in Oklahoma, in states that have the largest percentages of Native youth in their school populations. In Alaska and North Dakota, for example, 23% and 9% of public school youth are AIAN children, ranking first and sixth, respectively, among all states for percentage of AIAN populations. Yet, AIAN youth have representation indices of .34 and .26 in gifted programs, meaning they are only approximately one-third and one-fourth as common in gifted programs as they are in the general school population. This is severe underrepresentation (Gentry et al., 2019, Gray & Gentry, in press). It seems that underrepresentation and racism are at their worst in areas with large populations of AIAN youth. This is disconcerting and begs for better screening of educators, intensive training of those who are teaching, and efforts to include and enrich students who are being overlooked in droves. This leads to questions about identification procedures and definitions of giftedness and whether any consideration is given to Indigenous cultures, values, and ways of knowing. Intervention and change are warranted to end this trend and the pervasive and longstanding course of underrepresentation of Indigenous youth as gifted and talented.

Omission

Scholars frequently omit AIAN and Native Hawaiian or other Pacific Islander (NHPI) groups from their research and reports. This is due to the fact that they comprise such a small percentage of the population (at 1.04% and 0.39%, respectively), and such small numbers, especially with quantitative studies, do not yield stable statistical results. Therefore, researchers eliminate or combine these populations, and neither method captures whether what the researchers are studying works with or applies to these important, yet small populations. Their omission adds to their invisibility in research and society (Fryberg & Townsend, 2008). Second, diversity exists among Native nations, with 573 federally recognized tribes and villages in existence today (U.S. Department of the Interior, Indian Affairs, n.d.). That they exist is remarkable considering the concerted efforts by colonizers and their government to wipe out Indigenous populations.

There may be similarities across these different groups of Indigenous people, such as their being the original inhabitants and stewards of these lands known now as the United States, their beliefs in the importance of family and relationships, their respect for elders and their lived experiences, their respect for veterans and their sacrifices, as well as their historical and contemporary experiences with genocide, assimilation, marginalization, and invisibility. However, cultural generalizations across all AIAN peoples are wholly inappropriate and stereotypical. Yet, these types of generalizations are frequently made, with many seeing AIAN people as members of one group rather than members of many diverse cultures. Further, these generalizations across cultures result in a homogenized view of people devoid of any true understanding, nuance, or detail (Brady et al., 2020).

Mascots

For example, there exists a view by White people that it is somehow their right to use depictions and labels of AIAN people as their sports mascots. It is well documented that dehumanization of people, creating an us-and-them mentality, leads to lack of empathy, compassion, and even violence against these groups, be they Native, gay, Black, or Jewish, for instance. However, no one would even think about using a slur of any other group of humans as a sports mascot. And yet, according to the National Congress of American Indians (NCAI, 2020), there are almost 2,000 Indians, Warriors, Braves, Chiefs, and R*dsk*ns[2] as mascots among high schools and higher profile professional sports teams across the country today.

My high school, in Paw Paw, MI, was one of these places, and what was most disturbing was watching the teachers, administrators, and school board members argue vehemently for their right to be a "R*dsk*n." It was bad enough that members of the community, alumni, and current students were impassioned about the issue, but to hear from and watch the educators themselves speak with such insensitivity was gut-wrenching. One person told me in a heated debate on social media in 2015, "We use the term R*dsk*n as a term of honor and a point of pride, we don't mean anything bad or offensive by it, it is our heritage and right to be The R*dsk*ns." This statement embodies the absolute essence of privilege—when the person of privilege decides what is and is not offensive to minoritized people. Such sentiment, whether intentionally offensive or not, is racist to its core. (Another told me I "should die" because, when asked my opinion, I gave a view different from theirs.)

This story ended in 2020 (Miller, 2020a, 2020b) after several years of angry "debate," after budget cuts by the state, after a new superintendent, and after the board voted to "respectively retire" the offensive mascot. The board later voted to adopt the Red Wolves as the school's new mascot (Miller, 2020c). The Washington Redskins followed suit and finally agreed to retire their name, thanks in part to the Black Lives Matter protests of 2020 (you see, a rising tide really does lift all boats; Sanchez, 2020). But, make no mistake, the team retired the name, not because it was the right thing to do, but because the team was about to lose millions of dollars from sponsors. But there is a crack in the clay. Others may follow. However, in the state of Indiana, the Indianapolis Indians (minor league baseball) are alive and keeping their name, for now.

---

2   This term is so offensive to many Indigenous peoples that the NCAI spells it with asterisks. We have done the same. For a discussion on this term, see Cladoosby (2013).

Justyna's Story

Justyna is a senior at Navajo Preparatory School in Farmington, NM. This is a residential school, but like other schools, it has had to make changes due to the pandemic. As briefly described earlier, Justyna has attended schools in three different settings, a BIE school as an elementary student, a Midwestern middle and high school, and finally, Navajo Preparatory School as a junior and senior, where she is planning for her postsecondary school experiences. In between her BIE school and Navajo Prep, she attended a middle and high school near a major university in the Midwest, where she estimated 90% of her teachers were White and where there were few other Native youth. This is in direct contrast to her BIE school, which enrolled 99% Native youth and employed 80% Native teachers, and Navajo Prep with 97% Navajo students and 20% White teachers. Thus, her experiences in these public schools were, in some ways, shocking to her, and ultimately led to undermining her self-confidence and her love of learning, resulting in underachievement (Desmet et al., 2020). This undermining of her self-confidence began in middle school when the counselor decided to recommend her for a basic (rather than college preparatory) diploma for high school planning. This was despite a GPA greater than 3.0 and solid academic performance in her classes. In fact, at her BIE school, Justyna was identified as gifted. Fortunately, her parents intervened and ensured she was enrolled in college prep courses. She experienced marginalization, invisibility, and lack of understanding from her teachers at the middle school and the high school for a period of 5 years.

She recognized the toll being in the public school away from culture and understanding was taking on her performance, aspirations, and self-confidence.

In fact, without asking, her teachers routinely assumed she was Latina. And they often held low expectations for her, perhaps, she believes, because of her brown skin. Justyna described, once during speech class, asking if she could begin her speech in another language, as introducing yourself in Navajo is customary in her culture and something she wanted to share. Her teacher told her it "would be fine if she began her speech in Spanish." She also described having a substitute teacher in her ethnic studies class who told her and the rest of the class that Native Americans did not exist. She explained that when she would give her opinion as an Indigenous person from her perspective, many times teachers would "undermine or ignore" her input. For example, in a middle school social studies class, Justyna asked if they could discuss the Dakota pipeline, but her teacher shut that request down by telling her (and the class), "there was nothing to debate about." She recognized the toll being in the public school away from culture and understanding was taking on her performance, aspirations, and self-confidence, as she was routinely subjected to outright bias. Justyna asked to leave the public high school, from which she originally planned to graduate, and instead attend Navajo Preparatory School, the specialized residential school her older sister had attended prior to attending Brown University.

Justyna has applied to eight universities, and she aspires to work in the environmental sciences field to preserve the natural food webs of animal species indigenous to her Native nation's original lands. She will be the fourth of four girls from her family to attend college and the second to graduate from Navajo Preparatory School.

A Brief, Often Untold, History Worth Considering

So much of what is and was written in history books is limited and whitewashed. This is especially true concerning AIAN people. There are few lessons on Native nations, peoples, and cultures, and even fewer that reveal the role of the U.S. government and colonization in the genocide, broken treaties, spread of disease, deliberate destruction of resources, forced relocation, and ongoing trauma from abuse visited on Native children in boarding schools. Following are a few of the major events in the history of Indigenous people in the United States. It is beyond the scope of this essay to provide a complete history, but perhaps these snippets whet your curiosity to learn more, to be better, to be woke, and to consider your students differently and with compassion and understanding of centuries of marginalization as a backdrop to their cultures. (*Note.* For more on these topics, see the list of resources at the end of this chapter.)

In 1637, "peaceful pilgrims" massacred the Pequots, destroying their camps near Stonington, CT. Yet today, the dominant culture celebrates Thanksgiving as a peaceful treatise between White and Indian people. Thanksgiving is a myth, and many Indigenous people do not celebrate it for obvious reasons. Yet it is a holiday, in many ways as offensive as Columbus Day, and is routinely taught in schools from the perspective of the dominant-culture educators and curriculum writers.

Andrew Jackson was central to the extermination of Indians, proclaiming that the only good Indian was a dead Indian. He signed the Indian Removal Act on May 28, 1830, in order to open land to White settlers, which resulted in the Trail of Tears (1836–1838), affecting the Creek, Cherokee, Muscogee, Seminole, Chickasaw, and Choctaw nations, which cost in excess of 8,500 Indian lives. In 1864, the Navajo people experienced attempted ethnic cleansing as they were "deported" from their lands in Arizona to Bosque Redondo, in Eastern New Mexico. These forced relocations have been referred to as genocides and death marches. Countless others died in the internment or detention camps from overcrowding, disease, exposure, and starvation. Jackson's face is on the $20 bill today, and his picture hung behind the ceremony in the Oval Office when President Donald Trump "honored" three of the Navajo Code Talkers (Tatum & Merica, 2017). At the same meeting, Trump made disparaging comments about U.S. Senator Elizabeth Warren and Pocahontas. In 2019, Trump took Native American History Month, established in 1990 by President George H. W. Bush, and changed it to Native American History and Founders Month, thus undermining everything for which it stood.

Slavery is generally taught in schools with Abraham Lincoln portrayed as the hero who signed the Emancipation Proclamation. What is not mentioned, however, is that he allowed the largest mass execution in U.S. history to occur on December 26, 1862, in Mankato, MN, when 38 Dakota people were publicly hanged. These executions were in response to the Dakota uprising, violence brought on by treaty violations, hunger, and oppression of the Dakota people by the U.S. government. Lincoln commuted the sentences of 264 Dakota people, so he had knowledge of and the power to stop the executions, but he chose not to.

In 1860, the first Indian boarding school was opened. Assimilation was the goal, with Native children taken from their parents, given

White names, converted to Christianity, and forbidden to speak their language. It was not until 1978 with the passing of the Indian Child Welfare Act that Native American parents gained the legal right to deny their children's placement in off-reservation schools. The intent of these boarding school practices was to alienate Native children from their families, traditional cultural practices, and languages. Further Indian boarding school staff sought to indoctrinate children into White American "culture" and Christianity, thereby assimilating them into the dominant culture. Indian women were sterilized against their will, and Indian children were removed from their homes and placed with adoptive White families. And I could continue, as the atrocities are numerous, spanning centuries of colonization.

Finally, largely missing from the history books are the contributions of Indigenous people to society. For example, without the Navajo Code Talkers, the allies may have lost World War II. This is especially poignant, given the push by the U.S. government to eliminate Indigenous languages. A few examples of the countless contributions Indigenous peoples have made to society include cultivating cotton, rubber, beans, cranberries, chocolate, and corn; developing a framework for democratic governance; developing birth control, topical antiseptics, bottles, and syringes; and inventing suspension bridges, raised agricultural beds, baby bottles, toboggans, kayaks, canoes, and lacrosse. Finally, had the Pequot not shared food with the pilgrims and taught them cultivation techniques, it is likely that the pilgrims would not have survived.

Simple Changes and Awareness Can Make a Large Difference

As an educator, psychologist, counselor, administrator or other helping professional, what can you do? At a very basic level, you can begin by being open to learning about AIAN people and their history, cultures, and traditions. My own journey to where I am today has been one of growth, openness, and understanding. I have developed these through listening, observing, reading, asking questions, and—above all—caring about students.

When I asked Justyna what she wished her White teachers would do, she said, "I wish they would stomp down racism when it happens at school and they would realize the damage it can do to students around them." Kendi (2019) said you can't be a bystander and be antiracist. Justyna also said:

> I wish they wouldn't undermine or ignore the input I give in class discussions when it's about my point of view as an Indigenous person. I wish they would take into consideration that some students learn differently than others. Natives often learn better through hands-on learning and visual learning because of how we are taught our culture through storytelling.

Justyna went on to explain that she wished her White teachers would understand how she "grew up differently from other students, and that I have had experiences in life that they never had to experience. For example, I know what it is like to live without electricity. I wish they understood that being the one Brown student in your class can be unsettling." Finally, she offered this advice to her teachers, "Remember that everyone comes from a different background, and not everyone has the privileges they do."

Begin by being open to learning about AIAN people and their history, cultures, and traditions.

As I was doing another writing project, I came across an old reference, perhaps the first paper written by Rocky Robbins (1991) in which he described his observations and interactions with 125 gifted American Indian secondary students who attended a summer program, Explorations in Creativity, at the City campus of the University of Oklahoma. Despite the fact that this manuscript was published 30 years ago, I was struck by how the students' advice was applicable today and how aligned it was with Justyna's suggestions. For example, these students suggested that:

1. racism was overt and problematic, giving examples of the reenactment of the Oklahoma Land Run and celebration of Columbus day.

2. they were coerced to participate in school activities that violated Indian traditions such as the requirement to dissect animals in science class and the demand to cut hair in sporting activities.
3. and the stereotypical name calling such as "chief" "squaw," "quitter," and "lazy." (pp. 19–20)

Robbins (1991) also reported these students spoke of subtle prejudice (known as microaggressions today) consisting of cultural biases on achievement tests, denying Indian students places in gifted programs as well as scholarships. They commented on teacher ignorance about and insensitivity to Indian students as well as curriculum devoid of Indian writers, Indian language, or Indian history. Interestingly, they also commented on how they were left out when race was classified, as choices were Black or White.

Like Justyna, the students had suggestions for improvement (Robbins, 1991). These included having more Indian heritage events, using nonbiased tests, educating teachers about Indians, including Indians in books and curricula, and finally, enforcing the rights of Indian students in the schools. These students commented on high dropout rates for AIAN youth, suggesting a:

> long history of bad experiences of Indians with American education (language and cultural genocide); feelings of alienation due to cultural differences and physical appearance; an Anglo curriculum . . . and the absence of . . . Indian parents on school boards; high pregnancy rates with little support for pregnant students; the lack of Indian teachers; and drugs and alcohol. (Robbins, 1991, p. 20)

In addition to defining the problem, the students offered many solutions, most still germane today. Among these solutions were honoring Indian students, parents, and culture with banquets and field trips to historical Indian sites; creating Indian clubs; developing an Indian gifted academy school; including Indian teachers, counselors, daycare workers, and school board members; and offering parenting assistance. They also noted how important it is to help Indian students find pathways to postsecondary education and provide them with career counseling.

This advice is as good today as the day it was written, which shows how dire the situation still is for AIAN youth with gifts and talents.

As educators, held to the highest standard, with the care of youth in mind, it is important to see your AIAN students and to convey your support of them and your belief that they can do well. It is important to follow Kendi's (2019) suggestions about how to become an antiracist, to speak up, and to stand up. The language you use, the examples you choose, the manner in which you call on students, and more, all send powerful messages to your students. Make it a point to uncover students' interests, strengths, and talents, and resist the urge to take a deficit view of students different from you. Instead, learn about them, their culture, and what makes them special.

> *Make it a point to uncover students' interests, strengths, and talents, and resist the urge to take a deficit view of students different from you.*

Justyna and I would suggest you consider and watch your language, as everyday talk can be inappropriate even if not intended as such. Some people talk about "going off reservation," by which they mean leaving a place; or they talk about "having a pow wow," meaning a discussion or meeting; or they discuss their "spirit animal," maybe because they think it is cool; or they talk about "finding their tribe" when they find people to whom they connect and relate. These are just a few examples of language that should be reconsidered, as using these types of phrases trivializes and demeans Indigenous cultures. Similarly, dressing up as an "Indian" at Halloween or assuming that Thanksgiving, the Fourth of July, Presidents' Day, or Columbus Day holidays are reasons for celebration by all people are mistakes.

Finding and Nurturing
Giftedness Among AIAN Youth

First, educators must acknowledge that these youth are severely underrepresented in programs for youth with gifts and talents. This is, in part, due to the use of traditional measures that were not developed with or for use with AIAN youth. My and colleagues' recent analysis of the top 10 most frequently used ability measures to identify gifted youth revealed that only one included any AIAN youth in its development (Gentry et al., in press). Additionally, all Black and Brown youth are underidentified in gifted education and have been for decades, revealing systematic racism and exclusion from special programs designed to develop gifts and talents (Gentry et al., 2019). The thing is, students lucky enough to be identified and served in gifted education benefit from these services (e.g., Bernstein et al., 2020; Colangelo et al., 2004; Steenbergen-Hu et al., 2016), so exclusion of certain racial groups serves to keep these children from services and resources they deserve to develop their potential, thus contributing to maintaining a status quo of unequal opportunities, achievement gaps, and privilege.

As educators, we must also recognize the complexity of identifying giftedness within a culture, and acknowledge that if we are going to identify AIAN youth proportionally, then we must explore Indigenous conceptions of giftedness and expand programs and focus on developing these talents. There is much talk about multiple criteria (National Association for Gifted Children, 2019), multiple pathways (Peters et al., 2019), and local group norms (Peters et al., 2019), which are all good places to begin to address inequities in gifted education. But to these efforts we need to add multicultural conceptions of giftedness and talents. We also must recognize the diversity among AIAN peoples and resist the temptation to make finding and serving AIAN youth too simple. Instead, we need to invest the time and energy into understanding the cultural nuances that exist among different communities. Doing so has the potential to broaden the scope of gifted programming and enhance its value for all children. Imagine if the social studies teacher had engaged Justyna and her classmates in an earnest discussion about the Dakota Pipeline, rather than asserting his judgment of its lack of depth for discussion.

Lara-Cooper (2014) studied the Hupa, Yurok, and Karuk people who live on the Hoopa Valley Indian Reservation (HVIR) in Northern California. In addition to surveying 230 members of the tribes, she conducted in-depth interviews and focus groups with a variety of individuals ages 18 to 95. Based on her data, she underscored how they defined giftedness from a community perspective inclusive of indigenous knowledge, essential components of developing the gifts and talents of their youth. She offered the following definition of giftedness for these groups of people:

> Giftedness can be defined through k'winya 'nya:n-ma 'awhiniw ("the human way"), meaning to live in balance and harmony with the world by having honor and respect for community members, the environment, self, ancestors, and creation. The human way is guided by language and culture and it characterized by honor, humility, patience, gratitude, discipline, compassion, a good heart, and generosity, responsibility, and respect; maintaining relationships with the human, natural, and spiritual realms; understanding and valuing the HVIR worldview; and making a contribution to the HVIR community. (p. 6)

It is easy to appreciate the richness of this conception and understand how such conceptions could broaden thinking about what giftedness means within given cultures. Incorporating these views and understandings would strengthen programs, make them more inclusive, and more socially just. In fact, Lara-Cooper (2014) provided other researchers and practitioners a roadmap of methods for replicating her work with other cultures to develop similar understandings from which to build programs. Her definition contrasted with any number of official definitions of giftedness (e.g., various state definitions, NAGC) shows the dominant, and not necessarily better, view of giftedness. NAGC (2019), for example, has an official definition that includes verbiage about race, culture, and economics, and it reads in part, "Students with gifts and talents perform—or have the capability to perform—at higher levels compared to others of the same age, experience, and environment in one or more domains. They require modification(s) to their educational experience(s) to learn and realize their potential. . . ." Yet, according to all research, underrepresentation continues to be widespread, so clearly systemic changes are needed.

Afterword: Essential Resources

Obviously this is a large topic, but it is an important topic, and as educators, we owe it to our students to be the best we can be. This means being informed, compassionate, fair, open, and understanding. This means having high standards and teaching individual students in ways that they learn best. This means forging real connections with our students and mentoring and sponsoring them so that they can become successful. There is no more important job than that of an educator. So with these things in mind, here are a few suggested resources we hope you will find interesting as your embark on a journey to understand, teach, and relate to your AIAN youth—who, for far too long, have been excluded from gifted programs and, as some describe, are "invisible" in society and in education (Fryberg & Townsend, 2008).

Online Resources

American Indian College Fund. (n.d.). https://collegefund.org

Center for Native American Youth at the Aspen Institute. (n.d.). https://www.cnay.org

Gentry, M., Gray, A., Whiting. G. W., Maeda, Y., & Pereira, N. (2019). *System failure: Access denied. Gifted education in the United States: Laws, access, equity, and missingness across the country by locale, Title I school status, and race.* https://www.education.purdue.edu/geri/new-publications/gifted-education-in-the-united-states

History.com Editors. (2020, October 26). *Native American history timeline.* History. https://www.history.com/topics/native-american-history/native-american-timeline

Little, B. (2018, November 1). *How boarding schools tried to 'kill the Indian' through assimilation.* History. https://www.history.com/news/how-boarding-schools-tried-to-kill-the-indian-through-assimilation

National Congress of American Indians. (2020). *Tribal nations and the United States: An introduction.* https://www.ncai.org/about-tribes

National Indian Education Association. (n.d.). https://www.niea.org

Native American and Indigenous Studies Association. (n.d.). https://www.naisa.org

The Nihewan Foundation for Native American Education. (n.d.). http://www.nihewan.org

Project 562. (n.d.). *Changing the way we see Native America.* http://www.project562.com

Reclaiming Native Truth. (n.d.). *Reclaiming Native truth: A project to dispel America's myths and misconceptions.* https://rnt.firstnations.org

U.S. Department of Arts and Culture. (n.d.). *Honor Native land: A guide and call to acknowledgement.* https://usdac.us/nativeland

Books

Dunbar-Ortiz, R., Mendoza J., & Reese, D. (2019). *An Indigenous peoples' history of the United States for young people.* Beacon Press.

Tapahonso, L. (1998). *Blue horses rush in: Poems and stories.* University of Arizona Press.

Note. The Humanity Archive (https://www.thehumanityarchive.com/history/native-american-history-books-everyone-should-read) lists and annotates "Native American History Books Everyone Should Read." Among them are:

- » *A Short Account of the Destruction of the Indies* by Bartolomé de Las Casas
- » *1491: New Revelations of the Americas Before Columbus* by Charles C. Mann
- » *An Indigenous Peoples' History of the United States* by Roxanne Dunbar-Ortiz
- » *Bury My Heart at Wounded Knee* by Dee Brown
- » *Empire of the Summer Moon* by S. C. Gwynne
- » *Trail of Tears* by John Ehle
- » *American Indian Myths and Legends* by Richard Dedoes and Alfonso Ortiz

Articles

Gentry, M., Fugate, C. M., Wu, J., & Castellano, J. (2014). Gifted Native American students—Literature, lessons, and future directions. *Gifted Child Quarterly, 58*(2), 98–110. https://doi.org/10.1177/001 6986214521660

Gentry, M., & Fugate, C. M. (2012). Gifted, Native American students: Underperforming, under-identified, and overlooked. *Psychology in the Schools, 49*(7), 631–646. https://doi.org/10.1002/pits.21624

Gray, A., & Gentry, M. (in press). *American Indian Alaska Native youth identified as gifted: Access, equity, and missingness.*

Masta, S. (2018). Strategy and resistance: How Native American students engage in accommodation in mainstream schools. *Anthropology & Education Quarterly, 49*(1), 21–35. https://doi.org/10.1111/aeq.122 31

Wu, J., & Gentry, M. (2014). Summer residential experiences as perceived by gifted Diné youth. *Journal of American Indian Education, 53*(2), 66–84.

References

Bernstein, B. O., Lubinski, D., & Benbow, C. P. (2020). Academic acceleration in gifted youth and fruitless concerns regarding psychological well-being: A 35-year longitudinal study. *Journal of Educational Psychology.* Advance online publication. https://doi.org/10.1037/edu0000500

Bote, J. (2020, July 18). *'Get in good trouble, necessary trouble': Rep. John Lewis in his own words.* USA Today. https://www.usatoday.com/story/news/politics/2020/07/18/rep-john-lewis-most-memorable-quotes-get-good-trouble/5464148002

Brady, L. M., Strong, Z. H., & Fryberg, S. A. (2020). The mismeasure of Native American students. In R. T. Teranishi, B. M. D. Nguyen, C. M. Alcantar, & E. R. Curammeng (Eds.), *Measuring race: Why disaggregating data matters for addressing educational inequality* (pp. 131–153). Teachers College Press.

Cladoosby, B. (2013, October 31). *Would you call me a Redsk*in to my face?* HuffPost. https://www.huffpost.com/entry/redskins-name-change_b_4181199

Colangelo, N., Assouline, S. G., & Gross, M. U. M. (Eds.). (2004). *A nation deceived: How schools hold back America's brightest students* (Vol. 2). The University of Iowa, The Connie Belin & Jacqueline N. Blank International Center for Gifted Education and Talent Development.

Desmet, O. A., Pereira, N., & Peterson, J. S. (2020). Telling a tale: How underachievement develops in gifted girls. *Gifted Child Quarterly,* 64(2), 85–99. https://doi.org/10.1177/0016986219888633

Fryberg, S. A., & Townsend, S. S. M. (2008). The psychology of invisibility. In G. Adams, M. Biernat, N. R. Branscombe, C. S. Crandall, & L. S. Wrightsman (Eds.), *Commemorating Brown: The social psychology of racism and discrimination* (pp. 173–193). American Psychological Association.

Gentry, M., Desmet, O. A., Karami, S., Lee, H., Green, C., Cress, S., Chowkase, A., & Gray, A. (in press). Gifted education's legacy of high stakes ability testing: Using measures for identification that perpetuate inequity. *Roeper Review.*

Gentry, M., Gray, A., Whiting. G. W., Maeda, Y., & Pereira, N. (2019). *System failure: Access denied. Gifted education in the United States: Laws, access, equity, and missingness across the country by locale, Title I school status, and race.* https://www.education.purdue.edu/geri/new-publications/gifted-education-in-the-united-states

Grantham, T. C., Ford, D. Y., Davis, J. L., Frazier Trotman Scott, M., Dickson, K., Taradash, G., Whiting, G. W., Cotton, C. B., Floyd, E. F., Collins, K. H., Anderson, B. N., Fox, S., & Roberson, J. J. (2020). *Get your knee off our necks: Black scholars speak out to confront racism against Black students in gifted and talented education.* The Consortium for Inclusion of Underrepresented Racial Groups in Gifted Education.

Gray, A., & Gentry, M. (in press). *American Indian Alaska Native youth identified as gifted: Access, equity, and missingness.*

Grissom, J. A., & Redding, C. (2016). Discretion and disproportionality: Explaining the underrepresentation of high-achieving students of color in gifted programs. *AERA Open,* 2(1), 1–25. https://doi.org/10.1177/2332858415622175

Kendi, I. X. (2019). *How to be an antiracist.* Penguin Random House.

Lara-Cooper, K. (2014). "K'winya'nya:n-ma'awhiniw": Creating a space for Indigenous knowledge in the classroom. *Journal of American Indian Education, 53*(1), 3–22.

Miller, K. (2020a, March 9). *Michigan school scraps Redskins mascot, citing division.* Mlive. https://www.mlive.com/news/kalamazoo/2020/03/michigan-school-scraps-redskins-mascot-citing-division.html

Miller, K. (2020b, March 11). *Native American tribes applaud mascot change at Paw Paw schools.* Mlive. https://www.mlive.com/news/kalamazoo/2020/03/native-american-tribe-applauds-mascot-change-at-paw-paw-schools.html

Miller, K. (2020c, June 22). *Paw Paw schools announce new mascot Red Wolves.* Mlive. https://www.mlive.com/news/kalamazoo/2020/06/paw-paw-schools-announce-new-mascot-red-wolves.html

National Association for Gifted Children. (2019). *A definition of giftedness that guides best practice* [Position statement]. https://www.nagc.org/sites/default/files/Position%20Statement/Definition%20of%20Giftedness%20%282019%29.pdf

National Congress of American Indians. (2020). *National school mascot tracking database: The current numbers.* https://www.ncai.org/NCAI_School_Mascot_Tracking_Database_-_Overview_and_Numbers.pdf

Peters, S. J., Gentry, M., Whiting, G. W., & McBee, M. T. (2019). Who gets served in gifted education? Demographic representation and a call for action. *Gifted Child Quarterly, 63*(4), 273–287. https://doi.org/10.1177/0016986219833738

Robbins, R. (1991). American Indian gifted and talented students: Their problems and proposed solutions. *Journal of American Indian Education, 31*(1), 15–24.

Sanchez, R. (2020, July 13). *NFL's Washington Redskins to change name following years of backlash.* ABC News. https://abcnews.go.com/US/washington-redskins-change-years-backlash/story?id=71744369

Steenbergen-Hu, S., Makel, M. C., & Olszewski-Kubilius, P. (2016). What one hundred years of research says about the effects of ability grouping and acceleration on K–12 students' academic achievement: Findings of two second-order meta-analyses. *Review of Educational Research, 86*(4), 849–899. https://doi.org/10.3102/0034654316675417

Tatum, S., & Merica, D. (2017, November). *Trump holds event honoring Native American veterans in front of Andrew Jackson picture.* CNN. https://www.cnn.com/2017/11/27/politics/donald-trump-andrew-jackson

U.S. Department of the Interior, Indian Affairs. (n.d.). *Frequently asked questions.* https://www.bia.gov/frequently-asked-questions

Zack, N. (2017). *The Oxford handbook of philosophy and race.* Oxford University Press.

8

Poverty and the (Mis)Education of Black and Hispanic Gifted Students

Erinn Fears Floyd

> It is time for the politics of race and socioeconomic position to be removed from the processes needed to give children at poverty levels a chance to accomplish the best that they can. (Baldwin, 2007, p. 23)

Like the sprawling root system of a mature oak tree, the impact of poverty on the schooling of America's Black and Hispanic students has deep roots. Entangled in this web is the widely known fact that equitable identification of these traditionally marginalized students in gifted education programs across the nation is akin to faith in the biblical scripture—"the substance of things hoped for, the evidence of things not seen" (*King James Bible*, 1769/2017, Hebrews 11:1). There is a high concentration of Black and Hispanic students living in poverty. Together, they make up 92% of students in U.S. schools where poverty ranges from mid-low to high, with 25.1% to more than 75% percent of students eligible for free and reduced priced lunch (National Center for Education Statistics, 2019). Historically, especially for Black and Hispanic students living in poverty, labels of inferiority and problematic behavior have collectively placed them in the precarious position of being considered ineligible for or not worthy of gifted program participation. Although high-poverty schools are as likely as low-poverty schools to have gifted services, they exist with lower rates of Black and Hispanic students identified for participation.

The most recent data from the U.S. Department of Education's (2021) Office of Civil Rights Data Collection indicate that Black and Hispanic students comprise 8.5% and 18.1%, respectively, of students in gifted and talented programs, compared with 58.8% of White students who, on the contrary, are overrepresented in gifted education programs. These numbers represent the stark reality of the lack of diversity and racial equity in gifted education programs across the United States. That these numbers have remained constant for decades sends the glaring message that educators are comfortable with these statistics.

Poverty is characterized by a lack of basic resources and essentials for a minimum standard of living, such as food, clothing, shelter, healthcare, and transportation. Living in the absence of these essentials may lead to a multitude of other negative conditions for children and families. Lack of access to quality healthcare and medicine is attributed to chronic illness. Substandard and unstable housing may lead to homelessness. Food insecurity, another byproduct of poverty, may also contribute to poor prenatal health, inadequate nutrition, and poor physical and mental development. Living in unsafe neighborhoods may lead to behavioral and socioemotional problems, susceptibility to violence, physical health problems, and developmental delays.

Teachers and school leaders must understand the deep impact of culture on learning.

For students of color from low-income backgrounds, race, ethnicity, and language are distinct layers of the systemic racial injustices that are prevalent in education, but factoring even more heavily into the equation is the culture of poverty that plagues generations of families from diverse backgrounds. In schools across America, teachers and school leaders must understand the deep impact of culture on learning, and they must be keenly aware of the differences in the styles of communication, values, customs, and learning of students from diverse backgrounds (Trotman Scott & Moss-Bouldin, 2014). To this end, educators must not only address cultural variations among and between themselves and their students, but also confront the culture of poverty and its grip on the educational attainment of students of color.

Children living and attending school in poverty-stricken districts do not have the plethora of resources found in wealthier districts. Making matters worse, schools in poor neighborhoods and districts are typically underresourced with fewer curricular materials, have outdated technology (if any), and operate with a marginally credentialed teaching staff. Students are plagued with inexperienced teachers with out-of-field certifications. These conditions remain constant for students from lower income backgrounds because their parents typically are unaware of how to advocate for them and rarely seek resolutions for school-related matters, such as seeking advanced academic options or being overlooked during the gifted identification process. Many students living in poverty reside in single-parent homes or multifamily homes, are latchkey children, or remain largely unsupervised with parents who work rotating shifts or long hours. Further exasperating the experiences of children living in poverty is the lack of exposure to print-rich home environments, modeled reading, or quality opportunities for enrichment and exposure to the arts and music (Ford, 2007).

Cultural Disparity Between Educators and Students

All over America, students from racially diverse, particularly Black and Hispanic, backgrounds sit in classrooms led by predominately White educators whose historically disparate cultures, experiences, and perspectives place them in the challenging position to be able to authentically connect with and understand their students. These educators' demographics are starkly different from their students, thereby creating additional challenges for ethnically, linguistically, and racially diverse students when they have teachers who do not share their lived experiences. Without an acute awareness of the cultural beliefs and practices that occur within their students' homes and lives, teachers may mistake the behaviors of Black and Hispanic students as less than desirable or knowledgeable and not appropriate for participation in gifted education services (Trotman Scott & Moss-Bouldin, 2014).

To further encourage and inspire students living in poverty to excel and feel pride in themselves and improve performance and achievement, teachers must recognize and respect the differences that exist among diverse cultures represented in their classrooms and schools. One way to generate this awareness in primary grades is to develop a classroom collection of picture book biographies that celebrate the dialect and colloquial expressions of African American and Hispanic people in a sensitive yet authentic manner (Floyd & Hébert, 2010). In higher grades, biographies and curricular materials in varying genres should be available for students and serve as positive examples of success and achievement by people who resemble them. Teachers must be prepared with a thorough understanding of the specific cultures of the students they teach, how cultures affect student learning behaviors, and how they can change classroom interactions and instruction to embrace the differences.

Teachers must recognize and respect the differences that exist among diverse cultures represented in their classrooms and schools.

Constraints of Poverty on Academic Achievement

With the introduction of the No Child Left Behind Act (NCLB, 2001), high-stakes and accountability testing delineated subgroups that highlighted the performance of children from lower income backgrounds and became a major focus of every school in the country in the competition for federal dollars and a favorable school rating. Although the mantra declared no child would be forgotten or neglected, the mandate never addressed institutional or root causes of low student performance or actually improved the quality of services provided to students, especially Black and Hispanic students from low-income households.

In general education classrooms, there are instructional strategies, such as differentiated instruction, graphic organizers, and independent learning stations, to help students master the curriculum based on their respective learning style and ability level. To the contrary, despite the raging gaps (academic, wealth, health, etc.) between "the haves and the have nots," there is no mention of instructional differentiation or assessment that schools or districts provide for students from low-income households, especially during the gifted identification process. This systemic practice is antithetical to guidance in the definition of giftedness adopted by the National Association for Gifted Children (2019), which states:

> Students with gifts and talents perform—or have the capability to perform—at higher levels compared to others of the same age, experience, and environment in one or more domains. They require modification(s) to their educational experience(s) to learn and realize their potential. Student with gifts and talents:
> » Come from all racial, ethnic, and cultural populations, as well as all economic strata.
> » Require sufficient access to appropriate learning opportunities to realize their potential.
> » Can have learning and processing disorders that require specialized intervention and accommodation.
> » Need support and guidance to develop socially and emotionally as well as in their areas of talent. (p. 1)

Contrary to this definition, students from low-income households are not compared to their counterparts from low-income households; more specifically, they are not "compared to others of the same age, experience, and environment in one or more domains," but to their wealthier and more advanced peers, if even considered, for placement in gifted education programs. Further highlighting this disparity is that gifted education services are not equally accessible to students from all races and across all income levels, as poverty has exacerbated these students' consideration for placement. There is a long-standing practice of viewing students living in poverty from a deficit perspective. If organizations and district leaders actually followed the federally adapted definition to the letter and leveled the playing field for gifted students from economically diverse backgrounds, gifted programs would not continue to suffer from inequitable representation across ethnic and racial groups.

Reframing the Poverty Dynamic

Poverty is a societal barrier that has excluded students from low-income households from wholesome educational experiences that students from middle class and wealthy families have come to expect and enjoy. The systemic exclusionary practices that have relegated students from low-income households and marginalized populations to near nonexistence in gifted and talented programs must be confronted to help them succeed, regardless of their poverty-related issues. To this end, it is critical that gifted educators also shift the paradigm to create equity and excellence for gifted Black and Hispanic students who are economically disadvantaged. Teachers, despite their race, ethnicity, or gender, can help to alleviate the achievement gap between student groups through quality teaching and caring attitudes toward all students. Without addressing the specific needs of students who live in poverty, school districts put students from low-income households at further risk for academic failure. Thus, schooling alone may be insufficient for improving the lives of and access to quality education for most students living in poverty.

Increasingly diverse classrooms require educators to be cognizant of the different practices, beliefs, and needs of each student represented. By doing so, teachers will develop cultural competence and learn more about their cultural selves while exploring the visible and invisible differences among diverse student populations. In examining personal and institutional cultural beliefs and assumptions, educators begin to develop culturally responsive and more inclusive teaching practices. And to this end, according to Trotman Scott and Moss-Boudin (2014), culturally competent educators are able to distinguish between disability and cultural differences, thereby discounting discriminatory and exclusive practices that exclude Black and Hispanic students from participating in gifted education programs and result in their overrepresentation in special education programs.

> *As a nation, we must confront the perspectives that educators have of students living in poverty, especially those from diverse populations.*

The comprehensive goal of education should address the overwhelming need to increase the number of culturally competent educators who are appropriately equipped to serve in schools with high concentrations of students living in poverty and/or high concentrations of culturally or linguistically diverse students. At every level of teacher education, training, and experience, provisions must be established to guide teachers in recognizing the myriad challenges Black and Hispanic students from low-income households bring to school. Steps to accomplish this goal include collaborative partnerships with agencies and experts who specialize in diversity and equity; adding rigor, diversity, and cultural value to course content; providing ongoing professional learning for educators; creating intensive preservice teacher education internships; and establishing mentoring programs focused on meeting the needs of diverse learners. As a nation, we must confront the perspectives that educators have of students living in poverty, especially those from diverse populations. In profoundly addressing the overlooked rights of gifted students of color, Ford et al. (2018) focused on removing systemic barriers while mandating that gifted students of color have the right to be taught by culturally competent educators with unbiased culturally responsive philosophies and instructional practices.

Teacher education programs (both traditional and nontraditional) rarely provide the kinds of opportunities and professional learning necessary for teachers to examine what race and poverty are, and how prominent a role race and poverty play in their interactions with their students. A deeper understanding of racial/ethnic minority groups and students from low-income backgrounds is necessary for educators from dominant cultures. Additionally, gifted certification programs should require course content that provides the comprehensive and historical view of how gifted education practices have systemically excluded diverse students from low-income backgrounds. Further, courses should include diversity and culturally based gifted assessment training to support the belief that traditionally underrepresented students are also gifted.

With the enactment of the Every Student Succeeds Act (2015), federally funded dollars became available for districts to specifically provide professional learning to support the education, identification, and services to diverse gifted learners. Administrators and educators require specialized professional learning in cultural competence and leadership to comprehend the whole diverse gifted child. This specialized professional learning must be provided by someone who knows firsthand the experiences that affront people from diverse backgrounds and include discussions and real-world applications of how the culture of poverty affects the academic achievement of students whose access is limited to programs for the gifted.

Finding Promise in Poverty and a Pandemic

The Black Lives Matter movement and the COVID-19 pandemic concurrently pushed to the forefront the generational disparities in our society that are based on race and poverty in every realm—healthcare, education, politics, and the economy. Beyond the massive spread of the disease itself, the effects of COVID-19 have been detrimental across all domains. Unemployment rates have skyrocketed, businesses and schools have shut down, hospitals have become overcrowded, millions of lives have been lost, the sanctity of world peace is at stake, and the education, safety, and lives of people of color living in poverty have only worsened. The dual pandemics of racism and disease have exposed injustices at every turn and affected all communities, but they have especially wreaked havoc on diverse families living in poverty. The added stress of making ends meet while also having to manage or engage in virtual learning without stable Internet access or a technological device, along with other devastating personal or health challenges, have pushed people to the brink of despair.

Our global economy is at stake, racial unrest is at an all-time high, and poverty is quite a challenge to overcome. Despite daily reminders of doom and despair associated with poverty, it is not too heavy a task for all educators to dig up and disrupt its massive roots to help repair centuries of bias, maltreatment, and disregard. In doing so, they will uncover the masked talent there and begin to increase the numbers of Black and Hispanic students from low-income households who qualify for and participate in gifted education programs across the country.

References

Baldwin, A. Y. (2007). The untapped potential for excellence. In J. Van Tassel-Baska & T. Stambaugh, *Overlooked gems: A national perspective on low-income promising learners* (pp. 23–25). National Association for Gifted Children.

Every Student Succeeds Act, 20 U.S.C. § 6301 (2015). https://congress.gov/114/plaws/publ95/PLAW-114publ95.pdf

Floyd, E. F., and Hébert, T. P. (2010). Using picture book biographies to nurture the talents of young gifted African American students. *Gifted Child Today, 33*(2), 38–46.

Ford, D. Y. (2007). Diamonds in the tough: Recognizing and meeting the needs of gifted children from low SES backgrounds. In J. VanTassel-Baska & T. Stambaugh, *Overlooked gems: A national perspective on low-income promising learners* (pp. 37–41). National Association for Gifted Children.

Ford, D. Y., Dickson, K. T., Davis, J. L., Trotman Scott, M., & Grantham, T. C. (2018). A culturally responsive equity-based bill of rights for gifted students of color. *Gifted Child Today, 41*(3), 125–129. https://doi.org/10.1177/1076217518769698

King James Bible. (2017). King James Bible Online. https://kingjamesbibleonline.org (Original work published 1769)

National Association for Gifted Children. (2019). *A definition of giftedness that guides best practice* [Position statement]. https://www.nagc.org/sites/default/files/Position%20Statement/Definition%20of%20Giftedness%20%282019%29.pdf

National Center for Education Statistics. (2019). *Table 216.60. Number and percentage distribution of public school students, by percentage of students in school who are eligible for free or reduced-price lunch, school level, locale, and student race/ethnicity: Fall 2017.* Digest of Education Statistics. https://nces.ed.gov/programs/digest/d19/tables/dt19_216.60.asp

No Child Left Behind Act, 20 U.S.C. §6301 (2001). https://www.congress.gov/107/plaws/publ110/PLAW-107publ110.pdf

Trotman Scott, M., & Moss-Bouldin (2014). We need more drama: A comparison of Ford, Hurston, and Boykin's African American characteristics and instructional strategies for the culturally different classroom. *Interdisciplinary Journal of Teaching and Learning. 4*(2), 68–80.

U.S. Department of Education. (2021). *Civil Rights Data Collection (CRDC) for the 2015–16 school year.* https://www2.ed.gov/about/offices/list/ocr/docs/crdc-2015-16.html

Gender, Sex, and Sense of Self

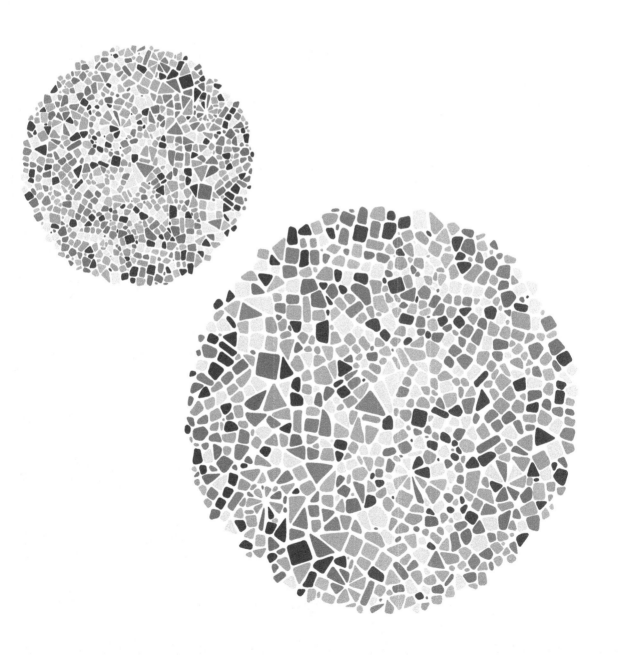

Introduction to Gender, Sex, and Sense of Self

Sally M. Reis

These essays are both enlightening and enriching, enabling readers to reflect on their knowledge. Even more important is the robust amount that we, as educators, need to learn in order to offer research-based, appropriate, and meaningful culturally responsive teaching, listening, and counseling practices to talented young people. It is especially important if we hope to develop their gifts and talents. Although we all share common paths in our learning experiences, we take completely unique journeys. What is critical for each of us to understand and make sense of is the impact of our own culture, biases, stereotypes, and experiences and the necessity for constant reflection about how our actions and intentions affect and influence the children and young adults we teach. We must be cautious not to generalize, or in some cases, over-generalize about any of these populations. When I teach my doctoral seminar in social and emotional development of gifted and talented students, I spend my first class discussing the fact that in too many articles and publications about giftedness, there are inaccurate generalizations about gifted students and adults. To set the record straight, there are some gifted LGBTQ+ students whose parents accept, love, and support them unconditionally. Some gifted transgender and nonbinary students also have extremely supportive parents and school cultures. Some gifted girls and boys do extremely well, having amazing support from parents and educators, as do students who are gifted and from culturally diverse backgrounds. Having said that, many do not, and that is one focus of this book. Another focus is the knowledge that we can *all* do better, every single day, about providing more culturally responsive and welcoming educational environments, and using culturally supportive and responsive teaching methods, many of which are discussed in this section.

We can all do better, every single day, about providing more culturally responsive and welcoming educational environments.

In the essays in this section, several common themes emerge. The authors understand the necessity of communicating high expectations and unconditional acceptance to the various populations they write about, while advocating for an understanding of the unique challenges and opportunities each group faces. Although the authors write about specific groups, these specific populations are heterogeneous groups, as they include a wide variety of abilities, talents, interests, personality traits, and strengths, as well as diverse challenges and needs these students encounter in their development.

The Essays

My own essay focuses on both current and previous research on gifted and creative girls and women who excel in various fields and domains. It illustrates the complex paths and directions they select, their diversity across multiple perspectives, and the different types of decisions that guide their paths, as well as the obstacles they face in their paths to creative productive work. In my research on gifted girls and women, I have found that the process of talent development in this population differs from the processes in men due to different psychological needs and environmental challenges. It is interesting, however, to note that in all essays in this section, support for talent development, both from parents and educators, is viewed as critically important. It is just that the type of support may vary based on both group and individual profiles and needs, as well as the resources necessary to support the individual process of talent development.

Also discussed are the different characteristics, traits, and gifted behaviors evidenced in males, as well as challenges that they experience. Six issues are addressed in this essay, including the experience of the empathic young male, self-inflected pressures that high-achieving males place upon themselves, identity development issues, image management, cultural expectations for young men of color, and differences in achievement orientations.

In the essay on Black males, the authors discuss what is necessary to support these students through the struggles and adversity that they face. The authors also discuss the various forms of ambiguity relating to the assumptions of others and those that Black males themselves hold regarding their racial and gender identities, particularly when being smart and achieving at high levels can be associated with acting White and emulating feminine traits. Further, the authors argue that these challenges can have a negative impact on academic achievement both in high school and as these young men prepare for college.

In the discussion of transgender and nonbinary gifted students, compelling points are highlighted about how this diverse population possesses gender identities and expressions that do not align with their sex assigned at birth and do not conform to the stereotypes of their assigned gender. The essay also discusses the daily pressures experienced by this group that demand our attention and support. In particular, to promote consistent application of best practices, schools and districts should not rely on individuals. The authors advise us to consider developing policies that support culturally responsive teaching. These policies should be enacted, documented, and made known to all stakeholders, and districts should encourage educators to accommodate gender expressions that may not conform to traditional social stereotypes.

Finally, the essay on students who are LGBTQ+ asks us to recognize the many sexual and gender identities that exist, and the need to understand that many of these students are a subculture within other subcultures, such as being gifted, Black, and LBGTQ+. Meeting the needs of this population may be daunting for educators and families of this group, as the young person begins a journey of discovering who they currently are and who they intend to be in the future.

Common Themes

Each of the authors of the compelling essays that follow provide insightful and interesting perspectives about the types of support and culturally appropriate teaching needed for some of the common experiences that the group has. Several themes emerge across essays regarding the needs and characteristics of these groups.

Inclusion and Support

One common theme that is found across these essays is the need for these students to be included in various ways and across various groups. Gifted students from each of these groups often fail to be identified for various reasons. Without broad and universal screening, many of the groups discussed will be overlooked for inclusion in gifted programs. Professional learning is necessary to understand the support that these young people need. Professional learning can enable educators to develop and enhance cultural competencies to create safe, welcoming, and productive environments for all of their students. In these safe environments, whenever possible, educators and parents should consider the types of strategies that support talent development, including those that welcome each student and those that develop the strengths and interests of all.

Pressure, Anxiety, Depression, and Sensitivities

The authors recognize the regular pressure and anxiety that some of these young people experience because they are both gifted and members of diverse populations. High-achieving males may experience self-inflicted pressures related to their identity development, image management, and cultural expectations. At the same time, many gifted girls face issues to excel across multiple areas and battle perfectionism. Black youth face additional anxiety and fear as a result of the current racial climate of our society. Teachers must be aware of the emotional anxiety gifted Black males and females carry within and try to understand and support them. Finally, gifted LGBTQ+ students may experience intense feelings of anxiety, self-isolation, and sensitivity regarding their decisions to come out. Transgender and nonbinary youth are more likely than cisgender peers to experience violent victimization, substance abuse, suicidal ideation, bullying, and feelings of being unsafe.

Search for Identity

All adolescents search for their identity, and indeed, the development of a stable sense of self is critical during this time period. Although one's identity development continues throughout adulthood, adolescence begins the process of considering how one's identity may emerge, affect life's most important decisions, and also change over time. We have to understand how young people who are gifted—Black or Brown; male, female, nonbinary, or transgender; gay or straight—search for compromises as they begin to understand that a journey in one direction, toward high levels of accomplishment, can take them on a different path from their friends and family. This journey affects their need for affiliation and acceptance, especially if the choices they make are not supported by their friends and family.

Defining Success

We must be aware that we cannot associate academic success with what we perceive to be assimilation into the dominant culture, despite the fact that the most successful individuals that most of us see on a regular basis are White men. Many glaring examples exist of the continuation of this outdated stereotype. As a society, we must endeavor to broaden our definition of success and expose students to more global and diverse examples of successful people. Providing peer and mentor support can help teachers and counselors become key advocates in identifying what success really means and can help gifted students transition from high school to take their place in college where they can continue to pursue their hopes and dreams.

Culturally Responsive Practices Across Diverse Groups

The authors suggest that educators need to recognize and support the development of different kinds of gifts and talents through strength-based pedagogy and planned talent development opportunities. Educators must continue to evolve and learn new strategies and information to support these groups and develop their talents. Teachers, administrators, and gifted coordinators should participate in professional learning that enables them to develop cultural competency and enhance the creation and sustainment of safe and productive environments for all gifted students to develop. Teachers who implement welcoming behaviors that support purposefully integrating students' strengths can create positive classroom and school environments.

9

Culturally Responsive Practices for Developing Gifts and Talents in Women

Sally M. Reis

What practices make a difference as educators strive to develop the innovative and creative talents of young girls and women in specific disciplines or domains? Do young women have adequate numbers of role models to develop their creativity and sense of creative self-efficacy? How do talented girls and women maintain their drive to create when they encounter obstacles that threaten their love of and passion for their work? How can educators, particularly educators of talented and gifted girls and young women, serve as agents of positive change to help these young women combat the boredom that they may encounter in some of their classes, and instead develop their creativity to make a positive impact and difference in the world? And most importantly, how do educators convince this population to pursue leadership opportunities in their professional fields or work?

Current and previous research on gifted and creative girls and women who excel in various fields and domains illustrates the complex paths and directions they select and the different types of decisions that guide their paths, as well as the obstacles they face in their pursuit of creative productive work. Creative and gifted girls and young women are an extraordinarily diverse group in every way. Their personalities vary, as do their interests and personal choices. The processes of developing their talents also vary (Reis, 1998, 2002, 2005). The process of talent development for this population is complex, due their heterogeneity, but some of the obstacles they face, both internally and externally, are similar.

Various theories have been offered by researchers, including Karen Arnold, Kate Noble, and Rena Subotnik's (1996) theory about "remarkable women," Barbara Kerr's (1985; Kerr & McKay, 2014) work about smart girls and women, and my own research and theories of talent development in women (Reis, 2002, 2005, 2021). This research documents the variations in talented girls' and women's personal and professional lives, home and work environments, parental and teacher support, creative processes, and some of the self-beliefs that guide their talent development and enable them to become eminent creative producers in their futures.

Why Concerns Linger On and On

Why do I remain worried about the creative futures of talented and creative women? Although the United States ranks first in women's educational attainment on the World Economic Forum's (2017) Global Gender Gap Index of 144 countries, it also ranks 26th in women's economic participation and opportunity, and 73rd in women's political empowerment. The Global Gender Gap Report benchmarks 144 countries on their progress toward gender parity across four thematic dimensions—economic participation and opportunity, educational attainment, health and survival, and political empowerment—finding that it will take more than 200 years to achieve gender parity in these areas (World Economic Forum, 2017).

Women's Creative Work and Leadership

Across the globe in 2019, 29% of senior management roles were held by women, the highest number ever on record (Catalyst, 2020), but this is still a depressingly low number. However, the same report shows that women working in male-dominated industries face a variety of challenges, including consistent stereotypes and sexual harassment.

And what about women's leadership positions? In 2013, women accounted for 8% of all national leaders and 2% of all presidential posts. In an analysis, the American Association of University Women (AAUW, 2016) noted that, "Despite gains in every profession, women remain underrepresented at all levels of leadership. In Congress, on corporate boards, and in our nation's colleges and universities, male leaders outnumber female leaders by considerable margins" (p. v).

Many obstacles prevent women from participating in leadership positions. They are less likely to have financial resources, they are likely to have more family responsibilities, and internationally, they usually have less education than men. In some countries, women's movements are restricted, or women are forbidden from appearing in public spaces so they cannot work or have the freedom needed to pursue higher education and training. During elections, women may be forced to vote for family-favored parties or individuals. In some cases, women don't even get to see their ballot, with male family members engaging in "proxy voting" to cast a vote in the name of women. Across the globe, discriminatory laws and institutions still limit women's options to become involved in leadership or run for office. And when they do, women are less likely than men to have the contacts and confidence to help them succeed.

Even when some women eventually do achieve leadership positions, they are in the minority, as fewer than 25 of the world's 196 countries have a woman leader. Women leaders often face prejudice, discrimination, harassment, and even violence because they represent a challenge to traditional gender roles and power relations. Women leaders, however, can be essential in helping other women's voices to be heard. For example, recent research analyzing data from democracies across the globe showed that greater political representation of women leads to overall higher importance being placed on issues such as gender equality in political and social rights, equality in marriage and divorce laws, as well as the availability of maternity leave (UN Women, 2021).

Has progress been made in women's leadership? In 2006, the average percentage of women in lower or single houses of 189 parliaments across the globe was 17% (Tremblay, 2007). This proportion varied greatly between countries. For example, an election for the Rwandan Chamber of Deputies resulted in a new record for women in national parliaments—48.8% were female members of parliament. This contrasts with data from other countries: 20.8% of the Canadian House of Commons (following the 2006 elections), 17.3% of the Italian Camera dei deputati (2006), 12.2% of the French Assemblée nationale (2002), 8.3% of the Indian Lok Sabha (2004), and 2.0% of the Egyptian Majlis Al-Chaab (2005). About 10 countries had no female member in their lower or single house (e.g., Micronesia, Nauru, Tuvalu, and the United Arab Emirates; Tremblay, 2007). Compare those figures with more current numbers, showing that 24.3% of all national parliamentarians were women as of February 2019, a slow increase from 11.3% in 1995. As of 2019, 11 women were serving as Head of State and 12 were serving as Head of Government (UN Women, 2021). Wide variations remain in the average percentages of women parliamentarians in each region. As of 2019, these were (single, lower, and upper houses combined): Nordic countries, 42.5%; Americas, 30.6%; Europe, including Nordic countries, 28.6%; Europe, excluding Nordic countries, 27.2%; Sub-Saharan Africa, 23.9%; Asia, 19.8%; Arab States, 19%; and the Pacific, 16.3% (UN Women, 2021).

Recent research also suggests that many female leaders begin their path to leadership early, engaging in various educational and leadership activities as adolescents (O'Neil et al., 2015). In several cases of leadership in other countries, such as India and Africa, case studies demonstrate that having women as leaders in communities can make a positive difference, driving policies and programs that improve family and community well-being (Abbott et al., 2008).

And what about other creative work? At one of the highest indicators of creativity, enormous gender differences exist. For example, only 5% of all Nobel prizes have been awarded to women, and despite the amazing progress made for women across the globe, they still achieve fewer awards, have fewer patents, and receive less recognition than men in all professional creative and leadership efforts (NobelPrize.org, 2021).

Cultural Obstacles to Talent Development in Women

All of the researchers mentioned in this chapter who have studied talented women over the decades have suggested that talent development in women may differ from that of men due to differences in psychological needs and drives, as well as in demands faced at home and at work, and in access to resources that encourage the development of gifts. Feminine models of talent development define gifted behavior differently than more traditional models. Talent can be expressed in many ways, such as through maternal giftedness—exemplified by women who nurture children well, build strong primary relationships, and create a safe and encouraging space for talent development in young girls and women.

Talent is important, but it is not the only factor that influences female achievement, as it is critical that talented women are able to withstand the cultural pressures of society to achieve their gifts.

High-achieving women must learn to overcome cultural and gender discrimination in whatever form they take, including cognitive and emotional flexibility, willingness to take risks and aim high, tolerance for making mistakes, persistence in the face of adversity, and the ability to resist the tendency to internalize limiting messages from the outside world. All of these play a role in female talent development. Talent is important, but it is not the only factor that influences female achievement, as it is critical that talented women are able to withstand the cultural pressures of society to achieve their gifts.

Smart Girls and Women

Barbara Kerr's writings on eminent women differ from other work discussed in this chapter in that Kerr conducted biographical research, rather than case study or experimental research (Kerr, 1985; Kerr & McKay, 2014). Kerr studied the lives of 33 eminent women in various domains, including Margaret Meade, Eleanor Roosevelt, Marie Curie, Maya Angelou, Katherine Hepburn, and Rigoberta Menchú, in order to draw conclusions about how female talent develops. In her review of the lives of successful actresses, scientists, activists, writers, and more, she found several themes. One of the most unique factors identified in Kerr's analysis of female talent development is time alone during girlhood. For some of these girls who later became eminent women, time alone was a choice; for others, it was a state forced upon them by circumstance. The eminent women Kerr studied were able to connect to others, such as mentors or partners, without losing their own identities or goals. Finally, in keeping with the idea that work was a huge part of the lives and relationships of these women, Kerr found that many joined work and love by marrying or partnering with others who shared their passions.

My previous work resulted in a theory of talent development, based on case study research, that continues to be refined (Reis, 2002, 2005). This theory includes abilities, certain personality and environmental factors, and personal perceptions, such as the social importance of the use of a woman's talent to make a positive difference in the world. Underlying this theory is the belief that talent development can occur in women of high potential through active choice, systematic work, and sustained individual effort.

My latest work in this area (Reis, 2021) continued my interest in studying creative, talented women to explore what both Ochse (1991) and Piirto (1991) asked—why are there so few women creators? I studied 15 talented, creative contributors in various fields or domains. Each woman was nominated to participate by either their deans, central administrators, leaders in their discipline, or university leadership because of her creative accomplishments or fame. They were all recognized as being at the top of their discipline and all elected to prestigious societies, academies, and associations in diverse areas, such as the arts, environmental sciences, physics, history, and other fields.

A brief case study of an African American scholar in this study is provided to illustrate some of the points made in this essay.

> F earned her BA in African American Studies from Princeton University and her doctorate from Yale. She served as director of African Studies and now teaches courses in precolonial, and colonial Africa, the history of South Africa, slavery, and the African diaspora. Since 2015, her teaching pedagogy has shifted to incorporate inquiry-based learning and human rights practice, resulting in highly creative and celebrated museum exhibits. She is well known for her scholarly work, and her books explore the relationship between African Christian converts, European missionaries, and the politics of land access, land alienation and the "civilizing" mission of African social and economic improvement in nineteenth century South Africa. She consults with various Historical Societies on oral history projects, including an exhibit documenting and recording the impact of 9/11 on Connecticut victims, families, and first responders. She organizes highly creative exhibits documenting the history of West Indian migrants and is engaged in a preservation and photo documentation project on Caribbean migration. She is frequently interviewed about her creative work, which is in great demand. She has won awards for her teaching and her creative scholarship and has had several articles written about her scholarship.

Eminent women I have studied learn over time to acknowledge their creativity and demonstrate confidence about their own creative work. Over time, they learn to express high creative self-efficacy, which has been found to be associated with creative personal identity, or the extent to which creativity makes up an individual's self-concept (Jaussi et al., 2007). The presence of both high creative self-efficacy and high creative personal identity is optimal for creative productivity and growth. But blocks continue to exist to this process and are the basis for understanding which culturally responsive practices make a difference in the lives of talented young women.

External Barriers or Blocks
That Impede Talent Development
in Girls and Women

The most important external barriers to the development of talent are the implicit biases and stereotypes talented girls and women face. New research (Storage et al., 2020) found that men are more likely than women to be regarded as "brilliant." The work concluded that these stereotyped views are an instance of implicit bias, revealing automatic associations that people cannot, or at least do not, report holding when asked directly. Across five different studies—with samples of American women and men, girls and boys ages 9–10, and women and men from 78 other countries—researchers consistently found evidence for an implicit stereotype associating brilliance with men more often than with women. The magnitude of the stereotypes found by these researchers is shocking. It is similar in strength to the implicit stereotype that associates men more than women with careers (and women more than men with the family). Previous work by Boston and Cimpian (2018) also found that women are underrepresented in careers where success is perceived to depend on high levels of intellectual ability (e.g., brilliance, genius), including those in science and technology. This certainly constitutes implicit bias and stereotyping.

The presence of both high creative self-efficacy and high creative personal identity is optimal for creative productivity and growth.

In my most recent study (Reis, 2021), almost all of the older women identified a similar external barrier when asked what the central barrier to their creativity was. For women, the most frequent and significant external block to creative productivity was finding time to focus on work. As gifted women mature and achieve higher levels of success, time is the most significant block identified by most of the women, but reasons for this block vary by age and marital status. For those who were younger and had children, it was time to focus on their family while passionately wanting to pursue their work. As a participant in my latest study explained:

> The most important challenge I have had as a creative woman is work life balance. My creative work does not come at a convenient time. The exciting content comes randomly at odd moments. I text myself ideas all the time but I also have to reel these in all the time If I am with my children, and I want to work or get a creative idea, I am called 'workaholic' and 'selfish' all the time, because I just want to do my work.

Internal Barriers and Blocks That Impede Talent Development in Girls and Women

My earlier work on talented women also focused on internal barriers that hindered the completion of high-level work and paths to productivity in younger gifted women and girls. Most experience self-doubt and the need to hide their abilities. Many gifted girls do not want to be considered different from their friends and same-age peers. And the problem becomes more difficult as they become women and their talents and gifts continue to set them apart from their peers and friends. If the school environment is one in which academics take a back seat to athletics or other activities, the issue can be exacerbated. Learning why smart girls mask or hide their ability is often critical to addressing the problem, and finding environments in which success is celebrated and individual differences are respected is crucial in helping females to resolve this issue.

Hiding Abilities and Self-Doubt

In addition to hiding abilities, many gifted and talented girls and women begin to doubt that they had advanced abilities, and gifted women often select gender stereotypic jobs, usually due to pressure from parents and teachers. A related issue occurs when females achieve high levels of success but then begin to experience what Clance and Imes (1978) and Clance (1985) called the "Great Impostor Syndrome." This syndrome describes the low sense of self-esteem that occurs when women attribute their successes to factors other than their own efforts and see their outward image of a bright, successful achiever as being undeserved or accidental. "I was lucky," "I was in the right place at the right time," "I really didn't do as well as it seems," and "I had a lot of help" are all statements made by talented females who are complimented on their successes.

Talented girls and women may attribute their successes to effort or external factors such as luck, while failures are explained as internal faults or as an absence of certain abilities. Arnold (1995) found, for example, that by the second year of college, more than a quarter of the female high school valedictorians she studied had lowered their self-rankings of their intelligence, indicating that they were merely average in intelligence. This phenomenon did not occur with the male valedictorians whose self-rankings remained consistent or improved. These women continued this pattern at graduation from college. None of the women placed themselves in the highest category of intelligence, while men, in sharp contrast, steadily increased their self-ratings.

Some talented women begin to believe that they have accomplished success because they have fooled other people or have been successful due to external factors, such as the right mentor or an act of chance. In some cases, this feeling has occurred because talented girls and women can often accomplish a great deal without the sustained effort often required from their less capable peers. If ability is high and less effort is warranted, many gifted girls and women begin to feel that they are lucky rather than academically gifted.

The academic self-efficacy of young men is enhanced based on their belief in their ability; during failures, they attribute failure to lack of effort. The same does not appear to be true for young women. Girls may accept responsibility for failure but not for success, and although girls may perceive themselves to be bright, they interpret any small failure quite negatively, believing that it is caused by lack of ability. Developing a strong belief in one's ability in the elementary and middle school years is important, as many gifted adolescent girls believe that possessing high ability means that they will achieve excellent grades without effort.

Students often believe that if they must work hard, they lack ability, and it is for this reason that I believe that educators must reinforce that gifted girls are smart and praise their abilities. In my research, I have found, for example, that culturally diverse young gifted girls who receive feedback complimenting their ability, rather than their effort, developed higher ability attribution, self-efficacy, and skills. This finding indicates that parents and teachers should praise girls for their ability and talents, thereby helping them understand that they have ability.

Confidence, Criticism, and Comparisons

Gifted girls have also been found to lack confidence when compared to boys of the same age. As gifted girls get older, they lower their self-rankings and seem to have more doubts about their own abilities, despite receiving higher grades throughout college. I found too many insecurities in smart Hispanic and Black girls and women I have worked with, at almost every age level, as they express doubt about their abilities, compare themselves more, and criticize themselves and others more.

Too many academically talented and high-achieving girls and young women from low-income and high-poverty backgrounds, for example, do not attend or even consider applying to selective colleges or universities for reasons that educators are only beginning to understand. Of the very small number who do apply or attend competitive colleges, some drop out quickly if they begin to feel isolated, different, or inferior. Others, like former first lady Michelle Obama, use their constant self-questioning of "Am I good enough?" and their self-doubt in every new setting as motivation to work harder. In her memoir, *Becoming*, Obama (2018) described how when she faced crippling self-doubt in new situations, she spoke quietly to herself, "Confidence, I'd learned then, sometimes needs to be called from within. I've repeated the same words to myself many times now, through many climbs. *Am I good enough? Yes, I am*" (p. 284).

Does this lack of confidence in smart girls seem to increase with females who are even more intelligent? Charmaine Gilbreath, formerly a rocket scientist at the Naval Research Laboratory in Washington, DC, led the electro-optics technology section. Her work involved shooting laser beams at rocket plumes to study reflected light and learn how particles in rocket fuel react with the atmosphere. After completing her first college degree in communications and humanities and deciding to become a lawyer, she changed her plans, deciding she liked physics and geometry. She recalled:

> it took me two years to get up the nerve to take a pre-calculus class. I was surprised that it wasn't that hard. I aced it. Then I took physics and calculus courses, and they weren't all that hard either. That's when I first realized I'd been buffaloed. (Cole, 1994, pp. 58–59)

When she returned to school to get her degree in physics and engineering, she found her biggest obstacle was her own lack of self-confidence. Therein lies the need to engage and support young gifted women in science, technology, engineering, and mathematics, especially young women of color and/or those from culturally diverse backgrounds.

Barriers to the Development of STEM Talents in Culturally Diverse Girls and Women

Enormous STEM talent gaps exist across race and gender (National Science Board, 2015). When one considers the absence of gifted students of color in STEM, they must consider the reasons these gaps exist. Several theories have been posited that provide insight on critical aspects of race, gender, and identity within STEM that impact all gifted girls, but in particular, Black girls (Collins et al., 2020). Although a comprehensive discussion of the many reasons that smart Black girls and women do not enter STEM fields is beyond the scope of this essay, complex reasons exist that include culture and socialization, as well as lack of support, encouragement, and opportunities—the three critical enrichment opportunities suggested in the Schoolwide Enrichment Model (Renzulli & Reis, 2014). Finding a welcoming educational environment is critical, as is mentorship and the reduction of the internal and external barriers that block the talents of Black girls and women, too often pertaining to self-doubt and negative stereotyping (Collins, 2017; Reis, 1998). For a comprehensive discussion of ways to reverse some of the challenges facing talented Black girls and women in STEM, see the excellent recent review by Collins et al. (2020).

Which Culturally Responsive Practices Encourage the Development of Gifts and Talents in Girls and Women?

Teachers of gifted girls and women must understand their own culture, biases, and stereotypes, and practice constant reflection of how these might affect the young women with whom they interact. They must communicate high expectations and, most importantly, ensure that they are identifying gifted girls, especially those from culturally diverse backgrounds, and then ensure that these girls participate in gifted and enrichment programs. The inclusion of culturally and linguistically diverse girls in programs is critical for their talent development and success in the future. This must happen!

Once these young women are identified, they need consistent encouragement and exposure to gifted women with whom they can identify and who are from various cultural groups. Active and engaging teaching practices, such as those associated with the Schoolwide Enrichment Model (Renzulli & Reis, 2014), also work well, as teachers can take a proactive role in identifying interests and strengths, and also identifying culturally and linguistically diverse enrichment (Type I, Enrichment Triad Model) speakers and role models. Offering Schoolwide Enrichment Model clusters that focus on students' strengths can also make a difference, as these are designed to develop interests, promote small-group interaction, and expose students to various topics, disciplines, and careers in which they may develop sincere interests. These are usually small-group instruction, which can also provide an encouraging, caring climate for discussions and opportunities for relationships to develop.

Getting to know students well is another area in which enrichment specialists and gifted education teachers can also make a difference, as they can demonstrate support and caring over many years. Over time, these opportunities can enable gifted education specialists and classroom teachers who are working with gifted girls to communicate both clear and high expectations, and let these talented students know that you also believe in their intelligence and abilities, helping to increase the young girls' confidence and their motivation to enroll in competitive classes and tackle challenging problems. Creating a sense of belonging and owning one's abilities are critical for these smart young women. That sense of belonging will help teachers to encourage girls to take as many STEM courses as possible and praise and reinforce their successes.

> *Creating a sense of belonging and owning one's abilities are critical for these smart young women.*

Once a sense of belonging can be established, and as I have advised for decades, teachers should help gifted girls create a written personal success plan for the future that includes their interests, goals, career plans, and college hopes and dreams, with specific tasks to accomplish over time. Having this type of plan will also help gifted girls understand, ameliorate, and challenge and avoid both the external and internal barriers that may impede their success. The Schoolwide Enrichment Model (Renzulli & Reis, 2014) helps encourage exposure, and gifted girls need to learn about the lives and successes of other gifted girls and women through direct and curricular experiences, including online video opportunities, TED Talks, lectures, field trips, seminars, role models, books, websites, videotapes, articles, and movies.

The Schoolwide Enrichment Model (SEM; Renzulli & Reis, 1985, 1997, 2014) is based on a foundational premise: *Schools should be places for talent development*. Our talent development approach has moved beyond various iterations of standards-based learning, no matter how advanced those standards and that curriculum may be, as our focus is different. Our focus in the SEM is on the development of creative productivity in students. The SEM is a product of almost 4 decades of research and field-testing, and it has been implemented in school districts worldwide (Reis & Peters, 2020). Prior and current research suggests that the model is effective at serving high-ability students in a variety of educational settings and that it works well in different types of schools across the globe (Reis & Peters, 2020).

It has been my experience that gifted girls can help and support each other for years, decades. For example, at the Renzulli Academy that I started with my colleagues in Hartford, CT, which provides services for culturally diverse gifted students, the gifted girls have strong caring relationships for each other that have lasted for more than a decade, as they support each other in classes, science and math clubs, and interest groups (e.g., robotics, journalism, creative writing).

Last, an exciting way to develop gifts and talents in young girls is to give opportunities for them to pursue a Type III experience based on their interests. In this experience, they conduct independent research and create original products to address personally relevant, real problems that do not have preexisting or unique solutions, are intended to cause change or to make a new contribution in the relevant field(s), and are of interest to a real audience (Renzulli & Reis, 2014). Renzulli and I believe that educators should implement strength-based programs to identify and develop individual gifts and talents, and when they do, gifted girls will thrive academically. The Type III process helps to develop self-reliance, independence, decision making, safe risk-taking, and an inclination for creative action, and in some cases, it will help to expose gifted girls to competition whenever possible so that they are better prepared for competitive situations in academics and in work. But most importantly, across all of these suggestions is the need for educators to develop a positive attitude about developing talents in girls in all areas, as well as become an unequivocal source of support, avoiding criticism as much as possible, as these young women will encounter too much of that from others in their lifetimes.

References

AAUW. (2016). *Barriers and bias: The status of women in leadership.* https://www.aauw.org/resources/research/barrier-bias

Abbott, P., Haerpfer, C., & Wallace, C. (2008). Women in Rwandan politics and society. *International Journal of Sociology, 38*(4), 111–125.

Arnold, K. (1995). *Lives of promise.* Jossey-Bass.

Arnold, K. D., Noble, K. D., & Subotnik, R. F. (1996). *Remarkable women: Perspectives on female talent development.* Hampton Press.

Boston, J. S., & Cimpian, A. (2018). How do we encourage girls to pursue and succeed in engineering? *Gifted Child Today, 41*(4), 196–207. https://doi.org/10.1177/1076217518786955

Catalyst. (2020, August 11). *Women in management: Quick take.* https://www.catalyst.org/research/women-in-management

Clance, P. R. (1985). The imposter phenomenon. *New World, 15*(7), 40-43.

Clance, P. R., & Imes, S. (1978). The imposter phenomenon in high achieving women: Dynamics and therapeutic intervention. *Psychology: Theory, Research, and Practice, 15*(3), 241–247. https://doi.org/10.1037/h0086006

Cole, K. C. (1994, March). Science discovers women. *Lears,* 56–61, 82–83.

Collins, K. H. (2017). From identification to Ivy League: Nurturing multiple interests in multi-potentiality in gifted students. *Parenting for High Potential, 6*(4), 19–22.

Collins, K. H., Joseph N. M., & Ford, D. Y. (2020). Missing in action: Gifted Black girls in science, technology, engineering, and mathematics. *Gifted Child Today, 43*(1), 55–63. https://doi.org/10.1177/1076217519880593

Jaussi, K. B., Randel, A. E., & Dionne, S. D. (2007). I am, I think, and I do: The role of personal identity, self-efficacy, and cross-application of experiences in creativity at work. *Creativity Research Journal, 19*(2–3), 247–258. https://doi.org/10.1080/10400410701397339

Kerr, B. A. (1985). *Smart girls, gifted women.* Ohio Psychology.

Kerr, B. A., & McKay, R. (2014). *Smart girls in the 21st century: Understanding talented girls and women.* Great Potential Press.

National Science Board. (2015). *Revising the STEM workforce: A companion to science and engineering indicators 2014.* https://nsf.gov/pubs/2015/nsb201510/nsb201510.pdf

NobelPrize.org. (2021). *Nobel Prize awarded women.* The Nobel Prize. https://www.nobelprize.org/prizes/lists/nobel-prize-awarded-women

Obama, M. (2018). *Becoming.* Crown.

Ochse, R. (1991). Why there were relatively few eminent women creators. *Journal of Creative Behavior, 25*(4), 334–343. https://doi.org/10.1002/j.2162-6057.1991.tb01146.x

O'Neil, T., Plank, G., & Domingo, P. (2015). *Support to women and girls' leadership: A rapid review of the evidence.* Overseas Development Institute.

Piirto, J. (1991). Why are there so few? (Creative women: Visual artists, mathematicians, musicians). *Roeper Review, 13*(3), 142–147. https://doi.org/10.1080/02783199109553340

Reis, S. M. (1998). *Work left undone: choices and compromises of talented females.* Creative Learning Press.

Reis, S. M. (2002). Toward a theory of creativity in diverse creative women. *Creativity Research Journal, 14*(3–4), 305–316. https://doi.org/10.1207/S15326934CRJ1434_2

Reis, S. M. (2005). Feminist perspectives on talent development: A research based conception of giftedness in women. In R. J. Sternberg & J. E. Davidson (Eds.), *Conceptions of giftedness* (pp. 217–245). Cambridge University Press. https://doi.org/10.1017/CBO9780511610455.014

Reis, S. M. (2021). Creative productive giftedness in women: Their paths to eminence. In R. J. Sternberg & D. Ambrose (Eds.), *Conceptions of giftedness and talent* (pp. 317–334). Palgrave MacMillan. https://doi.org/10.1007/978-3-030-56869-6_18

Reis, S. M., & Peters, P. (2020). Research on the Schoolwide Enrichment Model: Four decades of insights, innovation, and evolution. *Gifted Education International.* https://doi.org/10.1177/0261429420963987

Renzulli, J. S., & Reis, S. M. (1985). *The Schoolwide Enrichment Model: A comprehensive plan for educational excellence.* Creative Learning Press.

Renzulli, J. S., & Reis, S. M. (1997). *The Schoolwide Enrichment Model: A how-to guide for educational excellence* (2nd ed.). Creative Learning Press.

Renzulli, J. S., & Reis, S. M. (2014). *The Schoolwide Enrichment Model: A how-to guide for talent development* (3rd ed.). Prufrock Press.

Storage, D., Charlesworth, T. E. S., Mahzarin, M. R., & Cimpian, A. (2020). Adults and children implicitly associate brilliance with men more than women. *Journal of Experimental Social Psychology, 90,* 104020. https://doi.org/10.1016/j.jesp.2020.104020

Tremblay, M. (2007) Democracy, representation, and women: A comparative analysis. *Democratization, 14*(4), 533–553. https://doi.org/10.1080/13510340701398261

UN Women. (2021, January 15). *Facts and figures: Women's leadership and political participation.* https://www.unwomen.org/en/what-we-do/leadership-and-political-participation/facts-and-figures

World Economic Forum. (2017). *The global gender gap report 2017.* https://www.weforum.org/reports/the-global-gender-gap-report-2017

10

Supporting Gifted Males and Their Emotional Well-Being

Thomas P. Hébert

In working with gifted boys and young men, teachers, counselors, and coaches discover this population is a heterogeneous group with a wide variety of abilities, talents, and strengths, as well as diverse challenges they encounter in their development throughout adolescence. The following discussion offers an overview of different characteristics, traits, and gifted behaviors evidenced in males, along with challenges that they experience. Six issues addressed in this essay include the experience of the empathic young male, self-inflicted pressures that high-achieving males place upon themselves, identity development issues, image management, cultural expectations for young men of color, and differences in achievement orientations.

In the early stages of the COVID-19 pandemic, photos were circulating online of many exhausted doctors and nurses with bruises on their faces from wearing tight-fitting medical masks. Quinn Callander, a seventh grader, saw the photos and went to work creating ear guards—devices that help relieve some of the pressure felt by healthcare workers (Free, 2020). Quinn discovered a design on the Internet and began producing them with his 3-D printer.

His mother posted several photos of her son and his ear guard project on Facebook, and soon Quinn was inundated with requests. He extended his research and decided to program his printer to also produce a simple strap. The gadgets wrap around the back of the head and can be connected to mask straps, enabling people to adjust their masks and prevent them from rubbing against the back of their ears. Quinn's printer operates 24/7, hospital workers have been picking up the ear guards from his front porch, and orders have been sent to healthcare workers internationally. He said, "To me, this is something important I can do to help give back to people who are spending their time saving lives and trying to slow down the pandemic" (Free, 2020, para. 14). Quinn is a young man who personifies empathy, the ability to understand and share the feelings of others, a characteristic of gifted individuals (Piechowski, 2014). With empathic young men like Quinn, if another person is thought to be in need, then empathic emotions such as sympathy, compassion, and softheartedness evoke altruistic motivation to help the individual. Educators, counselors, and coaches celebrate this quality and want others to reflect deeply on how they can support students like Quinn to continue using their gifts in socially constructive ways to improve the lives of others.

Pressures Faced by Gifted Males

The empathy evident in Quinn's story is cause for pride; however, other emotional responses from gifted males may be worrisome. Consider the intense young man who places a tremendous amount of pressure upon himself to always be in control and to compete for excellence. Coleman's experience highlights this challenge. As a toddler,

Coleman was the joy of his mother's life. He spent many hours in her company chatting, reading, and playing imaginative games. As the oldest of three children, he was adored by his younger sisters. When he entered third grade, he was selected for a gifted and talented program, and after several months in the program, Coleman began complaining of stomachaches. When his parents suggested withdrawing from the program, Coleman readily agreed, and the stomachaches disappeared. When Coleman was a freshman in high school, his younger siblings heard a commotion in the family dining room. Investigating the scene, they found their older brother had thrown his Spanish textbook across the room where it crashed into the furniture. Coleman had brought home a grade of C on a weekly Spanish quiz and was furious with himself.

When he graduated from high school, Coleman had achieved a long list of accomplishments and a distinguished academic record. His family celebrated when he was accepted to a small, highly selective liberal arts college. Before leaving for school, however, Coleman confided to his grandfather that he was worried about whether he would make it in college and was concerned that the cost of the college was too high, especially because his father's engineering firm was struggling during the country's economic slump. He wondered if it were right for him to place his parents under additional financial strain and vowed to bring home a grade point average of 4.0 (Hébert, 1991).

Self-inflicted pressure involving the need to compete and the need to carry heavy responsibilities is an issue that may exact an emotional toll on gifted males. Many bright young men like Coleman internalize the societal belief that men must be in charge, and they place unnecessary pressures upon themselves to always be strong, and to always be the best. Men's work and career success are often measures of their masculinity (Howes, 2017), and young men like Coleman grow up believing that in order to be a man, they must constantly compete in a variety of areas.

Self-inflicted pressure involving the need to compete and the need to carry heavy responsibilities is an issue that may exact an emotional toll on gifted males.

Like Coleman, Garrett's developmental struggles were complex. His family moved from Pittsburgh, PA, to a suburban community in the South. When he arrived in the new community, he discovered that he and the students in his new high school shared very different adolescent experiences. To cope with his transition to his new community, he attempted to assimilate into the culture of his school: "I went through a clique a week trying to find somewhere to fit in, and I was everywhere but where I wanted to be. I was just bouncing off everything. I had no idea who I was."

That struggle to find his niche included Garrett's involvement on the track team, the swim team, ROTC, the cheerleading squad, and drama club. He served as the manager of the girls' basketball team and as a computer graphics artist for the school's yearbook, led the Spirit Squad, was involved in ballet and jazz dance troupes, and performed hip-hop routines at school pep rallies. Garrett's search for identity also incorporated drastic changes in appearance and style: "I tried to be preppy. Button-down shirts and khakis, but it didn't work because I listened to music like Anthrax and heavy metal." He said, "For 3 weeks during middle school, I was wearing jeans and T-shirts and carrying my dad's briefcase. Trying to be cool, I thought I was Alex P. Keaton. That was wild!" When asked to reflect on those years he described himself as "Captain Hormone" and explained, "My motive for everything was meeting girls" (Hébert, 2010).

All adolescents, including gifted young men like Garrett, undergo a search for identity. Researchers in gifted education who explore issues of identity development argue that because of their special talents and their advanced development, gifted adolescent males struggle with identity formation, and that search may be quite complex, as was evident in Garrett's experience (Hébert, 2010). For gifted males, in addition to facing the usual identity development tasks of adolescents, they have a role to play as the gifted student that other young men do not have to manage, making it more challenging for them to reach a clear understanding of who they are. For multitalented males, their identity search may involve even more experimentation with different roles associated with their multiple talents.

Social context may play an important role in identity development, as gifted males work to shape their emerging identity while also juggling conflicting social demands. These conflicting demands include the message that gifted males are unlike others, and their differences result in being praised or their strengths are disparaged. Another message is the belief that their exceptional talents should produce superior results at all times. They also may encounter others who only see them as "gifted students," and not as distinct individuals. When they succeed at getting other adolescents to regard them as intellectual males with other talents, they receive positive messages regarding other facets of their personalities (Hébert, 2020).

As gifted males negotiate their individual identities, they may also dedicate significant efforts at image management. Maintaining an image may require decisions that are detrimental to long-term adjustment. Gifted boys may be forced to mask their true identities to survive in a culture that incorporates a set of beliefs that influences what society regards as masculine. One feature of this mindset is the belief that vulnerabilities, weaknesses, and emotions are signs of femininity to be avoided at all costs. For a young man, being in control is often essential to proving one's masculinity (Orenstein, 2020). Consider the experience of Jon, a bright, personable, and charismatic teenager, who had a following of male friends and a constant circle of admiring eighth-grade females who suffered "major crushes." When his gifted education teacher planned a significant field trip to Washington, DC, students in the class spent much of the year involved in fundraising activities to cover the cost of the trip. Two weeks before departure, his teacher became aware that a problem was emerging among the young men in class. Several of the boys had quietly announced that Jon had chosen not to participate in the trip and they, too, would not be going. They claimed that they were not interested in visiting a bunch of "old museums," and that it was simply "a dumb trip for nerds."

> *Gifted boys may be forced to mask their true identities to survive in a culture that incorporates a set of beliefs that influences what society regards as masculine.*

A private conversation with Jon revealed that he suffered from motion sickness and simply could not tolerate the idea of a 16-hour long bus ride. The possibility of being physically sick while in the company of his peer group was unacceptable to this well-respected young man.

He explained that "tossing your cookies in front of your best friends" was not a cool thing to do. Although he realized that his decision to withdraw from the trip was influencing his friends and he sympathized with his teacher, the popular young man had an image to protect, and he chose not to travel to Washington.

Jon's dilemma highlights just how stifling a set of rigid peer group expectations can become for a talented young man. Even more challenging are the peer group rules for culturally diverse males with goals and high aspirations. Gifted young men of color often receive crippling messages from peers regarding academic achievement. These young men often experience conflicts between the values of their culture and those of the dominant culture, and members of their cultural peer group may discourage identity explorations that are at odds with the traditions of their group. By associating academic success with assimilation into the dominant culture, peers may direct abusive and derogatory remarks toward academically oriented young men, which may influence them to camouflage their intelligence. Whiting (2009) described a gifted Black male's experience that highlights this issue:

> School personnel were transporting Black students to an awards event in which students were to be honored for outstanding achievement. One Black male, a junior named Keith, approached the school van dressed in baggy pants, an overly large sweatshirt, and headband. Upon entering the van, he proceeded to pull off the outer layers of his outfit to expose a crisp dress shirt and creased khaki pants. He swapped tennis shoes for casual shoes. Before anyone could question him, the young man asserted: "I have an image to maintain." Being smart isn't part of that image. Not surprisingly, after the event and before returning to school, Keith went back into what his peers would accept him in, the original "urban" outfit. (p. 225)

By sharing Keith's experience, Whiting (2009) raised several significant questions that must be addressed if educators, counselors, and coaches are to support the emotional well-being of culturally diverse gifted males: How do young men of color make compromises in negotiating the need for achievement and the need for affiliation and social acceptance? How many gifted, high-achieving young men of color believe they must camouflage their intelligence and academic accomplishments? Moreover, how do gifted diverse males reconcile being young men of color in a society where racial injustices are widespread?

As many gifted young men of color overcome racial prejudice and injustices, other bright males often struggle with the challenge of maintaining an achievement orientation in their K–12 schooling. In comprehensive reviews of literature on underachievement in gifted males, researchers have highlighted studies that found personality, family, environmental, social, and school-related factors contribute to underachievement (Reis & McCoach, 2000; Siegle, 2013). Mindful of the multifaceted nature of underachievement, Schultz (2002) challenged the gifted education community to consider new approaches to research on this phenomenon. He maintained that rather than examine underachievement as a problem that needed to be fixed through interventions, researchers should investigate the perceptions of the young men bearing the underachiever label by examining their experiences and expectations. Speirs Neumeister and Hébert (2003) responded to the challenge, reflecting that, "To shed new insight on the problem, perhaps educators and researchers need to deconstruct the all-encompassing label of underachiever by looking beyond the underachieving behaviors and, instead, critically examine the attitudes that drive those behaviors" (p. 222).

Speirs Neumeister and Hébert (2003) reported the educational experiences of Sam, a gifted university student who had been labeled an underachiever by teachers and family members. Hébert and Schreiber (2010) extended this work by examining the experiences of Shannon and Greg, two additional gifted collegiate males. Conducting in-depth case studies of the three young men, these researchers were able to demonstrate that behaviors typically associated with underachievement are not always indicative of actual underachievement and, therefore, do not always require an intervention. The term *selective achiever* was coined and defined as "intrinsically motivated individuals whose performance matches ability only in specific areas that satisfy their interests and personal goal orientations" (Hébert & Schreiber, 2010, p. 570).

An examination of the themes uncovered across these two studies helps to explain the patterns of selective achievement within the three gifted males. Evidence of strong intrinsic motivation, combined with independence and resistance to conformity, played important roles in shaping their identities as selective achievers. Another theme in the data indicated that these young men demanded serious intellectual challenges that were associated with acquiring practical knowledge. To them, learning had to be challenging, practical, and applicable to reaching their personal goals. In addition, the young men saw an educator's personal character, teaching style, and expertise being critical to whether or not they would put forth effort in a course.

Resistance to conformity was evident in Shannon's efforts to get people noticing that he was marching to the beat of his own drum. In high school, when he enrolled in a local dance school and served on the cheering squad, he had a lot of explaining to do with his peer group. As a nonconformist, he enjoyed his rejoinders to the negative remarks made by other young men:

> When people found out that I did ballet and jazz dancing they were like, "What are you man? Kind of funny? What are you, a cheerleader? Dancer?" I came back with, "Look, dude, while you were showering with a whole team of nasty smelling guys, I'm hanging out with your girlfriend in tights! I didn't want to hear it!" Being able to say that really gave me a step up as the new freshman. (Hébert & Schreiber, 2010, p. 583)

The role of an educator's personal character, teaching style, and expertise being critical to whether or not the young men performed was significant. For example, when Sam encountered teachers who demonstrated characteristics he valued, such as respect for students, altruism, and authentic behavior, he was motivated to achieve. He described these teachers as the ones that seemed like they were doing good things in their lives. He saw these individuals as role models he admired: people who influenced his achievement motivation. He described his math teacher Mr. Osterman as a gentleman who was dedicated to serving others and being "a contributing member of society." He respected Mr. Osterman as a person and also admired him as a teacher. He described his creative approach to teaching and the fact that he respected students and treated them accordingly. Sam credited his experiences with Mr. Osterman as sparking his decision to become a high school math teacher (Speirs Neumeister & Hébert, 2003, p. 229).

The three young men demanded serious intellectual challenges that resulted in the acquisition of practical knowledge. For example, Greg viewed the university as a place to acquire the necessary skills to succeed as an engineer and saw little value in theoretical courses. He said, "If I have the knowledge in my head and I cannot move it to your head or to someone else's head, it's worthless" (Hébert & Schreiber, 2020, p. 586). Having met an engineer employed by the Tennessee Valley Authority, he had been influenced by this man's delineation between two different types of engineers. He explained that he now realized that there were engineers who were "really good at writing reports, engineers who could make things sound good but couldn't engineer themselves out of a wet paper bag." Greg saw the second group of engineers as "people who understand what's really going on, engineers who don't necessarily write flowery reports, but they can solve problems." Greg decided, "That's the kind of engineer I want to be" (Hébert & Schreiber, 2010, p. 586).

In conducting these two studies, my colleagues and I have helped to deconstruct the all-encompassing label of underachiever by looking beyond the underachieving behaviors and critically examining the attitudes that drive those behaviors in gifted males. Educators, counselors, and coaches who listen to the voices of gifted young men like Sam, Shannon, and Greg should appreciate their message and help guide other gifted males in the pursuit of their goals and aspirations.

Strategies for Educators and Counselors

In creating a culturally responsive environment to support the emotional well-being of gifted males, educators and counselors need a repertoire of appropriate strategies. The following discussion highlights several possibilities.

Side by Side, Heart to Heart, and Hands On

Adult males have reflected on their experiences as adolescents and realized how wise their parents had been. When a mother put one son to work chopping vegetables for beef stew, she learned what was really happening with his struggles in algebra. When she did the same with her younger son, she heard about the attractive girl who was flirting with him in his fifth-grade classroom. A father also developed strategies. When he decided to hold a man-to-man conversation with his son, it was during an evening walk around the neighborhood. Conversation was held side by side. If not a walk, Dad talked with his son as they washed and polished the family car or worked on outdoor chores together. These lessons from wise parents help enlighten teachers of gifted boys.

Psychologists who study and work with young men report that people are mistaken if they judge males' manner of communication as needing to be more like women's. Whereas females appreciate eye-to-eye communication, males prefer communication that precludes eye contact. Males might not be physically or emotionally expressive; however, they derive great support from authentic conversations that occur during hands-on activities (Hébert, 2017a). Glennon (2020) indicated that "boys build their emotional connection to others through activities" and maintained that "boys generally connect with others most easily by doing things together" (p. 62). Glennon's insights are valuable. If teachers or counselors want to help gifted boys unload their worries or share the highlights of their day, they need to consider doing something together with them. Educators have reported how they have accomplished this in their classrooms (Hébert, 2017b). Basketball coaches have described how athletes talk about their families, challenges with teachers, and girl problems while shooting baskets before practice begins. A mathematics teacher reported how she had meaningful conversations with gifted boys as they engaged in origami. As they folded paper and created geodesic domes, they shared their thinking on serious existential issues. Art teachers have described how boys have meaningful conversations with each other while involved in messy papier-mâché work, and science teachers have enjoyed meaningful conversations while conducting lab experiments. With some thoughtful planning, educators can infuse opportunities for supportive conversations with and among the gifted males in their classrooms. Taking time for side-by-side interaction, heart-to-heart conversation, and hands-on activities enables teachers to address concerns affecting the emotional well-being of intelligent boys in ways they can appreciate. Such an approach can be infused into school life in a variety of ways.

Movies as Discussion Facilitators

Using movies to facilitate discussions with gifted males about affective concerns in their lives can be helpful and effective. This strategy has been defined as guided viewing of film (Hébert & Sergent, 2005) and proposed as a method for teachers and counselors to help gifted students to develop insights to deal with personal challenges. Through guided viewing of film, educators and counselors can promote personal growth and development. This development occurs when young people identify with the film's character, reflect on that identification, gain new insights, and undergo emotional growth.

> *Through guided viewing of film, educators and counselors can promote personal growth and development.*

Movies are a therapeutic experience for young men in classrooms, as they are able to examine their issues from another perspective, allowing them to appreciate humorous aspects of situations and see alternative solutions for addressing their challenges. Moreover, a good movie can help to create a supportive understanding among a group of boys as they enjoy the film together. This strategy is especially appropriate for working with them because movies are an integral part of contemporary culture for bright adolescents and are particularly enjoyed when shown in a relaxed environment. As a result, gifted males are receptive to exploring personal issues safely through the discussion of a good film.

In facilitating guided viewing sessions, the discussion of difficult and potentially uncomfortable issues related to a film may elicit emotional responses in the students; therefore, it is important to incorporate enjoyable follow-up activities to provide the young men an opportunity to process their feelings. For example, activities that include artistic expressions, creative writing, technology, and music provide time for introspection and opportunity to continue the discussion of the issues explored in the film. During the follow-up activities, young men become more comfortable offering each other empathetic emotional support. Searching for high-quality movies appropriate for use in public school classrooms is enjoyable. Several to consider for use with gifted males include: *Blinded by the Light* (2019), *The Emperor's Club* (2002), *Endgame* (2015), *Finding Forrester* (2000), *42: The Jackie Robinson Story* (2013), and *Me and Earl and the Dying Girl* (2015).

Photo Elicitation

Photography offers gifted young men great opportunities to engage in hands-on learning, and with cell phones readily available, the possibilities are endless. One strategy to incorporate is a technique referred to as photo elicitation—the use of photographs to elicit conversation. A teacher or counselor may simply direct young men to respond to the following prompt: "Using your phone camera, shoot five pictures that represent your identity as a gifted male." The young men will need flexible time to reflect on how they would respond and shoot the pictures.

Kip, a highly creative boy, produced a collection of photographs that revealed several facets of his identity. He shared a photo of himself wearing a hat that covered his face, and attached to the hat was a sketch of Wile E. Coyote, the well-known cartoon figure. As he presented this photo, he wrote, "Wile E. Coyote is important to me because he represents the ideas that travel so fast through my head, my hyperactivity, and the creativity applied to my life." To let his teacher know that he saw himself as a creative student who preferred to learn through a hands-on approach, he took a picture of a baking soda and vinegar volcano model to which he added Hershey's chocolate powder. He pointed out, "The chocolate volcano represents my love of exploration, my curiosity, my deep need to research everything extensively, as well as all of my creative investigations." When he discussed his photo of an intersection of two paths in the woods where he jogged every morning, he wrote, "This is the path where I jog every day. It symbolizes the choices I've made in my life. I've often taken the road less traveled" (Hébert, 2020, p. 219).

Young men can enjoy sharing their photos in a variety of ways. Some may choose to add to the photographs a reflective written response, while others may prefer to present the photos in a technological format. Thoughtful discussions naturally evolve, and the young men learn a great deal about each other as well as about themselves.

Conclusion

Educating gifted young men is fulfilling. The relationships between educators and the bright boys in their schools may be mutually beneficial. Teachers and counselors working to support their emotional well-being realize early on that the boys have much to teach us. From their work with gifted males, educators gain a better understanding of the challenges they face and how to support them.

References

Free, C. (2020, April 16). *Nurses and doctors are posting photos of their faces bruised by masks. A boy stepped in to help.* The Washington Post. https://www.washingtonpost.com/lifestyle/2020/04/16/nurses-doctors-are-posting-photos-their-faces-bruised-by-masks-boy-stepped-help

Glennon, W. (2020). *Nurturing boys: 200 ways to raise a boy's emotional intelligence from boyhood to manhood.* Mango Publishing Group.

Hébert, T. P. (1991). Meeting the affective needs of bright boys through bibliotherapy. *Roeper Review, 13*(4), 207–212.

Hébert, T. P. (2010). [Unpublished raw data on gifted males as selective achievers]. University of Georgia.

Hébert, T. P. (2017a, May). Side by side, heart to heart, and hands on. *Teaching for High Potential*, 5–6.

Hébert, T. P. (2017b). Supporting the emotional well-being of gifted adolescent males. *TEMPO, 38*(2), 6–11, 30.

Hébert, T. P. (2020). *Understanding the social and emotional lives of gifted students* (2nd ed.). Prufrock Press.

Hébert, T. P., & Schreiber, C. A. (2010). An examination of selective achievement in gifted males. *Journal for the Education of the Gifted, 33*(4), 570–605. https://doi.org/10.1177/016235321003300406

Hébert, T. P., & Sergent, D. (2005). Using movies to guide: Teachers and counselors collaborating to support gifted students. *Gifted Child Today, 28*(4), 14–25. https://doi.org/10.1177/107621750502800405

Howes, L. (2017). *The mask of masculinity: How men can embrace vulnerability, create strong relationships, and live their fullest lives.* Random House.

Orenstein, P. (2020). *The miseducation of the American boy.* The Atlantic. https://www.theatlantic.com/magazine/archive/2020/01/the-mis education-of-the-american-boy/603046

Piechowski, M. M. (2014). *"Mellow out," they say. If only I could: Intensities and sensitivities of the young and bright* (2nd ed.). Royal Fireworks Press.

Reis, S. M., & McCoach, D. B. (2000). The underachievement of gifted students: What do we know and where do we go? *Gifted Child Quarterly, 44*(3),152–170. https://doi.org/10.1177/001698620004400302

Schultz, R. A. (2002). Illuminating realities: A phenomenological view of two underachieving gifted learners. *Roeper Review, 24*(4), 203–212.

Siegle, D. (2013). *The underachieving gifted child: Recognizing, understanding, and reversing underachievement.* Prufrock Press.

Speirs Neumeister, K. L., & Hébert, T. P. (2003). Underachievement versus selective achievement: Delving deeper and discovering the difference. *Journal for the Education of the Gifted, 26*(3), 221–238. https://doi.org/10.1177/016235320302600305

Whiting, G. M. (2009). Gifted Black males: Understanding and decreasing barriers to achievement and identity. *Roeper Review, 31*(4), 224–233. https://doi.org/10.1080/02783190903177598

11

Preparing Gifted Black Males for Transition to College[1]

Marques R. Dexter and Tarek C. Grantham

High school gifted Black males, many of whom develop heightened sensitivities to hostilities imposed by unsupportive social and political climates, need to be engaged by high school teachers in ways that can stimulate and affirm their sense of self and belonging. Nurturing a sense of self-efficacy is an important trait for Black males to be buoyant and resolute in the face of adversity (Whiting, 2009). Too often, gifted Black males have been found to face various forms of ambiguity relating to

---

the assumptions of others—and oftentimes themselves—have of their racial and gender identities (Henfield, 2012). Being smart and achieving at high levels is frequently associated with acting White (Grantham & Biddle, 2014), and emulating feminine traits (Martin & Harris, 2007), which can have grave effects on their levels of self-assertion as they prepare for college. We assume that high school teachers want to support and engage gifted Black males for college, but many may overlook the severity of gaps that exist.

Compounded by the pervasiveness of the encounters throughout society as described above, an increasing educational achievement gap exists between Black males and their White counterparts, paralleling the enrollment gap in gifted and advanced programs. Data from the 2013–2014 U.S. Department of Education's Civil Rights Data Collection show that of the 3.329 million public students enrolled in gifted/talented programs, only 4.45% (148,349) were identified as Black males, in comparison to 29.13% (970,191) who were identified as White males (Office for Civil Rights, 2016). Resultantly, gifted Black males struggle to find positive reflections affirming their racial, academic, and gendered identities within environments designed to instill agency within their teenage minds (Bonner, 2010).

The purpose of this article is to (1) encourage high school teachers to gain a better understanding of the intricate needs of gifted Black males, (2) provide a brief discussion of high school gifted Black males' experiences in a culture of fear, and (3) suggest reasons why high school teachers need to be proactive in their efforts to support gifted Black males' transition from high school to college.

Existing in a Culture That Fears You

As seen over the past decade, the racial climate of our society has become filled with an overabundance of acts of injustice and discrimination toward high school and college-aged Black males. Reports of fatal shootings have become the norm within visual and print media— Michael Brown, Tamir Rice, Jordan Edwards, and so many others. As such, it is imperative for high school teachers to be cognizant of the emotional baggage gifted Black males carry within and try to understand and support them.

Gifted Black males can be stifled in high school because of realities they face: Instead of being protected and provided with chances to succeed in high school and college, many Black males are perceived as a threat—criminalized without committing any crimes. For example, Lawrence Crosby, a Northwestern doctoral student accused of stealing his own car, was the victim of racial profiling. For Crosby, his only crime was having too nice of a car and "driving while Black" in an area where men who look like him are perceived as car thieves, not car owners.

Furthermore, high school teachers must understand that gifted Black males are also adversely impacted by the racial climates within many predominantly White high school classrooms and even more in today's predominantly White campuses. For example, at the University of Virginia, gifted Black males' sense of academic comfort has been recently threatened by White supremacy groups that disrupted and imposed their morals upon the campus, creating a severely hostile environment. Fortunately, thanks to the advocacy of several of the institution's cultural student groups, students of color responded to the messages of hatred with solidarity and affirmation. This illuminates the importance of the presence of cultural student centers and organizations, as they afford students with similar racial and ethnic identities the ability to support and affirm ways that cannot be found outside of their familial networks. By identifying such centers, these offices and student organizations provide safe spaces for students of color to voice instances of racial oppression. As a result, educators of gifted Black male students will afford these young men a strong chance of establishing a sense of belonging with their future institution much sooner.

> *To be young, gifted, and Black means to be different, an anomaly; to feel alone within a world that appears to be flooded by a sea of whiteness.*

It is no wonder that fewer Black males are attending, thriving, and graduating from postsecondary institutions than ever before. To be young, gifted, and Black means to be different, an anomaly; to feel alone within a world that appears to be flooded by a sea of whiteness.

Instead of having conversations about the latest episode of *Love & Hip Hop Atlanta*, many gifted Black males may feel forced to suffer through Kim's latest tantrum on *Keeping Up With the Kardashians*. With so many inescapable barriers expected of Black males to overcome in high school, it is imperative for teachers of gifted Black males to purposefully guide them in connecting with institutions and resources that can affirm and empower their holistic scholar identity.

High school teachers of gifted Black males can address their college preparatory needs by highlighting institutions that offer African American male initiatives. Teachers can better advocate for gifted Black males when they are purposive in exposing gifted Black males to institutions where these young men are able find a sense of community, benefit from structured systems of support that target the experiences of being Black and male, and are guided by peers who look and share similar cultural and racial values. High school teachers can be proactive and give gifted Black males guidance toward institutions that can help them to develop strategies for coping with the effects of any racial and gendered stereotypes, daily microaggressions, and ill-informed biases afflicting their sense of self-worth. The following sections provide high school teachers with an overview of one state's initiative to support and affirm African American males.

USG's African American Male Initiative

The University System of Georgia (USG) recognized the urgency to address barriers impacting African American males and implemented an innovative and unique statewide African American Male Initiative (AAMI, https://www.usg.edu/aami). After examination, the USG Board of Regents discovered a disparate gender gap among college-aged African American students (Perry-Johnson et al., 2003). African American females were found to attend college at twice the rate of their male counterparts. While mirroring national statistics, the data failed to represent the state's racial and ethnic demographics. The Board of Regents commissioned a task force in 2002 charged with uncovering barriers hindering African American males from matriculating to postsecondary institutions throughout the state (Grantham et al., 2018).

Composed of representatives from academic, educational, civic, and business backgrounds, the Task Force identified four primary questions to comprehend this phenomenon: (a) Were high school-aged African American males presented with equal opportunities for higher education? (b) Were their educational experiences unique at certain stages of the secondary or postsecondary ladder? (c) What were the barriers to African American male enrollment and retention in Georgia's public colleges and universities? Moreover, (d) why were women twice as likely to go to college than men? (Perry-Johnson et al., 2003).

College-aged African American males perceived their campus environments as lacking any sense of inclusion (Perry-Johnson et al., 2003). Most alarming was a belief that the (predominantly White) campuses denied them of opportunities to engage with other individuals who shared similar interests, representative of their racial and ethnic identity, and those with whom they could confide and relate. By obtaining a general understanding of the campus climate, high school teachers can assist these young men in making informed decisions on where they will choose to continue their educational journeys. Little is worse than having a graduating gifted Black male (GBM) student build up excitement over the summer only to have his world crushed when he discovers his predominantly White institution student body judges him unjustly.

College Prep for Gifted Black Males Considering Predominantly White Institutions

The majority of predominantly White institutions are filled with a deficit-orientation toward Black and Brown students. Grantham and Castenell (2016) found that many of the state flagship institutions throughout the Southeast have a range of 62%–84% enrollment of White students. Blacks males make up anywhere from 3%–11% of the total undergraduate student population. Succeeding academically when you are the only person that looks like you and having feelings of otherness and isolation can hamper the capacity for gifted Black males to prosper, despite their high intellectual abilities. Even if they are in tune with their Black culture and identity, swimming in seas of whiteness can have detrimental long-term effects on the students' sense of self, as well as their ability to obtain long-term success.

Suggestions for Preparing, Affirming, and Transitioning Gifted Black Males to College

1. **Ask them: Is you down or nah?** If GBM feel comfortable sharing their racialized thoughts about college climate with you, then this can enable you to better support and identify institutions that fit their desired academic, social, and demographic needs.
2. **Build your squad.** Establish a symbiotic partnership with institutions that offer AAMI-like programming. Not only can this support their recruitment efforts, but it will also allow for you to develop a network of alumni at those institutions who can serve as role models for your prospective GBM.
3. **Be REAL and upfront.** Inform GBM students and their families of the potential environments they will be in should they chose to attend a predominantly White institution. Do not hide or scare them with the issues of racism and discrimination, but let them know that not everyone will see them for who they truly are, that there are some who will have preconceived assumptions about who they are and what they are capable of. Additionally, inform them of potential resources available for guidance and support should they fall victim to these atrocities.
4. **Reaffirm success.** Remind them of their accomplishments and use that to empower them to continue their success in college and beyond. For example, you can create a list of accomplishments (awards, recognitions, scholarship offers, etc.) and search the Internet for other Black males who have similar accomplishments for each one. This will assist in providing a listing of names and faces that look like them and who they can aspire to be like.
5. **Begin establishing their Board of Directors (BoD).** Link high school GBM with potential representatives, mentors, and/

or individuals who can serve as a member of their support system before college and while at predominantly White institutions. Doing so can alleviate stress within the student and their family. This can also assist in ensuring they are supported with the transition from high school to college. Examples of individuals to have in a gifted Black male's BoD would be (a) student organization leader/officer, (b) faculty member, (c) academic support specialists, (d) admissions staff member, (e) an alumnus of the institution, and (f) a professional working in their desired field.

6. **Collectively make "Money Moves."** Work with your high school GBM on ways they can achieve their career goals and provide support in flushing out the appropriate benchmarks, barriers, and requirements for them to be successful. This may be in the form of obtaining additional degrees, certifications, work experiences, etc. A prime example would be encouraging your gifted Black male student to take Advanced Placement (AP) and/or college courses during high school. Doing so will allow them to save time and money by shortening the time they take to complete their degree. Additionally, this could also allow for them to pursue a dual major in another area, making them more marketable once they finish.

7. **Develop a backup plan with them.** This can provide reassurance that if something goes wrong at their initial college or university institution, they have alternative options. Examples would be: (a) other schools which may offer a similar major, (b) a trade or service job providing valuable skills and financial stability, or (c) local community college choices. The goal is to assure them that this decision isn't going to dictate the rest of their life; they have the agency to change their mind and pursue other endeavors. As long as they know there are options and those who will support them no matter their choice, they will be more confident in making future decisions.

8. **Remind them it's a GRIND.** College does not determine the remainder of their lives; it is just a step along the journey. Together with the racial and gendered stereotypes regarding Black males, your GBM may place unneeded stress upon themselves. Reassure them that it is okay to make mistakes and to feel

uncertainty but remind them of the numerous support systems at their disposal. They will be successful!

Conclusion

Ensuring gifted Black males' success is not solely the responsibility of the high school teacher. Yet, their efforts play a pivotal role in instilling and affirming a prolonged sense of determination that can motivate GBM students throughout their lives. Through teachers' intentional efforts to support, affirm, and prepare their high school GBM students early on for predominantly White institutional environments, they can develop their students' ability to adjust and find a sense of belonging in less diverse environments. Connecting brilliant young Black men and their families with institutions of higher learning with AAMIs, such as those with the University System of Georgia, can facilitate the affirmation of their cultural and gendered selves, while also providing peer and mentor support that many institutions do not offer. In the end, high school teachers are key advocates who can help gifted Black males transition from high school to take their place in college where they can be successful and continue pursuing their hopes and dreams.

References

Bonner, F. A., III. (2010). *Academically gifted African American male college students.* Praeger.

Grantham, T. C., & Biddle, W. H. (2014). From bystander to upstander teacher for gifted Black students accused of acting White. *Gifted Child Today, 37*(3), 178–187. https://doi.org/10.1177/1076217514530117

Grantham, T. C., & Castenell, L. A. (2016). *African American male enrollment trends in the Southeastern Conference (SEC) universities and The University of Georgia.*

Grantham, T. C., Castenell, L. A., Dexter, M., & Brewington, Q. (2018). Desegregating the University System of Georgia (USG) and establishing the African American Male Initiative at the University of Georgia (UGA): From USG shame to UGA GAAME. In L. A. Castenell, T. C. Grantham, & B. Hawkins (Eds.), *Recruiting, retaining, and engaging African-American males at select research universities: Challenges and opportunities in academics and sports* (pp. 59–80). Information Age.

Henfield, M. S. (2012). Masculinity identity development and its relevance to supporting talented Black males. *Gifted Child Today, 35*(3), 179–186. https://doi.org/10.1177/1076217512444547

Martin, B. E., & Harris, F., III. (2007). Examining productive conceptions of masculinities: Lessons learned from academically driven African American male student-athletes. *The Journal of Men's Studies, 14*(3), 359–378.

Office for Civil Rights. (2016). *Civil rights data collection (CRCD) for the 2013–14 school year.* https://www2.ed.gov/about/offices/list/ocr/docs/crdc-2013-14.html

Perry-Johnson, A., Papp, D., Butler, F, Hudson, C., Levine, S., Nickel, S., & Wolfe, J. (2003). *Summary and final recommendations for the University System of Georgia's African American Male Initiative.* University System of Georgia's African American Male Initiative, Matlock Advertising & Public Relations and Paul A Warner Associates.

Whiting, G. M. (2009). Gifted Black males: Understanding and decreasing barriers to achievement and identity. *Roeper Review, 31*(4), 224–233. https://doi.org/10.1080/02783190903177598

12

Transgender and Nonbinary Youth

Teresa Ryan Manzella and Jace Valcore

The previous essays in this section discussed cisgender youth, boys and girls whose sense of self does not contend with their sex assigned at birth and for whom daily life in their assigned gender is not seriously distressing or confusing. Transgender and nonbinary youth, however, possess gender identities and expressions that do not align with their sexes assigned at birth and do not conform to the stereotypes of their assigned genders. Trans youth, therefore, struggle in many ways to make sense of themselves and the world in which they live. As they grow and assert their independence and freedom of expression, they often violate deeply entrenched beliefs and stereotypes about sex and gender held by the adults responsible for raising and educating them, and challenge the norms and structures of social and public institutions (Meadow, 2018).

Before further delving into the lives and experiences of trans youth, we must pause and provide definitions for the terms and concepts that many may still be unfamiliar with. Gender is a social construct and multidimensional concept. It refers to the behaviors, indicators, and expectations associated with one's assigned sex. It refers to the assumptions of masculinity and femininity that are placed upon us because of the sex listed on our birth certificates.

Gender can be broken down into three distinctly measurable components: physical sex characteristics, gender identity, and gender expression/presentation (Englert & Dinkins, 2016). Physical sex characteristics include chromosomes, genes, hormones, gonads, internal and external genitalia, and secondary sex characteristics, all of which exist on a spectrum of male to female (Ainsworth, 2015). Gender identity is one's internal sense of self, one's personal sense of being a man, woman, both, or neither. Gender expression and presentation refers to our mannerisms, behaviors, and clothing, jewelry, and hair style choices—in other words, how we show or express our gender identity to others. Sex assigned at birth/assigned gender is simply the designation of male or female given to an infant at the time of birth based upon a physical examination of external genitalia (Adkins, 2016).

A BRIEF LIST OF GENDER IDENTITIES

- **Cisgender:** Anyone whose sense of personal identity and gender corresponds with their sex assigned at birth.
- **Trans:** Anyone who falls outside the gender binary; is not cisgender.
- **Transgender:** One whose gender identity differs from their sex assigned at birth.
- **Nonbinary:** A person who does not subscribe to the gender binary but identifies with neither, both, or beyond male and female; common nonbinary identities include genderqueer, agender, and gender fluid.

It is impossible to understand trans youth without proper acknowledgement of the society in which they live. The United States, like most Western and Global North nations, has structured its laws, institutions, and norms around the notion of a gender binary. It is assumed and embedded into the social order that human beings are categorized as either male or female, boy or girl, man or woman. And that categorization dictates nearly every aspect of our lives. It tells us what clothes to wear, how we are expected to behave, what jobs we are encouraged to pursue, what sports and activities we are allowed to participate in, what clubs we can join, how to address a stranger, how to express ourselves, and much else.

By now, we are all familiar with the traditional norms and stereotypes associated with the gender binary and their impact upon cisgender people. But perhaps not all are aware that those harms are self-inflicted. Prior to colonization, Indigenous people and cultures around the globe recognized and even celebrated those who existed outside of the binary, those who held a third gender, dual gender, or were two-spirit, meaning they possessed both masculine and feminine spirits (Lang, 2016). The insistence upon a rigid gender binary is an inherently neocolonial project that has dire consequences for transgender and nonbinary youth.

Both sexual- and gender-diverse people have long been pathologized, marginalized, and criminalized. Although lesbian, gay, bisexual, and queer people and communities are now widely accepted and their rights and relationships legally affirmed in many instances, trans people are still being targeted, scapegoated, and abused by politicians, the criminal legal system, and prejudiced cisgender people in every social institution and public space. During the Trump administration, advances that had been made for trans Americans were repealed or reneged upon, including implementation of a ban on transgender military service members, removal of guarantees for trans-affirming healthcare, refusal to hear civil rights complaints on behalf of trans students, and much, much more. These prejudicial administration positions were overturned through executive order by President Joe Biden in his first days in office. Still, at the state level, there have been, and continue to be, attempts to regulate access to public restrooms, to deny trans youth the right to participate in sports, and even to criminalize the provision of trans-affirming healthcare specifically for youth.

It is difficult to estimate how many trans youth exist because few institutions collect that data and few youth are in environments where they feel encouraged or supported in exploring and asserting their gender identity (Catalpa & McGuire, 2018), but a 2019 report from the Centers for Disease Control and Prevention (CDC) indicated that nearly 2% of U.S. high school students identify as transgender (Johns et al., 2019). All young people experience growing pains and continuously negotiate their independence and self-expression with parents and other adults in their lives. Trans youth, however, are not simply defying the wishes or expectations of their parents and teachers. They are defying societal norms, challenging the established order, and struggling simply to exist in the bodies which they have been given. At home, trans youth struggle to determine whether or not it is safe to come out to their families, and they may hide or conceal their true gender identities in order to avoid family conflict (Catalpa & McGuire, 2018). A large percentage of LGBTQ youth are homeless or experience housing instability because of parental rejection (The Trevor Project, 2020). One study found that 43% of transgender youth had experienced parental rejection and lasting family breaks, while most of the study participants (71%) expressed various forms of relational ambiguity initiated by their parents, including ambivalence, withdrawal of emotional support, misgendering, and even physical abuse (Catalpa & McGuire, 2018).

[Trans youth] are defying societal norms, challenging the established order, and struggling simply to exist in the bodies which they have been given.

At school, trans youth are frequently subjected to bullying, harassment, and verbal and physical abuse. They may also experience emotional exhaustion from pretending to be their assigned sex during school hours (Meadow, 2018). Parents of trans youth describe meeting with concerned teachers or being confronted by family members who are upset by the nonnormative behavior of their children. It seems that schools are often the first place in which trans youth truly feel forced to conform to rigid, binary gender expectations, especially feminine children who were assigned male at birth. Classmates and teachers alike police their choice of playmates, toys, and use of free time (Meadow,

2018). Many trans youth develop anxiety and depression and become socially isolated as a result.

A CDC study found that trans students are more likely than cisgender students to report violent victimization, substance use, and suicide risk; 35% of trans high school students reported being bullied at school, 27% felt unsafe at school or traveling to/from, and 35% had attempted suicide in the previous year (Johns et al., 2019). A review of the mental health literature also revealed that trans youth experience higher rates of depression, eating disorders, suicidality, and self-harm than their cisgender peers (Connolly et al., 2016). But medical intervention and/or social support can drastically decrease those rates and prevent harm. According to the 2020 National Survey on LGBTQ Youth Mental Health, transgender and nonbinary youth who reported having pronouns respected by all or most people in their lives attempted suicide at half the rate of those who did not. Additionally, having access to gender-affirming clothing, binders, and shapewear decreased the likelihood of suicide attempts. Although most LGBTQ youth reported having at least one affirming space or adult in their lives, those who did not were, not surprisingly, more likely to report suicide attempts (The Trevor Project, 2020).

This introduction provides background necessary to understand the students being discussed in this essay, as well the lived experiences that they bring with them into the classroom. In the sections that follow, we leverage this background to illustrate what constitutes culturally responsive teaching when working with trans and nonbinary students.

Implicit Bias

Before discussing how implicit bias manifests itself with regard to nonbinary, trans, and gifted identities, a definition of the concept, as used in this context, may be useful:

> Also known as implicit social cognition, implicit bias refers to the attitudes or stereotypes that affect our understanding, actions, and decisions in an unconscious manner. These biases, which encompass both favorable and unfavorable assessments, are activated involuntarily

and without an individual's awareness or intentional control. Residing deep in the subconscious, these biases are different from known biases that individuals may choose to conceal for the purposes of social and/or political correctness. Rather, implicit biases are not accessible through introspection. (The Kirwan Institute, 2012, para. 1)

It is human nature to favor the familiar. Not everyone in education is familiar with nonbinary and trans identities, which contributes to the perpetuation of implicit bias toward students who appear not to comply with societal norms of gender expression. As discussed in the introduction, gender may be viewed as more of a continuum than a binary. This is not a new development; however, increases in trans and nonbinary people's attempts to be their authentic selves in the public sphere make some people uneasy, as reflected in the statistics provided earlier.

The result is that gifted nonbinary and trans students can trigger implicit biases in the people whose mission it is to help them receive an appropriate education. Thus, not only may these youth encounter bias as members of the general student body, but also their nonconforming appearance and behaviors may interfere with ever even getting identified for gifted programs. Such bias may prevent them from receiving the level of services their needs demand. This is especially true in states/districts where universal screening is not implemented—where teacher and/or parent nomination systems in place may present barriers to identification. If parents are disengaged from their trans or nonbinary kids, for example (as described in the introduction), it is unlikely that those parents will be inclined to advocate for their children's needs as gifted students or to nominate them for gifted programs.

Recent literature on gifted youth discusses the intensities that make up the whole gifted person, drawing on Kazimierz Dabrowski's theory of positive disintegration. Intensified feeling (physical and emotional), thinking, and imagining can guide a gifted person through a process of transformation that can be painful, but that can lead to greater creativity, self-knowledge, and joy, which can ultimately result in ongoing inner growth. At the heart of these intensities is a nervous system more attuned to one's surroundings, and what Dabrowski called the "higher pitch of felt experiences"—overexcitabilities (OEs)—which Michael

Piechowski, a renowned Dabrowski scholar, said "ring loud and clear in gifted children" (Piechowski, 2008, p. 22).

Researchers have specifically observed heightened sensitivity and concern for justice and fairness in gifted children. The more highly gifted a student is, the greater the degree to which this concern manifests itself, with 90% of exceptionally gifted students (IQ of 160+) involved in a study conducted by the Gifted Development Center in Denver demonstrating these sensitivity and concern characteristics (Meckstroth & Kearney, 2013). This strong sense of justice is often coupled with "empathy for those who are mistreated" and can set the stage for conflict between gifted students and adults who wield authority in their lives—especially if the students perceive that "those adults use their authority unfairly" (Piechowski, 2014). Actions rooted in implicit bias, as they are inherently unjust (even if unconscious), can activate students' sensitivities.

These characteristics, part of the broader spectrum of OEs common to gifted people, can create vulnerabilities in students and exacerbate the other status of gifted youths (Manzella, 2012) among both classmates and teachers—again triggering actions based on implicit biases.

Challenges and Opportunities

Gender is "among the first elements of self-knowledge," and a sense of incongruity between "who they are told they are and who they sense they are" can establish itself in children as young as 3 or 4 (Solomon, 2013). Self-knowledge is key to establishing one's sense of self. Unfortunately, trans and nonbinary students are consistently harassed about what they know to be true about themselves, which can be damaging to their developing sense of self.

Consider the potential impact of attitudes expressed by fellow students, faculty, and staff on a sensitive trans or nonbinary gifted student's sense of self, as illustrated by the following statistics, drawn from the 2015 National School Climate Survey, conducted by GLSEN (2016):

» 95.7% of LGBTQ students heard negative remarks about gender expression (not acting "masculine enough" or "feminine enough"); 62.9% heard these remarks frequently or often.

» 85.7% of LGBTQ students heard negative remarks specifically about transgender people, like "tranny" or "he/she"; 40.5% heard these remarks frequently or often.
» 63.5% of students reported hearing negative remarks about gender expression from teachers or other school staff.

Consider also the challenges created by school and district policies related to programs that gifted students often participate in, such as music, theater, art, debate, and academic competitions. Engaging with other gifted students in these activities helps nourish students' academic and artistic needs, as well as their social and emotional needs (Friedrichs et al., 2018). However, travel arrangements, uniforms, role assignments, etc., may carry gender-based restrictions. Gifted students who are trans or nonbinary may be denied these opportunities due to rules rooted in implicit bias.

What many of us take for granted linguistically can be a source of great challenge and pain for gifted trans and nonbinary students. A conversation with parents of such children revealed numerous instances of fellow students, teachers, and specialists engaging in dismissive behaviors when asked to use nonbinary pronouns (personal communication, August 12, 2020):

» A high school English teacher repeatedly denied a student's request for use of "they" and "them" and persisted in using wrong pronouns.
» High school students were allowed to tease a student about pronouns, with no intervention from the classroom teacher.
» A middle school math teacher claimed not to know what pronouns are and misused a student's requested pronouns so frequently as to trigger panic attacks in the student.
» A middle school speech therapist advised a student to "pick your battles" and give up on asking for the appropriate gender pronouns.

The challenges described (and this is not an exhaustive list) generate important and varied opportunities for educators who are committed to culturally responsive teaching.

Best/Promising Practices

Find out what your district is doing to support students in each of these areas, in terms of identification, curriculum, training, policy, and overall school environment. The practices outlined here offer educators a variety of strategies for countering implicit bias, enhancing culturally responsive teaching, and increasing representation for nonbinary and trans students in gifted programs.

Universal Screening Tied to Local Norms

According to an article published by the Minnesota Department of Education (MDE, n.d.), "universal screening is always best" (p. 1). Assessing all eligible students—not just those nominated by teachers and/or parents—to determine whether they qualify for gifted programs will remove barriers for students who may not present as the ideal gifted student. In addition, using local, rather than national, norms in this assessment is best, as this establishes students as gifted as compared to their peers at school, not as compared to students across the country (MDE, n.d.).

Underrepresented students, including trans and nonbinary youth, are well served by universal screening. Because some of the difficulties they face (including insufficient academic challenge) may result in behaviors that do not reveal their full potential or that seem noncompliant (Mitchell-Hutton, 2013), these students may—without universal screening—be overlooked for inclusion in gifted programs.

> *Underrepresented students, including trans and nonbinary youth, are well served by universal screening.*

Mandated Training in Trans and Nonbinary Inclusion

Teachers, administrators, and gifted coordinators should participate in professional development that allows them to develop cultural competency and enhance the creation and sustainment of safe and productive environments for gifted trans and nonbinary students (National Association for Gifted Children [NAGC], 2015). Educators and administrators at all school levels should purposefully distinguish between tolerance (which implies enduring the differences of others) and integration (which supports welcoming and integrating the strengths of all students) when pursuing strategies to create positive classroom and school environments (Danuta Walters, 2014).

Documented Policies to Support Inclusion

To promote consistent application of best practices, schools and districts should not rely on individuals, who may move on to another location, as the foundations of these approaches. Policies that support culturally responsive teaching should be enacted, documented, and made known to all community stakeholders—including parents (Manzella, 2018). In particular, policies to accommodate gender expression that may not conform to social stereotypes must be established and enforced (NAGC, 2015).

Inclusive Curriculum and Activities That Create Visibility

Teachers should seek opportunities to incorporate diverse figures (in general, and trans and nonbinary, specifically) in all subjects (NAGC, 2015), to illustrate the importance of nondominant culture contributors to society—past and present. Schools and districts should plan events that feature the work and viewpoints of trans and nonbinary people. Offering students consistent opportunities to see their identities acknowledged and validated in school is critical to supporting their developing sense of self (Manzella, 2018).

This selection of best practices is not comprehensive; rather, it is intended as a departure point from which educators are encouraged to develop ideas and strategies to support culturally responsive teaching for gifted trans and nonbinary students. In addition, NAGC (2017) has launched an online LGBTQ Diversity Toolbox with suggestions and resources specifically tailored to nonheteronormative students. Please see the references section for a link to the toolbox.

References

Adkins, D. (2016). Expert Declaration of Deanna Adkins, MD, Carcano v. McCrory, No. 1:16-cv-00236, 2016 WL 4256691 (M.D.N.C. May 13, 2016).

Ainsworth, C. (2015). Sex redefined. *Nature, 518*(539), 288–291.

Catalpa, J. M., & McGuire, J. K. (2018). Family boundary ambiguity among transgender youth. *Family Relations: An Interdisciplinary Journal of Applied Family Science, 67*(1), 88–103. https://doi.org/10.1111/fare.12304

Connolly, M. D., Zervos, M. J., Barone, C. J., II, Johnson, C. C., & Joseph, C. L. M. (2016). The mental health of transgender youth: Advances in understanding. *Journal of Adolescent Health, 59*(5), 489–495. https://doi.org/10.1016/j.jadohealth.2016.06.012

Danuta Walters, S. (2014). *The tolerance trap: How god, genes, and good intentions are sabotaging gay equality.* New York University Press.

Englert, P., & Dinkins, E. G. (2016). An overview of sex, gender, and sexuality. In H. F. Fradella & J. M. Sumner (Eds.), *Sex, sexuality, law, and (in)justice* (pp. 1–30). Routledge.

Friedrichs, T., Manzella, T., & Seney, R. (2018). *Needs and approaches for educators and parents of gifted gay, lesbian, bisexual, and transgender students.* National Association for Gifted Children.

GLSEN. (2016). *The 2015 National School Climate Survey: Executive summary.* https://www.glsen.org/research/2015-national-school-climate-survey

Johns, M. M., Lowry, R., Andrzejewski, J., Barrios, L. C., Demissie, Z., McManus, T., Rasberry, C. N., Robin, L., & Underwood, J. M. (2019). Transgender identity and experiences of violence victimization, substance use, suicide risk, and sexual risk behaviors among high school students—19 states and large urban school districts, 2017. *Morbidity and Mortality Weekly Report, 68*(3), 67–71.

The Kirwan Institute. (2012). *Understanding implicit bias.* The Ohio State University, Kirwan Institute for the Study of Race and Ethnicity. https://kirwaninstitute.osu.edu/article/understanding-implicit-bias

Lang, S. (2016). Native American men-women, lesbians, two-spirits: Contemporary and historical perspectives. *Journal of Lesbian Studies, 20*(3–4), 299–323. https://doi.org/10.1080/10894160.2016.1148966

Manzella, T. R. (2012). *Twice other: Cultural challenges faced by gifted and GLBTQ adolescents* [Unpublished master's thesis]. Metropolitan State University.

Manzella, T. R. (2018). *See me: Increasing two-way visibility of gifted LGBTQ students to support academic success* [Conference session]. 65th Annual Convention of the National Association of Gifted Children, Minneapolis, MN, United States.

Meadow, T. (2018). *Trans kids: Being gendered in the twenty-first century.* University of California Press.

Meckstroth, E., & Kearney, K. (2013). Indecent exposure: Does the media exploit highly gifted children? In C. S. Neville, M. M. Piechowski, & S. S. Tolan (Eds.), *Off the charts: Asynchrony and the gifted child* (pp. 282–291). Royal Fireworks Press.

Minnesota Department of Education. (2019). *Identifying under-served student populations for gifted programs: Some methods and frequently asked questions.* https://education.mn.gov/MDE/fam/gifted/index.htm

Mitchell-Hutton, B. (2013). I'll bet your teacher training didn't prepare you for this: Responding to asynchrony in the classroom. In C. S. Neville, M. M. Piechowski, & S. S. Tolan (Eds.), *Off the charts: Asynchrony and the gifted child* (pp. 398–411). Royal Fireworks Press.

National Association for Gifted Children. (2015). *Supporting gifted students with diverse sexual orientations and gender identities* [Position statement]. https://www.nagc.org/sites/default/files/Position%20Statement/GLBTQ%20(sept%202015).pdf

National Association for Gifted Children. (2017). *Diversity toolbox.* https://www.nagc.org/resources-publications/resources/timely-topics/including-diverse-learners-gifted-education-program-1

Piechowski, M. M. (2008). Experiencing in a higher key: Dabrowski's theory of and for the gifted. In M. W. Gosfield (Ed.), *Expert approaches to support gifted learners: Professional perspectives, best practices, and positive solutions* (pp. 19–42). Free Spirit.

Piechowski, M. M. (2014). *"Mellow out," they say. If only I could: Intensities and sensitivities of the young and bright* (2nd ed.). Royal Fireworks Press.

Solomon, A. (2013). *Far from the tree: Parents, children, and the search for identity.* Scribner.

The Trevor Project. (2020). *National survey on LGBTQ youth mental health 2020.* https://www.thetrevorproject.org/survey-2020

13

Culturally Responsive ABC's for Gifted LGBTTIQQ2SA+ Students

PJ Sedillo

Being culturally responsive to students who are gifted and LGBT-TIQQ2SA+ (lesbian, gay, bisexual, transsexual, transgender, intersexual, queer, questioning, two-spirit, and asexual) means being able to identify bias in oneself and others toward these students. For the remainder of the essay, I will refer to the more familiar acronym of LGBTQ+. It is important to understand that many of these students are part of a subculture within other subcultures, including those of different racial, ethnic, religious, ability, and disability groups. Responses of gay men that I interviewed for a 2013 study about their lived experiences as gifted students are included within this essay to provide personal reflections of their diverse journeys.

When confronting one's own bias, Henry David Thoreau noted, "The question is not what you look at, but what you see." Meeting the needs of this population can be daunting for educators, counselors, parent(s), family, friends, and most importantly, the gifted student who is discovering their identity. Gifted students working to understand their sexuality often find success by utilizing their comprehensive knowledge and intelligence (Sedillo, 2013). Aided by superior intelligence, these learners are often able to locate the facts, data, and foundational research to help them understand their feelings. In the words of one student, "In elementary [school] I asked my best friend if she liked me. She said she liked me like a brother because I was gay. She had confirmed what I was feeling. It is that outing that put me on my path to research a lot of information that described who I was" (Sedillo, 2013, p. 155). It should be noted, however, that the massive amount of information available online can lead to "analysis paralysis," a situation in which the student is unable to distinguish factual from inaccurate, and potentially harmful, information.

Knowing that gifted students who are gay often begin their journey of self-discovery alone, cultural competency and understanding is necessary for educators of this population. The importance of being able to identify our own bias, as well as the biases of others, cannot be overemphasized. Ultimately, a support network is needed to address the needs of this population. However, we must be sensitive to students' fears of the potential consequences of coming out to others (e.g., self-disclosure of a person's identities, behaviors, beliefs, affiliations, tastes, and interests).

Knowing that gifted students who are gay often begin their journey of self-discovery alone, cultural competency and understanding is necessary for educators of this population.

Gifted LGBTQ+ students may spend months, years, or decades questioning, understanding, and comprehending their sexual identities.

When these students are ready to "come out," they have painstakingly selected the person to trust with their disclosure. The person entrusted with this information, many times a teacher, must be mindful that this gifted LGBTQ+ student took an important step toward living their true life. Questions such as, "Why didn't you tell me sooner?" should be avoided, as they may come across as a judgment. One must realize that the student who makes the decision to come out did not just wake up one day and say, "Today I am going to be gay." They have already been on a deep emotional journey. It is important to recognize that the student may have struggled with accepting themselves, and as a gifted student, they may have thought through every possible consequence that may result from their disclosure. The emotional, and even physical, exhaustion that this process may have caused should be considered and acknowledged. Additionally, the person granted the trust of the student who has come out to them may also feel similar exhaustion and should take time to digest this information. Both the student and teacher to whom they have come out need time to process the information.

Gifted LGBTQ+ students may experience intense feelings during the coming out process, including overwhelming impatience, self-isolation, overthinking, extreme heightened sensitivity, and constant thoughts about the potential consequences of their decision. The resulting anxiety and behaviors may intensify and, in extreme cases, have the potential to become life-threatening (Sedillo, 2013). One participant stated, "I had a feeling of nonexistence, and breakdowns of depression." Yet another remembered feeling like "life would be easier if I didn't exist because I was gay" (Sedillo, 2013, p. 152). Therefore, the person who they have come out to should immediately take on an advocacy role. If an educator is unprepared, or unable, to provide the level of support needed, they should work with the student to identify another individual who is both knowledgeable and a willing advocate. Time is of the essence for providing social-emotional support, as these students' needs are different because of their combined giftedness and sexual identity.

As educators, we must be sensitive to, and respectful of, student privacy. We must be ready to listen and, when appropriate, ask questions. Remember, the student has taken the time to embrace their true identity before entrusting you with this very personal information. Statements such as, "I am, and will be, here for you with whatever you need" express to the student that you have their best interests at heart. Avoid making assumptions based on personal biases related to how they look, talk, or act. Most importantly, listen. If they ask for a response, then respond with any meaningful questions you may have—but make sure that your questions are limited and allow the student to answer as they choose. Do not make this an overwhelming, awkward situation by forcing them to answer questions they may not be ready to answer at this time. Respectful "asks" might include, "What pronouns do you prefer (him, her, they, etc.)?", "Do you have a girlfriend/boyfriend?", and most importantly, "How do you identify?" Some students may have become saturated with the information they have uncovered and are bursting at the seams to share. As one student shared, "I really enjoyed learning and [had] an insatiable curiosity. My curiosity kept me alive when I finally, logically knew I was gay—it's that pursuit of knowledge" (personal communication, March 20, 2011).

The heightened sensitivities of gifted LGBTQ+ students and their well-being should always be the focus during your conversation. Too many questions might cause students to "close up" and feel that they are being interrogated. Emotions may also be intensified. Educators can help by acknowledging students' feelings and assuring them of your availability and acceptance. The following steps can help you support gifted LGBTQ+ students:

» Understand the importance of the questions you are asking and how they will be perceived.
» Use wait time to allow students to think about their responses.
» Give students time to ask questions.
» Consider your responses and how they will be interpreted.
» If you are not sure about a response, answer any part of the question you can and let them know that you will get back to them with additional information.
» Change "you" statements to "I" statements to let them know that you are there to support them.
» Provide students with some control. For example, you might say, "I understand that you are upset. Would it be helpful if I shared some information?"
» Manage your tone and body language.
» Offer to attend meetings as appropriate to advocate and/or provide support for the student.
» Be aware of signs that a student may need a referral for outside mental health counseling.

As an allied advocate, it is your responsibility to educate yourself and locate resources pertaining to gifted LGBTQ+ students. By providing support through resources, mentors, self-advocacy techniques, and counselors/therapists, you can support and encourage these students to develop their own voice. This heightened level of self-actualization of their own coming out experience may help them become a role model for other students and allies.

When to Refer Students for Counseling

Gifted LGBTQ+ students are as likely as their peers to experience heightened levels of anxiety or depression. Although they are not more likely to engage in suicidal behaviors than other students, they do have unique risk and protective factors. At times, risk factors may outweigh protective factors (Cross & Cross, 2020). In instances in which the student expresses thoughts of self-harm, appears disconnected with reality, or is unable to function in school or at home, a referral to a mental health professional may be required. A basic mental health risk assessment will assess risk factors, such as ideation or planning to cause harm to oneself or others. A comprehensive risk assessment may reveal other risk behaviors (e.g., cutting, substance abuse, bullying, or child abuse). Educators should be trained to recognize symptoms of common mental health issues and behavioral clues to ensure all students receive mental health referrals when needed.

Opportunities and Challenges

Being gifted and LGBTQ+ comes with a unique set of opportunities and challenges. Characteristics of gifted students can include intellectual curiosity, advanced critical thinking skills, preferences for independence in work and study, unusual emotional depth and intensity, insatiable curiosity, and a heightened self-awareness, accompanied by feelings of being different (Clark, 2008). For these reasons, gifted students might be struggling with their own identities or just wanting to understand more about others who identify differently from themselves. Do not assume that a student with a gay pride flag on their backpack identifies as LGBTQ+; they might instead be showing their empathy and support for other students who identify as gay and who may be bullied at school (Sedillo, 2018).

Gifted students who struggle with their self-esteem often feel different from their peers. If they are also struggling with their own sexual identity, these feelings can be unbearable. As one student noted:

> I reached the point where all I wanted to do was die . . .
> I felt completely isolated, like nobody could ever understand me or what I was going through and that I would never find anyone that could or would want to. (Sedillo, 2013, p. 148)

Be aware of negative self-talk and extreme mood swings. Some gifted students who are struggling with their sexual identity might worry "in the back of their minds" that peers, family, and/or teachers friends, and the school environment will be hostile, aggressive, and unreceptive in accepting this dissimilar sexual identity. These intensified feelings of differentness—as a result of their giftedness and their sexual identity—can cause intense feelings of loneliness. As one gay gifted individual noted, "I was losing interest in people. I started thinking of myself as useless" (Sedillo, 2013, p. 149). These feelings of loneliness can cause these students to question whether they should, would, or could disclose their true self to another person, or even themselves: "When I was young, I was comfortable coming out to random people. It was later made clear to me that some people didn't like or agree with that. I became more withdrawn" (Sedillo, 2013, p. 154). Their uncertainty about the consequences of revealing who they are, as well as their overexcitabilities, can be frightening for gifted students (Whitney & Hirsh, 2011).

Ultimately, gifted LGBTQ+ students have unique emotional support needs (Clark, 2008), but what if that support is not there or even available? Friedman (2014) noted that as many as 50% of LGBTQ+ teens experience a negative reaction from their parents when they come out; 30% experience physical abuse, and 26% are kicked out of their homes. LGBTQ+ children comprise 40% of all homeless youth, and family rejection is the primary cause (Friedman, 2014). According to one individual, "It would have been a difficult adjustment for my family if I came out; there would be family shame" (Sedillo, 2013, p. 151). If the coming out experience is negative, then the student may remain "closeted" and be more prone to suicide and suicidal ideation: "There was a total stigma for being gay. I wish I could have embraced who I was. I really was in a dark place when I was in the closet" (Sedillo, 2013, p. 148). The question of whether or not they will be accepted at home or at school can weigh heavily on the mind of the gifted LGBTQ+ student and can have real consequences.

Steps for Creating Culturally Responsive Classrooms for LGBTQ+ Students

Supporting and assisting students who are gifted and LGBTQ+ requires teachers, counselors/therapists, family, and friends to be culturally responsive. This requires that they are person-centered, eliminate barriers to learning and achievement, and support these students so that they reach their full potential. Furthermore, being culturally responsive means proactively working to respect, understand, and meet the needs of gifted LGBTQ+ students who come from different cultural and subcultural backgrounds through the positive emphasis of their values, beliefs, habits, customs, and traditions.

> *Educators need to develop a culturally responsive philosophy in their classrooms related to the needs of gifted LGBTQ+ students.*

Society's mindset toward those who are LGBTQ+ varies greatly across different cultures. All cultures have their own values regarding appropriate and inappropriate sexual identity. Some might sanction and affirm same-sex love and sexuality, while others might despise and disapprove of those who identify as LGBTQ+. Educational systems can sometimes stifle the cultural responsiveness of educators among this population in the school environment. On a positive note, in June of 2020 the U.S. Supreme Court ruled that firing a person on the basis of sexual orientation or gender identity was unlawful. The result of this ruling could have a profound effect on the course of educators' beliefs and attitudes about teaching and supporting gifted LGBTQ+ students specifically, as the fear of retaliation from administrators is lifted. Even so, there is still much work to be done.

Educators need to develop a culturally responsive philosophy in their classrooms related to the needs of gifted LGBTQ+ students. Some questions to start this process might be the following: Are you enthusiastic and eager to work with gifted LGBTQ+ students? Do you hold high expectations for all of your students regardless of their sexual identity and giftedness? What changes need to occur in your classroom to effectively meet the needs of your gifted LGBTQ+ students? The limited number of standards-based practices, resources, mentors, curricula, and research conducted about LGBTQ+ students hinder their support (Sedillo, 2015). Although these areas of need exist, some strategies for developing a culturally responsive philosophy include the following.

Establish a Culturally Responsive Learning Environment

As with your teaching philosophy, the learning environment sets the context and climate for the classroom. At its essence, the learning environment is about relationships, communication, and expectation while focusing specifically on students' sense of membership and belonging. The following questions will assist in developing a culturally responsive learning environment:

» Are my visuals or displays nonstereotypical?
» Do all of the visuals, materials, or displays represent different cultural groups in my classroom? Do they include those who are gifted, LGBTQ+, and gifted and LGBTQ+?
» Do all of my students feel a sense of appreciation, support, and belonging?
» Are all of my students encouraged and expected to work collaboratively?

» What steps have I taken to prevent bullying of gifted LGBTQ+ students and others in my classroom and school?

Utilize Culturally Responsive Curricula

The utilization, design, and implementation of culturally responsive curricula and materials or resources build upon differentiating instruction for gifted students with an emphasis on rigor and relevance (Banks, 2008; Ford, 2005; Ford & Harris, 1999; Ford & Milner, 2005); this includes those who are gifted LGBTQ+. The curriculum should not stand out as a separate subject, but it should be integrated throughout the day. To this end, professional learning should be introduced at the start of the year. Inclusive curricula provide support for all to empathize, connect, and collaborate with culturally different peers, which leads and encourages all to respect others, including their gifted LGBTQ+ peers. Interestingly enough, in the past few years a few states have mandated that schools teach LGBTQ+-inclusive curriculum. The following questions will assist educators in reflecting on their support of culturally responsive curricula:

» Am I ensuring that all students are engaged, interested, and motivated by what is being taught?
» Do I find relevant information, biographies, videos, and resources about noteworthy gifted LGBTQ+ individuals and integrate these resources within the current curriculum?
» Are the LGBTQ+ topics, issues, and/or events presented in the classroom balanced, comprehensive, and multidimensional?
» Are different viewpoints shared, discussed, and welcomed?
» Have I addressed LGBTQ+ stereotypes, distortions, and omissions in the curriculum (Banks, 2008)?

Additional Considerations

Additional considerations for schools to consider in support of gifted LGBTQ+ students include the following.

1. Start with the implementation of LGBTQ+ culturally responsive conversations to build confidence between district leaders and educators.

2. Provide professional learning to promote safer school environments for the gifted LGBTQ+ children (Friedrichs & Sedillo, 2019).

3. Develop and evaluate lessons during grade-level or subject area meetings to ensure that they include positive representations of LGBTQ+ culture, people, history, and events, and to ensure that bias is avoided.

4. Supply readily available books in the classroom or library that highlight historically famous gifted, LGBTQ+, and gifted LGBTQ+ persons.

5. Introduce LGBTQ+ History Month (October) and LGBTQ+ Pride Month (June). Remember, if this is the only time this curriculum is made available during the year, it can lead to curriculum isolation. Having only one month on this topic, the curriculum can fail to connect to other big ideas and topics being studied.

6. Positively shift school culture by introducing schoolwide days of action and visibility, such as No-Name Calling Week (January), Day of Silence (April), and GLSEN's Ally Week (September).

7. Address name-calling, bullying, or harassment immediately.

8. Use teachable moments.

9. Provide a support network for gifted, LGBTQ+, and gifted LGBTQ+ students, and hold students accountable. GLSEN provides a Safe Space Kit on how to do this at https://www.glsen.org/activity/glsen-safe-space-kit-solidarity-lgbtq-youth.

Final Thoughts

Being culturally responsive to students who are gifted and LGBT-TIQQ2SA+ means being able to identify bias toward these students in oneself and others. Most individuals in our society are cisgender (denoting or relating to a person whose sense of personal identity and gender corresponds with their birth sex) and heteronormative (denoting or relating to a world view that promotes heterosexuality as the normal or preferred sexual orientation). Realizing this privilege, educators need to be more sensitive and understand the linear differences related to sexual identities and orientations. To do so means confronting and challenging one's own implicit bias. These biases can become a barrier to the positive growth for gifted LGBTQ+ individuals and their culture. Again, when a student chooses to come out to you, they are entrusting and honoring you with their decision to be part of a raw declaration of their being. As one individual said:

> If I didn't have my intelligence as a strength, as a positive, I would have been more worse off. It helped me deal with being gay. Because my parents did not accept me, I realized if I took classes to graduate early, I would have an "escape plan" to get out of this situation. I finally realized that it always gets better. When I came out to a few select people I first needed them to just listen . . . and now going through this experience I pride myself on how I moved forward and believed in myself that I can get through this and any other obstacles that come my way. (Sedillo, 2013, p. 150)

Cultural responsiveness ensures that educators have the ability to facilitate and guide those who are gifted and LGBTTIQQ2SA+, demonstrating respect and acceptance so that these students can continue to grow, thrive, survive, and live.

In closing, the following lists provide some advice as you move toward a more inclusive and culturally responsive environment.

WHAT **NOT** TO DO WHEN SOMEONE COMES OUT

1. Do *not* ignore the revelation.
2. Do *not* state, "I knew all along."
3. Do *not* ask, "Why didn't you tell me sooner?"
4. Do *not* tell them "this is just a phase."
5. Do *not* use religion to shame them.
6. Do *not* judge.

7. Do *not* be too serious.

8. Do *not* assume in advance that you know what it means to be gifted and LGBTTIQQ2SA+.

9. Do *not* push.

10. Do *not* blow things out of proportion.

11. Do *not* allow the individual to become isolated.

WHAT TO DO WHEN SOMEONE COMES OUT

1. Do tell them you believe in them.

2. Do tell them "thank you" for sharing this part of their life with you.

3. Do ask about what kind of support they need.

4. Do commit and become an ally to the LGBTTIQQ2SA+ community.

5. Do be patient.

6. Do provide confidentiality and respect for their privacy.

7. Do acknowledge the risk they took coming out.

8. Do say, "Thank you for trusting me." Or say, "It does not change how I feel about you."

9. Do allow them the integrity to share what they want, when, and how they want to.

10. Do call frequently during the time right after they have come out to you. This will let them know you are still there for them.

11. Do what you have always done together.

12. Do talk about other LGBTTIQQ2SA+ people you know.

13. Do learn about the LGBTTIQQ2SA+ community.

GOOD QUESTIONS TO ASK

1. How long have you known you are LGBTTIQQ2SA+?

2. Has it been hard for you carrying this secret?

3. Is there any way that I can help you?

4. If I have ever offended you unknowingly, please let me know.

5. What do you expect from me (confidentiality, of course)?

6. What can I do to improve?

7. Do you want me to just listen?

WHAT TO SAY WHEN
SOMEONE COMES OUT

1. Thank you for trusting me.

2. I will leave the door open for any future communication.

3. I support you.

4. I am here for you to help me understand what you may need.

5. If/when you are ready, let us talk more.

6. Let us look into resources.

7. Thank you.

8. You have a lot of courage to share this with me.

9. I understand that if I have a question, you might not know all of the answers.

References

Banks, J. A. (2008). *Teaching strategies for ethnic studies*. Allyn & Bacon.

Clark, B. (2008). *Growing up gifted* (7th ed.). Pearson Prentice Hall.

Cross, T. L., & Cross, J. R. (2020). An ecological model of suicidal behavior among students with gifts and talents. *High Ability Studies*. https://doi.org/10.1080/13598139.2020.1733391

Ford, D. Y. (2005). Welcoming all students to room 202: Creating culturally responsive classrooms. *Gifted Child Today, 28*(4), 28–30, 65.

Ford, D. Y., & Harris, J. J., III. (1999). *Multicultural gifted education*. Teachers College Press.

Ford, D. Y., & Milner, H. R. (2005). *Teaching culturally diverse gifted students*. Prufrock Press.

Friedman, M. (2014). *The psychological impact of LGBT discrimination: How the LGBT community is being harmed each and every day*. Psychology Today. https://www.psychologytoday.com/us/blog/brick-brick/201402/the-psychological-impact-lgbt-discrimination

Friedrichs, T. P., & Sedillo, P. J. (2019). Professional learning standards and practices for educators of gifted GLBTQ youth. In A. M. Novak & C. L. Weber (Eds.), *Best practices in learning and teacher preparation: Special topics for gifted professional development* (Vol. 2, pp. 31–50). Prufrock Press.

Sedillo, P. J. (2013). *A retrospective study of gay gifted, young adult males' perceptions of giftedness and suicide* [Unpublished doctoral dissertation]. University of New Mexico, Albuquerque.

Sedillo, P. J. (2015). Gay gifted adolescent suicide and suicidal ideation literature: research barriers and limitations. *Gifted Child Today, 38*(2), 114–120. https://doi.org/10.1177/1076217514568557

Sedillo, P. J. (2018). Why is there a gay pride flag on my 9-year-old's backpack? *Parenting for High Potential, 7*(2), 2–4.

Whitney, C. S., & Hirsch, G. (2011). *Helping gifted children soar: A practical guide for parents and teachers* (2nd ed.). Great Potential Press.

Section IV

A Call to Action

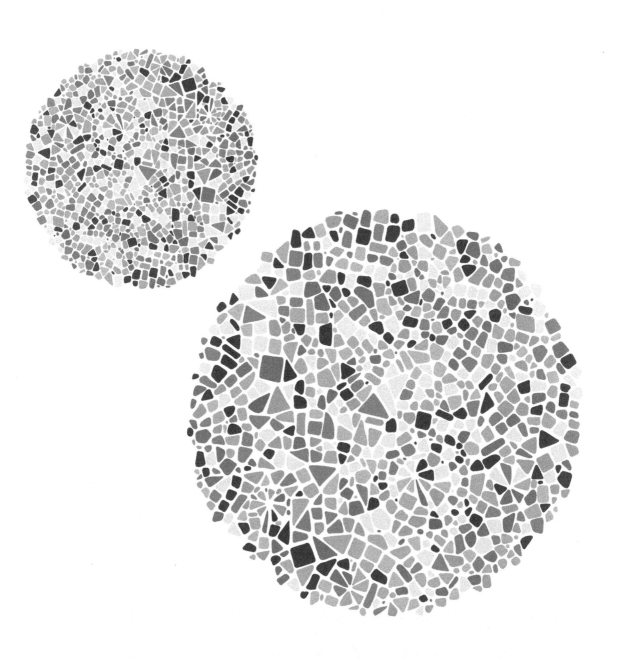

A Call to Action

Supporting Equity, Diversity, and Access for Gifted Students[1]

The Association for the Gifted, Council for Exceptional Children

Society continues to become more diverse. For that reason, it is critical that we find and develop the gifts and talents of all children and youth in our nation. Equity, diversity, access, and excellence are essential to high-level academic achievement. Diversity has been a topic of discussion in America for decades. Embedded in discussions of equity, diversity, access, and excellence are race, culture, class, ethnicity,

---

1 *Note.* This section is from *A Call to Action: Supporting Equity, Diversity, and Access for Gifted Students*, by The Association for the Gifted, Council for Exceptional Children, 2020, http://cectag.com/resources/a-critical-call-to-action-supporting-equity-diversity-and-access-for-gifted-students. Reprinted with permission.

income, gender, sexual orientation, linguistic differences, and learning differences.

Our Mission Statement speaks directly to this:

The Association for the Gifted (TAG), a division of the Council for Exceptional Children (CEC), embraces and supports the needs of students with gifts and talents, focusing on multi-exceptional and other diverse learners, through advocacy, professional learning, and resources.

CEC-TAG values working collaboratively and respectfully to advocate for quality education and service for all children with gifts and talents, especially those who are twice-exceptional (2e) and from other diverse populations. Given TAG's emphasis on equity, diversity, and inclusion, this document is a call to action for all stakeholders, as there is shared responsibility for providing schools where all students thrive, including gifted and talented students from racially, culturally, ethnically, and linguistically different (RCELD) populations who are too often underrepresented. In order to achieve diversity, equity, and inclusion, action is required in six areas:

» professional learning,
» equitable access,
» culturally responsive curriculum and instruction,
» research in equity and diversity,
» parent and community partnerships, and
» policy.

This call to action presents key data points, recommendations, resources to learn more, and research references in each of the six action areas. Developing the strengths of all gifted and talented and high-ability learners requires purposeful actions by all stakeholders to ensure a bright future for our nation and our world.

Please note, researchers often use the terms "Hispanic" and "Latinx" interchangeably. For consistency, the term "Latinx" is used more frequently in this resource. In addition, the authors believe the phrase "racially, culturally, ethnically, and linguistically diverse" (RCELD) student is the most inclusive of the populations most often underrepresented in gifted and talented services and advanced courses.

Professional Learning

After earning a certificate, licensure, or endorsement in gifted education, educational professionals typically participate in annual professional learning to increase their effectiveness and enhance learning for students with gifts and talents. Professional learning should bring awareness to disparities in identification and services and suggest actions to overcome them. Ideally, preservice teachers and all other educators would be offered similar professional learning because these students are gifted and talented all day long, every day.

The Data

The underrepresentation of racially, culturally, ethnically, and linguistically different (RCELD) students, as well as students who are twice exceptional (2e), has been an ongoing discussion in gifted education for decades. The underrepresentation data are persistent, pervasive, and overwhelming; underrepresentation is a loss, not only for the students, but also for the nation. Effective, ongoing professional learning focused on equity, diversity, and inclusiveness proves critical to move the nation's schools toward increasing these populations' participation in gifted education services.

» Only five states require gifted coursework as part of preservice teacher and administrator training, and only four states require gifted coursework as part of counselor training (Plucker et al., 2018).

» A 2019 survey conducted by Education Week Research found that "most . . . general education teachers receive training on working with gifted students but only a minority report that the training is mandatory" (p. 4).

» There is a "cultural mismatch between our predominantly White, female, middle-class teaching force and our increasingly culturally diverse population of students" (Davis, 2019, p. 52).

» Many educators feel unprepared to serve and teach students from diverse backgrounds even after having one or two courses on the topic (Nieto, 2013). If giftedness is added to the equation, educators feel even less prepared.

» According to the National 2e Community of Practice, "working successfully with this unique population [2e students] requires specialized academic training and ongoing professional development" (AEGUS, n.d., para. 4).

Recommendations

What professional learning strategies for gifted and general education personnel can improve identification, enrollment, and retention of students receiving gifted services, particularly students who are RCELD or have multiple exceptionalities? Gifted education researchers, theorists, authors, practitioners, and advocates committed to this question have identified recommendations:

» Develop system-wide equity, diversity, and inclusion policies and frameworks for professional learning for schools and districts.
» Provide quality foundational training in special and gifted education to increase the chance of educators meeting the needs of students who are twice exceptional (2e) (Baldwin et al., 2015).
» Incorporate gifted education, particularly training and experiences in differentiating for high-ability learners, in educator preparation programs so that preservice teachers are better prepared to address the needs of students with gifts and talents (Brevik et al., 2018).
» Design professional learning experiences for teachers, counselors, and administrators about identifying and serving RCELD gifted students that are specific to the school's and district's student body and includes culturally relevant content, a safe space for candid conversations, and a collaborative approach (Lewis et al., 2018).
» Conduct an annual evaluation of gifted professional learning practices, including an equity audit.

Resources to Learn More

» "Reframing Professional Learning to Meet the Needs of Teachers Working With Culturally Diverse Gifted Learners" (a chapter by Joy Lawson Davis in *Best Practices in Professional Learn-*

ing and Teacher Preparation Series: Special Topics for Gifted Professional Development [Vol. 2])

» "Administrative Leadership in Gifted Education" (a chapter by Tarek Grantham, Kristina Collins, and Kenneth Dickson in the second edition of *Critical Issues and Practices in Gifted Education: What the Research Says*)

» Learning Forward (https://learningforward.org)

References

Association for the Education of Gifted Underachieving Students. (n.d.). *Our work.*

Baldwin, L., Baum, S., Pereles, D., & Hughes, C. (2015). Twice-exceptional learners: The journey toward a shared vision. *Gifted Child Today, 38*(4), 206–214. https://doi.org/10.1177/1076217515597277

Brevik, L. M., Gunnulfsen, A. E., & Renzulli, J. S. (2018). Student teachers' practice and experience with differentiated instruction for students with higher learning potential. *Teaching and Teacher Education, 71*(1), 34-45. https://doi.org/10.1016/j.tate.2017.12.003

Davis, J. L. (2019). Reframing professional learning to meet the needs of teachers working with culturally diverse gifted learners. In A. M. Novak & C. L. Weber (Eds.), *Best practices in professional learning and teacher preparation: Special topics for gifted professional development* (Vol. 2, pp. 51–70). Prufrock Press.

Education Week Research Center. (2019). *Gifted education: Results of a national survey.*

Lewis, K. D., Novak, A. M., & Weber, C. L. (2018). Where are gifted students of color? Case studies outline strategies to increase diversity in gifted programs. *The Learning Professional, 39*(4), 50–58. https://learningforward.org/wp-content/uploads/2018/08/where-are-gifted-students-of-color.pdf

Nieto, S. (2013). *Finding joy in teaching students of diverse backgrounds: Culturally responsive and socially just practices in U.S. classrooms.* Heinemann.

Plucker, J. A., Glynn, J., Healey, G., & Dettmer, A. (2018). *Equal talents, unequal opportunities: A report card on state support for academically talented low-income students* (2nd ed.). Jack Kent Cooke Foundation. https://www.jkcf.org/research/equal-talents-unequal-opportunities-second-edition-a-report-card-on-state-support-for-academically-talented-low-income-students

Equitable Access

Despite considerable academic conversation and study, underrepresentation of racially, culturally, ethnically, and linguistically different (RCELD) students and those with multiple exceptionalities persists in gifted and talented services and advanced courses. Although a few programs across the country are making strides in this area, the problem continues to be pervasive, and the performance divide is growing.

The Data

Educators and the public tend to be aware of the Achievement Gap, but few are well versed in the Excellence Gap. According to Plucker and Peters (2016), "Excellence Gaps are differences between subgroups of students performing at the highest levels of achievement" (p. ix). Despite an increase in the number of students scoring at advanced levels on the National Assessment of Educational Progress, there has not been an increase in students from low-income backgrounds scoring at advanced levels. Therefore, the Excellence Gap has continued to increase over time and is present at all educational levels (Jack Kent Cooke Foundation [JKCF], 2019). Patrick et al. (2020) found several factors contributing to this disparity. Their research focused specifically on students who are Black and Latinx, but what they learned applies to all students who are RCELD or have multiple exceptionalities.

» Students who are Black, Latinx, or from low-income backgrounds are underrepresented in gifted and talented services.
» Many schools offer little to no advanced coursework, such as Algebra I for eighth graders, Advanced Placement, International Baccalaureate, and dual credit courses.
» Students who are Black and Latinx are disproportionately less likely to be in advanced courses even when their schools offer it. Schools that predominantly serve Black and Latinx students have fewer seats in advanced courses, and other schools that offer advanced courses do not enroll Black and Latinx students in those courses in representative numbers.

The JKCF (2020) reported that despite scoring in the top quartile academically, one quarter of students from the bottom economic quartile do not take college entrance exams or apply to college.

Recommendations

The inequity illustrated by the Excellence Gap must be addressed in numerous ways. All stakeholders play a role in solving this educational crisis. The following recommendations may help a community address the Excellence Gap:

» Employ best practices in the identification of children and youth as gifted and talented.
  › Utilize local norms in schools in which few children are identified as gifted and talented (Plucker & Peters, 2016).
  › Utilize universal screening to cast a wide net for the identification of children as gifted and talented (Patrick et al., 2020; Plucker & Peters, 2016).
  › Utilize multiple measures, including alternative assessments, to ensure opportunities for advanced learning (Plucker & Peters, 2016).

» Employ open enrollment/access to advanced coursework within a school and district, and ensure the policy is well known to students and parents.
» Prepare students to participate in advanced learning opportunities by frontloading, which includes scaffolding skills and concepts (Plucker & Peters, 2016).
» Increase the number and sections of Advanced Placement courses to accommodate larger numbers of students (Patrick et al., 2020).

Resources to Learn More

» Acceleration Institute at the Belin-Blank Center (https://www.accelerationinstitute.org)
» Jack Kent Cooke Foundation (https://www.jkcf.org)
» The Education Trust (https://edtrust.org)

References

Jack Kent Cooke Foundation. (2019, July). *New research brief: The Excellence Gap is growing.* https://www.jkcf.org/our-stories/research-brief-excellence-gap

Jack Kent Cooke Foundation. (2020). *What is the Excellence Gap?* https://www.jkcf.org/our-research/what-is-the-excellence-gap

Patrick, K., Socol, A., & Morgan, I. (2020, January). *Inequities in advanced coursework: What's driving them and what leaders can do.* The Education Trust. https://edtrust.org/resource/inequities-in-advanced-coursework

Plucker, J. A., & Peters, S. J. (2016). *Excellence Gaps in education: Expanding opportunities for talented youth.* Harvard Education Press.

Culturally Responsive Curriculum and Instruction

RCELD refers to students who are racially, culturally, ethnically, and linguistically different—all historically underserved groups of children in the U.S. educational system (Artiles et al., 2010). They include students who are Black, Latinx, and Native American descent; English learners; and those from low-socioeconomic backgrounds. Their academic achievement in gifted services relies on instructional and curricular support provided by classroom teachers. RCELD students and students who are twice exceptional (2e) need curriculum and instruction that develop and hone their strengths. Current research, action steps, and resources can be used to incorporate culturally responsive curriculum and instructional support for diverse populations receiving gifted services.

The Data

Culturally responsive curriculum and instruction within gifted services afford RCELD students opportunities to experience academic success because the curriculum and instruction utilize cultural knowledge, prior experiences, and product and performance preferences of diverse students to make learning more appropriate and effective for them.

> » Researchers have concluded that culturally responsive practices are helpful for all students and should not just be targeted towards RCELD students in schools within special programs like gifted education (Ford, 2014; Gay, 2010; Ladson-Billings, 2014).
> » Culturally responsive educators are adept at motivating all students, including those with gifts and talents, and understand that students of color may face more challenges than their White classmates and peers (Wright et al., 2017).
> » Gifted students of color want, need, and deserve to see themselves mirrored in curriculum and literature (Ford et al., 2018).
> » In order to appropriately serve culturally and linguistically diverse exceptional students, educators must demonstrate cul-

tural responsiveness when interacting with the learners and families (Obiakor, 2012).

» A culturally responsive curriculum benefits all children, including those with gifts and talents, by building on the richness of varied lived experiences and cultures to make learning more meaningful (Bergeron, 2008).

Recommendations

The inequities experienced by RCELD students and students who are twice exceptional (2e) must be addressed. The following recommendations may help stakeholders address those inequities:

» Implement culturally responsive curriculum which is characterized by the following:
  › thematic organization (Nieto, 2013);
  › real-world application and relevant current event integration (Gay, 2010);
  › ongoing and diagnostic assessment (Ladson-Billings, 1995);
  › high expectations for all groups with support to mirror the expectation (Ladson-Billings, 2014); and
  › cultures incorporated into the curriculum (Ford et al, 2018).

» Implement culturally responsive instructional practices, which include the following:
  › modeling and scaffolding (Gay, 2010);
  › cooperative and flexible grouping (Santamaria, 2009);
  › inquiry-based classroom environment (Linan-Thompson et al., 2018);
  › graphic organizers and highly visual creative student outputs (Nieto, 2013); and
  › student ownership of the learning process (Gay, 2010).

Resources to Learn More

» Teaching Tolerance Lesson Plans and Teacher Guides (https://www.tolerance.org/frameworks)

> » A Culturally Responsive Equity-Based Bill of Rights for Gifted Students of Color (https://www.nagc.org/blog/culturally-responsive-equity-based-bill-rights-gifted-students-color)

References

Artiles, A., Kozleski, E., Trent, S., Osher, D., & Ortiz, A. (2010). Justifying and explaining disproportionality, 1968–2008: A critique of underlying views of culture. *Exceptional Children, 76*(3), 279–299. https://doi.org/10.1177/001440291007600303

Bergeron, B. S. (2008). Enacting a culturally responsive curriculum in a novice teacher's classroom: Encountering disequilibrium. *Urban Education, 43*(1), 4–28. https://doi.org/10.1177/0042085907309208

Ford, D. Y. (2014). Why education must be multicultural: Addressing a few misperceptions with counterarguments. *Gifted Child Today, 37*(1), 59–62. https://doi.org/10.1177/1076217513512304

Ford, D. Y., Dickson, K. T., Davis, J. L., Scott, M. T., & Grantham, T. C. (2018). A culturally responsive equity-based bill of rights for gifted students of color. *Gifted Child Today, 41*(3), 125–129. https://doi.org/10.1177/1076217518769698

Gay, G. (2010). *Culturally responsive teaching practices: Theory, research, and practice* (2nd ed.). Teachers College Press.

Ladson-Billings, G. (1995). Toward a theory of culturally relevant pedagogy. *American Educational Research Journal, 32*(3), 465–491. https://doi.org/10.3102/00028312032003465

Ladson-Billings, G. (2014). Culturally relevant pedagogy 2.0: Aka the remix. *Harvard Educational Review, 84*(1), 74–84. https://doi.org/10.17763/haer.84.1.p2rj131485484751

Linan-Thompson, S., Lara-Martinez, J. A., & Cavazos, L. O. (2018). Exploring the intersection of evidence-based practices and culturally and linguistically responsive practices. *Intervention in School and Clinic, 54*(1), 6–13. https://doi.org/10.1177/1053451218762574

Nieto, S. (2013). *Finding joy in teaching students of diverse backgrounds: Culturally responsive and socially just practices in U.S. classrooms.* Heinemann.

Obiakor, F. E. (2012). *Multicultural special education: Culturally responsive teaching.* Pearson.

Santamaria, L. J. (2009). *Culturally responsive differentiated instruction: Narrowing gaps between best pedagogical practices benefiting all learners.* Teachers College Record, 111(1), 214–247.

Wright, B. L., Ford, D. Y., & Young, J. L. (2017). Ignorance or indifference? Seeking excellence and equity for underrepresented students of color in gifted education. *Global Education Review, 4*(1), 45–60.

Research in Equity and Diversity

Renzulli (1999) identified the lack of equity in gifted education as "a time bomb ticking away in our field" (p. 129), and added that this time bomb would "erode political support" for gifted education and that the field needed to act on these concerns in "specific and concrete ways" (p. 130). We see this prediction coming to fruition. Equity and diversity in gifted education are currently in the limelight as states are restructuring or even eliminating gifted education services altogether. Claims that services are inequitable and facilitate racial and ethnic segregation in education are the crux of the issue. Misdiagnosis and underidentification of children and youth with gifts and talents, in general, occur for many reasons and are especially prevalent among learners from RCELD populations and students who are twice-exceptional (2e). Dreilinger (2019) reported that "in addition to the 3.3 million U.S. public school children identified as gifted, there are as many as 3.6 million gifted children being overlooked in school" (para. 1). Although these issues are clearly known within the field of gifted education, there is little research establishing evidenced-based practices to address them.

The Data

There is a critical need for research regarding strategies to support equitable identification and services.

» Plucker and Callahan (2014) stated that the current status of research in the field of gifted education "involves theory and model generative essays, research studies, and applied/advice pieces; . . . within the research category, the bulk of the research is gifted education has been descriptive and correlational" (p. 393).

» In a content analysis of the literature relevant to 2e students, Hughes-Lynch and Troxclair (2019) found very limited research-based data.

» Ford and colleagues (2008) stated, "Little attention, if any, has focused on the concept of 'racially, culturally, and linguistically responsive research'" (p. 82). This is a significant issue related to cross-cultural research.

Recommendations

The lack of research focused on identifying evidence-based practices to better serve RCELD students and students who are twice-exceptional (2e) must be addressed. The following recommendations may help stakeholders address those inequities:

» Increase replication of existing studies on the Excellence Gap and the use of nonverbal assessments to identify RCELD students (Plucker & Callahan, 2014).
» Increase experimental research on interventions, assessment that aligns with outcomes, the use of new designs and statistical analyses, and involvement of government regarding data collection (Plucker & Callahan, 2014).
» Partner with local school districts, universities, and educational support organizations to study the effectiveness of program changes made to better identify and serve gifted RCELD students and 2e students.
» Evaluate every aspect of research projects from a cross-cultural perspective and utilize strategies that are appropriate for diverse groups (Ford et al., 2008).
» Develop cross-cultural competence by being self-aware, socially responsible, culturally aware, and recognizing researcher biases (Ford et al., 2008).

Resources to Learn More

» Council for Exceptional Children, The Association for the Gifted (http://cectag.com)
» Journal for the Education of the Gifted (https://journals.sage pub.com/home/jeg)
» National Center for Research on Gifted Education (https://nc rge.uconn.edu)
» Research on Giftedness, Creativity, and Talent Special Interest Group, a part of the American Educational Research Association (https://www.aera.net/SIG091/Research-on-Giftedness-Crea tivity-and-Talent-Development)

References

Dreilinger, D. (2019, November 26). *Up to 3.6 million students should be labeled gifted, but aren't.* The Hechinger Report. https://hechinger report.org/up-to-3-6-million-students-should-be-labeled-gifted-but-arent

Ford, D. Y., Moore, J. L., Whiting, G. W., & Grantham, T. C. (2008). Conducting cross-cultural research: Controversy, cautions, concerns, and considerations. *Roeper Review, 30*(2), 82–92. DOI:10.10 80/02783190801954924

Hughes-Lynch, C., & Troxclair, D. (2019, July 24-28). *Preaching to the choir: Twice-exceptional gifted literature analysis* [Conference Session]. 23rd World Council for the Gifted and Talented Children Conference, Nashville, TN, United States.

Plucker, J., & Callahan, C. (2014). Research on giftedness and gifted education: Status of the field and considerations for the future. *Exceptional Children, 61*(4), 390–406. DOI:10.1177/0014402914527244

Renzulli, J. (1999). Reflections, perceptions, and future directions. *Journal for the Education of the Gifted, 23*(1), 125–146.

Parent and Community Partnerships

Potential giftedness in racially, culturally, ethnically, and linguistically different (RCELD) children as well as children who are twice-exceptional (2e) are often overlooked or misinterpreted (Henfield et al., 2014). As a parent, then, being aware of common gifted characteristics is especially important (Luckey Goudelock, 2019) as is understanding the nature and needs children with gifts and talents. Seminal research by Dr. Mary Frasier and her colleagues at the University of Georgia explain how traits and behaviors can look different in different populations (Frasier et al., 1995). Parent and community members need to understand the nature and needs of RCELD and 2e children in order to partner with schools more effectively.

The Data

Parents play a critical advocacy role for their RCELD and 2e children, and they need support to fulfil this role.

» Children need exposure to peers who share their interests and passions, which further ignites their intellectual growth and love of learning (Amend & Joerg, 2019).

» Most gifted children socialize and make friends with those more related to their mental age rather than their chronological age (Cross, 2011).

» Parents and teachers do not always see eye-to-eye when it comes to behavior concerns because behavior may vary depending on the environment (Thompson & Winsler, 2018).

» Families of gifted children often feel that they do not relate to families of nongifted children mainly due to their unique academic needs. Consequently, parents of gifted children may find it difficult to access support groups within gifted or other communities (Jolly & Matthews, 2013).

Recommendations

Children can grow socially, emotionally, and cognitively in settings intentional in supporting RCELD and 2e students with policies, procedures, and instruments (Ford, 2015). Parents can use the following recommendations to identify creative and personal strategies to better support their children's growth:

» Model and explain how to move forward after making mistakes (Amend & Joerg, 2019).
» Reflect on the stressful moments with other parents of gifted and 2e children. This interaction may provide comfort in talking to other parents with similar experiences (Zanetti et al., 2019).
» Demonstrate a comfort with personal strengths and weaknesses to help children become comfortable with their own giftedness and areas of weakness (Amend & Joerg, 2019).
» Enroll their children in enrichment programs to broaden interests within a community where students feel emotionally safe and accepted. Invitational learning is culturally responsive; it includes compassion, empathy, and a focus on justice for students (Ford, 2015).

Resources to Learn More

» Supporting the Emotional Needs of the Gifted (https://www.sengifted.org)
» National Association for Gifted Children Parent TIP Sheets (Timely Information for Parents) (https://www.nagc.org/resources-publications/resources-parents/parent-tip-sheets)
» Our Gifted (https://ourgifted.com)
» Hoagies' Gifted Education Page (https://www.hoagiesgifted.org/parents.htm)

References

Amend, E. R., & Joerg, M. (2019). *Talking with your child about giftedness.* National Association for Gifted Children. http://www.nagc.org/sites/default/files/Parent%20CK/NAGC%20TIP%20Sheet-Talking%20with%20Your%20Child%20About%20Giftedness.pdf

Cross, T. L. (2011). *Competing with myths about the social and emotional development of gifted students.* https://www.sengifted.org/post/competing-with-myths-about-the-social-and-emotional-development-of-gifted-students

Ford, D. (2015). Culturally responsive gifted classrooms for culturally different students: A focus on invitational learning. *Gifted Child Today, 38*(1), 67–69. https://doi.org/10.1177/1076217514556697

Frasier, M. M., Martin, D., Garcia, J., Finley, V. S., Frank, E., Krisel, S., & King, L. L. (1995, September). *A new window for looking at gifted children.* https://nrcgt.uconn.edu/wp-content/uploads/sites/953/2015/04/rm95222.pdf

Henfield, M. S., Washington, A. R., & Byrd, J. A. (2014). Addressing academic and opportunity gaps impacting gifted Black males: Implications for school counselors. *Gifted Child Today, 37*(3), 147–154. https://doi.org/10.1177/1076217514530118

Jolly, J. L., & Matthews, M. S. (2013). Homeschooling the gifted: A parent's perspective. *Gifted Child Quarterly, 57*(2), 121–134. https://doi.org/10.1177/0016986212469999

Luckey Goudelock, J. D. (2019). Parenting high-ability African American children: Navigating the two-edged sword of giftedness. *Parenting for High Potential, 8*(2). https://www.nagc.org/sites/default/files/Parenting%20for%20High%20Potential%20June%202019.pdf

Thompson, B., & Winsler, A. (2018). Parent-teacher agreement on social skills and behavior problems among ethnically diverse preschoolers with autism spectrum disorder. *Journal of Autism and Developmental Disorders, 48*(9), 3163–3175. https://doi.org/10.1007/s10803-018-3570-5

Zanetti, M. A., Gualdi, G., & Cascianelli, M. (Eds.). (2019*). Understanding giftedness: A guide for parents and educators.* Routledge.

Policy

Effective policies can make a significant impact on closing Excellence Gaps and increasing access so that students from all populations can thrive. States and districts that have implemented specific policies to address access have seen marked progress toward their goals in advancing equitable access to students who are racially, culturally, ethnically, and linguistically different (RCELD) or students who are twice exceptional (2e) (Patrick et al., 2020).

The Data

The Jack Kent Cooke Foundation regularly completes a state-by-state review of policies that support advanced learners. The latest report (Plucker et al., 2018) assigned states a grade based on 15 indicators that address both excellence in supporting advanced learning outcomes and closing Excellence Gaps. In addition, The Education Trust (Patrick et al., 2020) studied RCELD students' access and success in advanced coursework.

» Regarding excellence, states' grades ranged from B+ to D (Plucker et al., 2018).

» Regarding closing Excellence Gaps, states' grades ranged from C+ to F (Plucker et al., 2018). "Every state in the nation has Excellence Gaps—in grade 4, grade 8, and high school; in math and in reading" (Plucker et al., 2018, p. 8).

» Only 7 states required universal screening for at least one grade level, despite universal screening being a key step toward closing Excellence Gaps (Plucker et al., 2018).

» Black and Latinx students are not fairly represented in advanced courses due to systemic barriers (Patrick et al., 2020).

Recommendations

Numerous recommendations could be made to impact closing Excellence Gaps and increasing access. A few of those recommendations are included here:

» Enact policy at the highest level possible in order to affect more students.
» Disaggregate achievement data and participation in advanced coursework by subpopulation, so that all stakeholders, including decision-makers, are informed (Patrick et al., 2020). This should include students with multiple exceptionalities.
» Be cognizant of state regulations and policies as well as district policies that may impact children with gifts and talents. Also be knowledgeable about policies that cross district departments such as the special education department and English Learners.
» Establish a state accountability system that focuses on growth (Plucker et al., 2018).
» Before passing policy, ask these two questions:
  › "How will this affect our brightest students?
  › How will this help other students begin to achieve at high levels?" (Plucker et al., 2010, p. 30)

Resources to Learn More

» Jack Kent Cooke Foundation includes specific state data as well as other information and resources (https://www.jkcf.org)
» The Education Trust (https://edtrust.org)
» National Association for Gifted Children, Gifted by State (https://www.nagc.org/information-publications/gifted-state)

References

Patrick, K., Socol, A., & Morgan, I. (2020, January). *Inequities in advanced coursework: What's driving them and what leaders can do.* The Education Trust. https://edtrust.org/resource/inequities-in-advanced-coursework

Plucker, J. A., Burroughs, N., & Song, R. (2010, February 4). *Mind the other gap: The growing Excellence Gap in K–12 education. Center for Evaluation and Education Policy.* https://files.eric.ed.gov/fulltext/ED531840.pdf

Plucker, J. A., Glynn, J., Healey, G., & Dettmer A. (2018). *Equal talents, unequal opportunities: A report card on state support for academically talented low-income students* (2nd ed.). Jack Kent Cooke

Foundation. https://www.jkcf.org/research/equal-talents-unequal-opportunities-second-edition-a-report-card-on-state-support-for-academically-talented-low-income-students

Concluding Thoughts

As educators, continual reflection upon our own implicit biases and understanding of how these affect our interactions with students and colleagues is critical for our personal and societal growth. At the beginning of this book, we asked you to read with the purpose of self-reflection. We present these questions again here, as well as the Reflections on Classroom Practice Survey in Appendix A, and selected books we each suggest for your consideration as you continue on your journey in Appendix B.

1. In what ways do I acknowledge and address my own implicit bias?

2. In what ways do I address biases that are present in my school?
3. In what ways do I help students understand their own cultural biases?
4. In what ways do I advocate for the diverse representation of students in my school environment?
5. In what ways do I make sure all students have a voice in shaping the school environment?
6. In what ways do I communicate high expectations for all students?
7. In what ways do I make my instruction relevant to students' experiences?
8. In what ways do I encourage students to be respectful of others and their perspectives?
9. In what ways do I foster collaboration among students?
10. In what ways do I engage students in their learning, and in my own learning?
11. In what ways do I encourage students to become problem solvers in their own and the global community?
12. In what ways do I engage the agency of family and community?
13. In what ways do I increase access to opportunities for students both inside and outside of school?
14. In what ways do I incorporate students' lived experiences into my own personal growth?

Appendix A
Reflections on Classroom Practice Survey

A printable version of the Reflections on Classroom Practice Survey is available on this book's webpage at https://www.prufrock. com/Culturally-Responsive-Teaching-in-Gifted-Education-Resources.aspx.

Reflections on Classroom Practice Survey

Directions: This tool is intended to assist you as you reflect on your current classroom practices by using the descriptors as a guide for where you are on your journey toward culturally responsive practices for your students. This is *not* intended to be all-encompassing but rather a snapshot of where you are on your personal and professional journey.

REFLECTIONS ON CLASSROOM PRACTICE SURVEY, continued

Descriptor	Novice: Starting the journey and gaining awareness	Developing: On the journey with increased understanding	Practitioner: Putting into practice the lessons learned on the journey	Lifelong Learner: Applies in-depth knowledge for novice, developing, and practitioner levels, continues the learning journey
Characteristics	Searches for in-depth knowledge of culturally relevant practices	Continues learning with culturally relevant practices that impact personal growth synthesizing multiple viewpoints	Creates lessons that reflect study of culturally relevant practices, relationships with students, and understanding of others' perspectives	Mentors educators new to culturally relevant practices and continues learning about practices to enhance personal growth
I ensure that my classroom is a safe place in which all students have a choice and voice.				
I build on the assets of all of my students (e.g., strengths, culture, traditions, and norms) within my classroom.				

REFLECTIONS ON CLASSROOM PRACTICE SURVEY, continued

I incorporate students' lived experiences in my classroom.				
I encourage students' use of their heritage language in my classroom.				
I communicate high expectations for all of my students.				
I find ways to engage all of my students in the curriculum.				
I ensure that all students are meeting the learning goals.				
I encourage my students to look at learning from various points of view.				
I encourage my students to demonstrate their understanding in multiple ways.				
I provide all of the necessary materials for students to complete their work in my classroom (e.g., assignments, projects).				

Appendix B

Suggested Reading for Developing Culturally Responsive Practices

Matt's Top 10 List
Selected Books to Support Cultural Responsiveness and Diversity

Alexie, S. (2007). *The absolutely true diary of a part-time Indian*. Little, Brown.

Blackburn, M. V., Clark. C. T., & Schey, R. (2018). *Stepping up!: Teachers advocating for sexual and gender diversity in schools*. Routledge.

Chugh, D. (2018). *The person you mean to be: How good people fight bias*. HarperCollins.

Jones, G. W., & Moomaw, S. (2002). *Lessons from Turtle Island: Native curriculum in early childhood classrooms*. Redleaf Press.

Kendi, I. X. (2016). *Stamped from the beginning: The definitive history of racist ideas in America*. Bold Type Books.

Kerr, B. A., & McKay, R. (2014). *Smart girls in the 21st century: Understanding talented girls and women*. Great Potential Press.

Reichard, W. (2011). *American tensions: Literature of identity and the search for social justice*. New Village Press.

Sadowski, M. (2016). *Safe is not enough: Better schools for LGBTQ students*. Harvard Education Press.

Seale, D., & Slapin, B. (Eds.). (2005). *A broken flute: The Native experience in books for children*. AltaMira Press.

Tatum, B. D. (2017). *Why are all the Black kids sitting together in the cafeteria?: And other conversations about race*. Basic Books.

Wendy's Top 10 List
Selected Books for Creating Culturally Responsive Schools

Aguilar, E. (2020). *Coaching for equity: Conversations that change practice.* Jossey-Bass.

Blankstein, A. M., & Newsome, M. J. (2021). *Breakthrough leadership: Six principles guiding schools where inequity is not an option.* Corwin.

Delpit, L. D. (2006). *Other people's children: Cultural conflict in the classroom.* The New Press.

Gay, G. (2000). *Culturally responsive teaching: Theory, research, and practice.* Teachers College Press.

Hammond, Z. (2015). *Culturally responsive teaching and the brain: Promoting authentic engagement and rigor among culturally and linguistically diverse students.* Corwin.

Khalifa, M. (2018). *Culturally responsive school leadership.* Harvard Education Press.

Plucker, J. A., & Peters, S. J. (2016). *Excellence gaps in education: Expanding opportunities for talented students.* Harvard Education Press.

Stembridge, A. (2020). *Culturally responsive education in the classroom: An equity framework for pedagogy.* Taylor & Francis.

Wells, A. (2020). *Achieving equity in gifted programming: Dismantling barriers and tapping potential.* Prufrock Press.

Wormeli, R. (2018). *Fair isn't always equal: Assessment and grading in the differentiated classroom* (2nd ed.). Stenhouse.

Cecelia's Top 10 List
Selected Books to Support Cultural Responsiveness for Hispanic/ Latinx Students and Students From Rural Populations

Hispanic/Latinx Resources

Kogan, E. (2001). *Gifted bilingual students: A paradox?* Lang.

Fajardo-Anstine, K. (2020). *Sabrina and Corina: Stories.* One World.

Ferrera, A. (2019). *American like me: Reflections on life between cultures.* Gallery Books.

Hammond, Z. (2015). *Culturally responsive teaching and the brain: Promoting authentic engagement and rigor among culturally and linguistically diverse students.* Corwin.

James, L. (2019). *Definitely Hispanic: Growing up Latino and celebrating what unites* us. Atria Books.

Morales, E. (2019). *Latinx: The new force in American politics and culture.* Verso.

Reynoso, N. (2020). *Fearless trailblazers: 11 Latinos who made U.S. history.* Con Todo Press.

Rural Resources

Davidson, O. G. (1996). *Broken heartland: The rise of America's rural ghetto.* Free Press.

Haas, T., & Nachtigal, P. (1998). *Place value: An educators' guide to good literature on rural lifeways, environments, and purposes of education.* ERIC Clearinghouse on Rural Education and Small Schools.

Stambaugh, T., & Wood, S. M. (Eds.). (2015). *Serving gifted students in rural settings.* Prufrock Press.

Joy's Top 10 List
Selected Books to Address Diversity, Equity, and Antiracism in Schools

Castellano, J. (2018). *Educating Hispanic and Latino students: Opening doors to hope, promise, and possibility.* Learning Sciences International.

Coates, T.-N. (2015). *Between the world and me.* One World.

Davis, J. L. (2010). *Bright, talented, and Black: A guide for African American families of gifted learners.* Great Potential Press.

Ford, D. Y. (2013). *Recruiting and retaining culturally different students in gifted education.* Prufrock Press.

Kendi, I. X. (2019). *How to be an antiracist.* Penguin Random House.

Ladson-Billings, G. (2009). *The dreamkeepers: Successful teachers of African American children* (2nd ed.). Jossey-Bass.

Love, B. L. (2019). *We want to do more than survive: Abolitionist teaching and the pursuit of educational freedom.* Beacon Press.

Nieto, S., & Bode, B. (2018). *Affirming diversity: The sociopolitical context of multicultural education* (7th ed.). Pearson.

Stevenson, B. (2014). *Just mercy: A story of justice and redemption.* Spiegel & Grau.

Winters, M.-F. (2020). *Black fatigue: How racism erodes the body, mind, and spirit.* Berrett-Koehler.

About the Editors

C. Matthew Fugate, Ph.D., is assistant professor in Educational Psychology and Assistant Chair of Urban Education at the University of Houston-Downtown. He received his doctorate in Gifted, Creative, and Talented Studies at Purdue University. Prior to this, Matthew worked as an elementary teacher in the Houston Independent School District, where he also served as a gifted coordinator and magnet coordinator. During this time, Matthew received his Master's in Educational Psychology, Gifted Education from the University of Connecticut. His research has examined the relationship between working memory and levels of creativity in gifted students who also have characteristics related to ADHD. He has also examined the coping mechanisms of twice-exceptional girls in secondary school as they navigate both their academic studies and interpersonal relationships. Matthew was also part of a team that looked at the benefits of the Total School Cluster Grouping Model, a Javits Grant funded project. He has presented to parents, teachers, and schools across the United States and internationally on topics such as creativity, curriculum compacting, identification, twice-exceptionality, underserved populations, and Total School Cluster Grouping. Matthew currently serves on the Board of the Texas Association for the Gifted and Talented and as Chair of the Special Populations Network for the National Association for Gifted Children. Additionally, he serves as a reviewer for several journals and is the associate editor of *Teaching for High Potential*. He has published several articles, book chapters, and books related to his work.

Wendy A. Behrens, M.A. Ed., a graduate of Bradley University and Hamline University, is the Gifted and Talented Education Specialist for the Minnesota Department of Education, where she advises educators, administrators, parents, and policymakers. Prior to her service to the state, Wendy worked as a district K–12 gifted services coordinator and a consultant for the Science Museum of Minnesota. In 2009, her vision for professional learning led to the creation of the Hormel Foundation Gifted and Talented Education Symposium, an annual event attracting attendees from around the country and the world. Recently, Wendy was the director of Project North Star, a Jacob K. Javits grant designed to elevate the identification and programming approaches provided for disadvantaged and underserved rural populations. Her current Javits grant work, Universal Plus, focuses on creating a two-step process for equitably identifying computer talent. Wendy is a past-president of the Council of State Directors of Programs for the Gifted and currently serves as the President-Elect of The Association for the Gifted (CEC-TAG). In 2013, she received the President's Award from the National Association for Gifted Children. Wendy is an active member of, and has held leadership roles in, NAGC, the Council of Exceptional Children, CEC-TAG, and the World Council for Gifted and Talented Children. Additionally, Wendy serves on several education-related advisory councils and the *Gifted Child Today* editorial board. She has published several books, chapters, and articles related to the education of gifted learners and frequently presents to national and international audiences on comprehensive service design, acceleration, underserved populations, and policies that support highly able learners.

For 17 years, **Cecelia Boswell, Ed.D.,** taught migrant and gifted students in a rural school. During that time, she was a finalist for Texas Migrant Teacher of the Year. After public school, Cecelia began work for a Texas Education Service Center (ESC) as the Director of Gifted Education and State Director of AP/IB Projects. She received the award for Gifted Advocate of the Year and, upon completion of her doctorate, the National Rural Education Association's award for Dissertation of the Year. She founded Austin Creek Education Systems, developed curriculum for the Texas and Florida Departments of Education, led research projects for International Baccalaureate, and audited gifted programs across the state. During this time, she served on the board and as president of the Texas Association for the Gifted and Talented (TAGT). Cecelia next became the executive director of advanced academics in an urban school. While there, she developed a middle school academy for gifted learners. She was awarded the Texas Administrator of the Year by TAGT and was elected to the board and became president for CEC-TAG. Cecelia has published in juried journals and written teacher guides for children's novels. She has coauthored five books on gifted education. Cecelia also has co-conducted a rural research study with a colleague, and an article is at press. Currently, she works with a school district to revamp services for the gifted students, facilitates online classes, contracts with TAGT, and presents sessions for teachers of the gifted.

Joy Lawson Davis, Ph.D., is an award-winning author, scholar, professional learning trainer, and independent consultant. Her areas of expertise include culturally responsive teaching, cognitive diversity, and equity and access in gifted education programs with a focus on meeting the needs of Black gifted students and their families. She holds two degrees in gifted education from William & Mary. She has provided training (for educators and families) across the nation and internationally—in South Africa, the Caribbean, Dubai, and Turkey. Her earlier experiences include serving for 5 years as the K–12 Gifted Education Specialist for the state of Virginia; as an assistant professor in the School of Education at the University of Louisiana, Lafayette, where she taught coursework in teacher education and gifted education; and as an associate professor and chair of the Department of Teacher Education at Virginia Union University. She also served for 5 years on the Board of Directors of the National Association for Gifted Children. Davis is the author of numerous publications, including two books, *Bright, Talented, and Black: A Guide for Families of African American Gifted Learners* and *Gifted Children of Color Around the World* (coedited with J. L. Moore). In addition to her work as an independent consultant, Dr. Davis also serves on the Duke Precollegiate Programs advisory board and the Board of Trustees of The Roeper School for the Gifted in Michigan.

About the Authors

Nina Barbieri, Ph.D., is an assistant professor of criminal justice and director of the Lab for Equity in Action at the University of Houston-Downtown. She teaches and publishes on topics relating to the intersectionality of the criminal justice system and other social institutions, as well as on understanding the resulting social harms of racialized social systems. She has published in *Aggression and Violent Behavior, Criminal Justice and Behavior, Crime & Delinquency, Deviant Behavior,* and other outlets.

Kristina Henry Collins, Ph.D., is the core talent development faculty at Texas State University. She earned her Ph.D. in educational psychology and Ed.S. in gifted and creative education from the University of Georgia. Dr. Collins currently serves as president for Supporting Emotional Needs of the Gifted (SENG) and a member-at-large for the National Association for Gifted Children (NAGC) board of directors. Her research foci include multicultural gifted education, culturally responsive STEM identity, and talent development. Dr. Collins is the proud recipient of the 2020 NAGC Special Population Early Career Award, the 2020 Bridges 2e Education "Person to Watch" Award, and the Georgia Association for Gifted Children's 2011 Mary Frasier Equity and Excellence Award presented for her work in advancing educational opportunities for underrepresented students in gifted education.

Jeff Danielian is the director of the La Salle Scholars Program in Providence, RI. He received his master's degree in educational psychology from the University of Connecticut and currently holds the position of Teacher Resource Specialist for NAGC, serving as editor-in-chief for *Teaching for High Potential.* He has authored four books for Prufrock Press and four volumes of poetry. Jeff has presented at local, national, and international conferences on topics including the affective needs of gifted and talented students, creativity and eminence, and the school/home connection. He is the codirector of Edufest, a summer professional development conference held at Boise State.

Marques R. Dexter, M.S., is a doctoral candidate at the University of Georgia's Mary Frances Early College of Education. He serves as the Assistant Director of Student Initiatives within the Office of Institutional Diversity. Additionally, Dexter is the assistant director of the Georgia African American Male Experience program, UGA's African American Male Initiative. Dexter's research centers around the experiences and factors contributing to academically and athletically high-achieving Black male athletes' success. He is an executive committee member of the Georgia Association of Diversity Officers in Higher Education and a former NCAA track and field athlete and coach.

Erinn Fears Floyd, Ph.D., a gifted education, diversity, equity, and inclusion scholar, is Director of Training and Partnership Development for The Consortium for Inclusion of Underrepresented Racial Groups in Gifted Education. She is former Director of Professional Learning for the National Association for Gifted Children and Gifted Education Director for the Alabama Department of Education. She has more than 28 years of experience as a classroom teacher, gifted and school improvement specialist, literacy coach, district gifted coordinator, and school administrator. She is an inaugural recipient of NAGC's Dr. Mary Frasier Teacher Scholarship for Diverse Talent Development. Dr. Floyd serves on the Board of Trustees for the Alabama School of Fine Arts and is founder of Equity and Excellence in Education, LLC, which provides professional learning and academic support to educators and students.

Michelle Frazier Trotman Scott, Ph.D., is the College of Education's Director of Graduate Affairs and Professor of Special Education at the University of West Georgia. Dr. Scott's research interests include the achievement gap, special education overrepresentation, gifted education underrepresentation, dual exceptionalities, culturally responsive teaching, and family involvement. She conducts professional development workshops and facilitates community dialogs about educational practices and reform. She has written and coauthored several articles and chapters, has made numerous presentations at professional conferences, and has coedited six books. She is also on the editorial board for multiple journals and has served in leadership roles in professional organizations.

Marcia Gentry, Ph.D., directs the Gifted Education Research and Resource Institute at Purdue University where she enjoys working with doctoral students and engaging in research and gifted education professional development. She remains active in the field through service to NAGC and AERA and by writing, reviewing, and presenting research aimed to improve education for children, youth, and teachers. She focuses on underserved populations and on creating an equitable, socially just field.

Tarek C. Grantham, Ph.D., is a professor of educational psychology at the University of Georgia. He serves as coordinator for the Gifted and Creative Education Graduate Program, and he codirects the University-School Partnerships for Achievement, Rigor, and Creativity initiative. Dr. Grantham's research addresses equity for underrepresented groups in advanced programs, gifted Black males, motivation, and creativity policy. He is a member of the Board of Directors for NAGC and a recipient of the Dr. Alexinia Baldwin "Gifted & Special Populations" Award and the Georgia Association for Gifted Children's Mary M. Frasier Excellence and Equity Award.

Justyna Gray is Diné, lives on the Navajo Nation, and has three older sisters. She is a senior at Navajo Preparatory School and plans to study environmental sciences in college. For the past 10 years, Justyna has spent her summers at a camp in northern Minnesota and has a passion for canoeing in the Boundary Waters Canoe Area.

Thomas P. Hébert, Ph.D., is a professor of gifted and talented education at the University of South Carolina. Dr. Hébert has more than a decade of K–12 classroom experience working with gifted students and 25 years in higher education training graduate students and educators in gifted education. He has also conducted research for the National Research Center on the Gifted and Talented (NRC/GT) and served on the Board of Directors of NAGC. He received the 2012 Distinguished Alumni Award from the Neag School of Education at the University of Connecticut and the 2019 Distinguished Scholar Award from NAGC.

Javetta Jones Roberson, Ed.D., serves as the District Coordinator of Secondary Advanced Academics & Gifted and Talented in McKinney Independent School District in McKinney, TX. She also serves as an adjunct professor in the Teacher Education and Administration department at the University of North Texas-Denton campus. Her research interests include diverse gifted and Advanced Placement populations, blended learning, culturally responsive and antiracist pedagogy (teaching, leadership, and curriculum), and professional learning of teachers (special education and gifted). Javetta serves on the Board of Directors for the Council of Exceptional Children, The Association for the Gifted and the Texas Association for the Gifted and Talented. She is also active with NAGC and serves on the following committees: Diversity, Education, Standards, and Online Community. She is also active with the NAGC Special Populations Network and is G-RACE special interest group co-chair.

Teresa Ryan Manzella, M.A., is a founding member of the NAGC GLBTQ Network. She has authored numerous articles, book chapters, and online resources on gifted LGBTQ topics, published by NAGC and other gifted organizations. She serves on the American Mensa/MERF National Gifted Youth Committee, the Minnesota Department of Education Committee on Gifted and Talented Education, and the Minnesota Council for the Gifted and Talented Connections (diversity and equity) Committee. She has been invited, by organizations across the United States, to present on strategies to address the complex challenges facing gifted LGBTQ youth.

Luciana C. de Oliveira, Ph.D., is Associate Dean for Academic Affairs and Professor in the School of Education at Virginia Commonwealth University. Her research focuses on issues related to teaching multilingual learners at the K–12 level, including the role of language in learning the content areas and teacher education, advocacy, and social justice. She has authored or edited 24 books and has more than 200 publications in various outlets. Dr. de Oliveira served as President (2018–2019) of TESOL International Association and was a member of the Board of Directors (2013–2016). She was the first Latina to ever serve as President of TESOL.

Nielsen Pereira, Ph.D., is Associate Professor of Gifted, Creative, and Talented Studies at Purdue University. His research interests include conceptual and measurement issues in the identification of gifted and talented populations, design and assessment of learning in varied gifted and talented education contexts, and understanding gifted and talented student experiences in talent development programs in and out of school. He was the recipient of the 2018 Hollingworth Award and the 2020 Early Scholar Award from NAGC and the 2019 Pathbreaker Award from the American Educational Research Association Research on Giftedness, Creativity, and Talent Development special interest group.

Bernardo Pohl, Ed.D., is an associate professor in the Department of Urban Education and joined the University of Houston-Downtown (UHD) in 2013. He currently teaches social studies methods and special education courses. His expertise is in social studies methods and disability studies. Before joining UHD, he taught social studies and special education for more than 10 years. His research interests include teacher retention and attrition, social studies pedagogy, cross-curricular literacy, and moral/ethical issues in special education and disability studies. Dr. Pohl has presented and published his research nationally and internationally.

Sally M. Reis, Ph.D., holds the Letitia Neag Chair in Educational Psychology, is a Board of Trustees Distinguished Professor, and is the former Vice Provost for Academic Affairs at the Neag School of Education at University of Connecticut. She was a classroom teacher in public education as well as an administrator before her work at UConn. She has authored and coauthored more than 270 articles, books, book chapters, monographs, and technical reports, and worked in a research team that has generated more than $100 million in grants in the last 2 decades. She is also the codirector of Confratute, the summer institute on gifted education and talent development.

PJ "Paul James" Sedillo, Ph.D., an associate professor for the Special/Gifted Education Department at New Mexico Highlands University, is published in *Gifted Child Today, Journal of Education & Social Policy*, Prufrock Press, *Parenting for High Potential*, and ABQ Press, where his book *Solidarity Through Pride* won best book in Arizona/ New Mexico for 2018. PJ has a new chapter coming out in a forthcoming Prufrock Press book tentatively titled *Identifying and Serving Diverse Gifted Learners: Meeting the Needs of Special Populations in Gifted Education*, which introduces stages of identity for LGBTQ+ gifted persons. He served as President for the New Mexico Association for the Gifted, Communication Member and Chair-Elect for the NAGC GLBTQ Network, NAGC State Affiliate Leadership and Advocacy member, cochair for the 2019 NAGC annual convention in Albuquerque, and currently is an at-large board member for NAGC.

Jace Valcore, Ph.D., is an associate professor of criminal justice at the University of Houston-Downtown. He researches hate crimes and hate speech, policing, queer criminology and methodology, and trans issues in the criminal legal system. He strives to be a critical, antiracist, anticolonial scholar and educator. He is a founding board member of the Division on Queer Criminology of the American Society of Criminology, serves on the Houston Independent Police Oversight Board, and conducts queer competency trainings for educators, community leaders, and police professionals.